LEARN, TEACH...
SUCCEED...

With **REA's PRAXIS II®️ Special Education**
test prep, you'll be in a class all your own.

WE'D LIKE TO HEAR FROM YOU!
Visit **www.rea.com** to send us your comments

PRAXIS II®

SPECIAL EDUCATION

(0353, 0354, 0543, 0545)

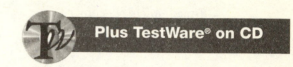

Plus TestWare® on CD

Esther Langer, M.S.Ed.
Special Educator
New York City Board of Education
New York, New York

Kymberly Harris Drawdy, Ph.D.
Department of Teaching and Learning
Georgia Southern University
Statesboro, Georgia

Research & Education Association

www.rea.com

Research & Education Association
61 Ethel Road West
Piscataway, New Jersey 08854
E-mail: info@rea.com

PRAXIS II®: Special Education Assessments (0353, 0354, 0543, 0545) with TestWare® on CD

Published 2014

Copyright © 2012 by Research & Education Association, Inc.
All rights reserved. No part of this book may be reproduced in
any form without permission of the publisher.

Printed in the United States of America

Library of Congress Control Number 2011945802

ISBN-13: 978-0-7386-0872-3
ISBN-10: 0-7386-0872-6

Cover image: JGI/Blend Images/Getty Images

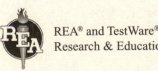

About Research & Education Association

Founded in 1959, Research & Education Association is dedicated to publishing the finest and most effective educational materials—including study guides and test preps—for students in middle school, high school, college, graduate school, and beyond.

Today, REA's wide-ranging catalog is a leading resource for teachers, students, and professionals. Visit *www.rea.com* to see a complete listing of all our titles.

Acknowledgments

In addition to our authors, we would like to thank REA's Larry B. Kling, Vice President, Editorial, for supervising development; Pam Weston, Publisher, for setting the quality standards for production integrity and managing the publication to completion; John Paul Cording, Vice President, Technology, for coordinating the design and development of REA's TestWare®; Kathleen Casey, Senior Editor, for project management and editorial preflight review; Alice Leonard, Senior Editor, and Diane Goldschmidt, Managing Editor, for post-production quality assurance; Heena Patel, software project manager, for her software testing efforts; Weymouth Design and Christine Saul, Senior Graphic Artist, for cover design; and S4Carlisle Publishing Services for typesetting.

About the Authors

Esther Langer has an M.S.Ed. in Special Education from Duquesne University, and has serviced exceptional students in grades K-8 in diverse locations ranging from a large urban public school to a small private religious school. She completed her internship in the Pittsburgh Public Schools and is currently a special educator with the New York City Board of Education. Becoming certified in three states required that she complete several standardized tests, so she knows just how students feel when taking the Praxis exams! She scored 197 out of 200 on the Praxis 0354.

Kymberly Harris Drawdy, Ph.D., is an associate professor of special education at Georgia Southern University. Dr. Drawdy's research interests include identifying best practices for including students with disabilities in general education math classrooms, preservice teacher preparation at the graduate and undergraduate level, preservice teacher math efficacy, and curriculum matching of state math standards to common math practices at the secondary level.

CONTENTS

CHAPTER 4
DELIVERY OF SERVICES TO STUDENTS:
INSTRUCTION AND ASSESSMENT
59

CHAPTER 5
INSTRUCTION AND ASSESSMENT
73

CHAPTER 6
FOUNDATIONS AND PROFESSIONAL RESPONSIBILITIES
95

PRACTICE TEST 1 (0353)
113

PREFACE

The information tested on the Praxis is very broad—it covers the gamut of special education, from early intervention to assisted employment to legal history. There is a lot of information you'll be expected to know. But don't fret—you can easily create a personalized study plan that will help you to do your best on the Praxis exam. This book will help show you how.

The book has been organized by competencies covered on the key tests in the Praxis II Special Education battery of tests. When you begin studying, don't try to memorize the whole book. Instead, begin by reading over the table of contents and glancing over each section. Decide whether each topic is new material you'll need to learn, material you'll need to review, or material you already know well. You may be surprised by how much you remember from your lectures and books.

The bold headings provided throughout the book will make your studying easier. Place bookmarks in or highlight sections you will want to review. You may want to use sticky bookmarks, such as Post-its, to provide easy reference to information you'd like to stress for review. Remember when highlighting not to highlight the entire section, but only the section containing information you wish to reinforce. Then, be sure to go back and review that information so you consolidate your gains. You may want to take your own notes about subjects you are unfamiliar with.

Key terms have been put in italics. You should work to add these terms to your special education vocabulary. You are likely to see these terms on the Praxis exam within the questions and answers.

Often, information has been provided in list form. Look over these lists carefully—they typically contain information you will need to memorize. The lists make it easy for you to create flashcards to facilitate studying. This will give you easy access to your study materials wherever you are.

And now—why not begin studying?

—**Esther Langer**

Introduction

ABOUT THIS BOOK AND TESTWARE®

If you're looking to secure certification as a special education teacher, you'll find that many states require one or more of the four tests covered in this test prep. Think of this book as your toolkit to pass your exam(s).

Deciding to pursue a teaching career already speaks volumes about you. You would not have gotten to this point without being highly motivated and able to synthesize considerable amounts of information.

But, of course, it's a different matter when you have to show what you know on a test. That's where we come in. We're here to help take the mystery and anxiety out of the process. We're here to equip you not only with the nuts and bolts, but, ultimately, with the confidence to succeed alongside your peers across the United States.

We've put a lot of thought into this, and the result is a book that pulls together all the critical information you need to know to pass any one of these Praxis tests:

- Education of Exceptional Students: Core Content Knowledge (0353)

- Special Education: Core Knowledge and Applications (0354/5354)

- Special Education: Core Knowledge and Mild to Moderate Applications (0543/5543)

- Special Education: Core Knowledge and Severe to Profound Applications (0545/5545)

In this test prep, REA offers our in-depth, up-to-date, objective coverage, with test-specific modules devoted to targeted review and true-to-format practice exams. Practice Tests 1 and 2 for Education of Exceptional Students: Core Content Knowledge (0353) and Special Education: Core Knowledge and Applications (0354/5354), respectively, are included in two formats: in printed form in this book and on the enclosed TestWare® on CD. Practice Tests 3 and 4 will help prepare you to take the Special Education: Core Knowledge and Mild to Moderate Applications (0543) and/or the Special Education: Core Knowledge and Severe to Profound Applications (0545) exams, respectively. Even if you're not planning to take either the 0543 or the 0545 exams covered in this book, you will doubtless benefit from additional practice in these areas. This is because, while the subject matter focus may vary somewhat, the format in which you'll be tested is identical.

We strongly recommend that you begin your preparation with the TestWare® practice tests on CD. The software provides the added benefits of timed testing conditions and instantaneous, accurate scoring, which makes it easier to pinpoint your strengths and weaknesses.

ABOUT THE PRAXIS SERIES

Praxis is Educational Testing Service's (ETS) shorthand for Professional Assessments for Beginning Teachers. The Praxis Series is a group of teacher licensing tests that ETS developed in concert with states across the nation. There are three categories of tests in the series: Praxis I, Praxis II and Praxis III. Praxis I includes the paper-based Pre-Professional Skills Tests (PPST) and the Praxis I Computer-Based Tests (CBT). Both versions cover essentially the same subject matter. These exams measure reading, mathematics, and writing skills and are often a requirement for admission to a teacher education program.

Praxis II embraces Subject Assessment/Specialty Area Tests, including the Praxis II Special Education and Exceptional Education series, of which these exams are a part. The Praxis II examinations cover the subject matter that students typically study in teacher education courses—such content as human growth and development, school curriculum, methods of teaching, and other professional development courses. In most teacher-training programs, students take these tests after having completed their classroom training, the course work, and practicum.

Praxis III is different from the multiple-choice and essay tests typically used for assessment purposes. With this assessment, ETS-trained observers evaluate an instructor's performance in the classroom, using nationally validated criteria. The observers may videotape the lesson, and other teaching experts may critique the resulting tapes.

The Praxis II Special Education and Exceptional Education series covers the spectrum of content areas that affect the special education or exceptional student. This test prep addresses each of these broader content areas and the subareas as delineated in the following table.

REVIEW-AT-A-GLANCE	0353	0354 5354	0543 5543	0545 5545
Chapter 2: Understanding Special and Exceptional Students				
Human development and behavior as related to students with disabilities	✔	✔		
Language development and behavior	✔			
Cognition	✔			
Physical development, including motor and sensory	✔			
Characteristics of students with disabilities	✔	✔		
Affective and social-adaptive factors	✔			
Genetic, medical, motor, sensory, and chronological age factors	✔			
Basic concepts in special education	✔	✔	✔	✔
Definitions of all major categories and specific disabilities	✔			
The causation and prevention of disability	✔			
The nature of behaviors	✔			
The classification of students with disabilities	✔			
The implications of the classification process for the persons classified, etc.	✔			
The influence of level of severity and presence of multiple exceptionalities on students with disabilities	✔			
Co-occurring (dual diagnosis) conditions		✔	✔	✔
How family systems contribute to the development of individuals with disabilities		✔	✔	✔
Environmental and societal influences on student development and achievement		✔	✔	✔
Impact of disabilities on individuals, families, and society across the life span		✔	✔	✔
Impact of language, cultural, and gender differences on the identification process		✔	✔	✔
Influence of (an) exceptional condition(s) throughout an individual's life span	✔			
Chapter 3: Planning and the Learning Environment				
Characteristics of good lesson plans		✔	✔	✔
Basic elements of effective lesson plans		✔	✔	✔
Learning objectives that are measurable and appropriately challenging		✔	✔	✔
Means of providing access to the curriculum		✔	✔	✔
Organizing the learning environment		✔	✔	✔
Theory and practice of positive behavior supports		✔	✔	✔
Theory and practice of effective classroom management		✔	✔	✔
Design and maintenance of a safe and supportive classroom environment		✔	✔	✔
Chapter 4: Delivery of Services to Students: Instruction and Assessment				
Background knowledge	✔			
Placement and program issues	✔	✔	✔	✔
Integrating best practices	✔	✔	✔	✔

(continued)

REVIEW-AT-A-GLANCE	0353	0354 5354	0543 5543	0545 5545
Chapter 5: Instruction and Assessment				
Appropriate instructional strategies/techniques		✔	✔	✔
Instructional strategies for ensuring individual academic success in one-to-one, small group, and large group settings		✔	✔	✔
Instructional strategies that facilitate maintenance and generalization of concepts		✔	✔	✔
Selection and implementation of research-based interventions for individual students		✔	✔	✔
Selection and implementation of supplementary and/or functional curriculum		✔	✔	✔
Options for assistive technology		✔	✔	✔
Instructional strategies/techniques that support transition goals		✔	✔	✔
Preventive strategies and intervention strategies for at-risk learners		✔	✔	✔
Evidence-based assessments that are effective and appropriate		✔	✔	✔
Defining and using various assessments		✔	✔	✔
Interpreting assessment results		✔	✔	✔
Understanding and using the results of assessments		✔	✔	✔
Chapter 6: Foundations and Professional Responsibilities				
Historical movement/trends	✔	✔	✔	✔
Federal definitions	✔	✔	✔	✔
Federal requirements for the pre-referral, referral, and identification	✔	✔	✔	✔
Federal safeguards of the rights of stakeholders	✔	✔	✔	✔
Components of a legally defensible individualized education program	✔	✔	✔	✔
Major legislation	✔	✔	✔	✔
Major legal cases	✔	✔	✔	✔
Roles and responsibilities of the special education teacher	✔	✔	✔	✔
Roles and responsibilities of other professionals	✔	✔	✔	✔
Strengths and limitations of various collaborative approaches	✔	✔	✔	✔
Communication with stakeholders	✔	✔	✔	✔
Potential bias issues	✔	✔	✔	✔
Practice Test 1 (Education of Exceptional Students: Core Knowledge) 60 multiple-choice questions 1 hour	✔			
Practice Test 2 (Special Education: Core Knowledge and Applications) 120 multiple-choice questions 2 hours		✔		
Practice Test 3 (Special Education: Core Knowledge and Mild to Moderate Applications) 90 multiple-choice questions 3 integrated constructed-response questions 2 hours			✔	
Practice Test 4 (Special Education: Core Knowledge and Severe to Profound Applications) 90 multiple-choice questions 3 integrated constructed-response questions 2 hours				✔

Who Takes the Test?

Most people who take these tests are seeking initial licensure, although an experienced teacher may seek additional certification in special education at another time in his/her career. In any case, you should check with your state's education agency to determine which Praxis examination(s) you should take; the ETS Praxis website (*www.ets.org/Praxis/*) and registration bulletin may also help you determine the test(s) you need to take for certification. You should also consult your education program for its own test requirements. Remember that colleges and universities often require Praxis examinations for entry into programs, for graduation, and for the completion of a teacher certification program. These requirements may differ from the baseline requirements the state has for teacher certification. You will need to meet both sets of requirements.

When Should I Take the Test?

The Praxis II Special Education and Exceptional Education series of tests are for those who plan to teach special education at any grade level from preschool through grade 12. Each state establishes its own requirements for certification; some states specify the passing of other tests. Some states may require the test for initial certification; other states may require the test for beginning teachers during their first months on the job. Generally, each college and university establishes its own requirements for program admission and for graduation. Some colleges and universities require certain tests for graduation and/or for completion of a teacher education program. Check with your college and the state teacher certification agency for details.

When and Where Can I Take the Test?

ETS offers these exams seven times a year at a number of locations across the nation. The usual testing day is Saturday, but examinees may request an administration on an alternate day if a conflict—such as a religious obligation—exists.

How Do I Get More Information on the ETS Praxis Exams?

To receive information on upcoming administrations of the Praxis II 0353, 0354/5354, 0543/5543, or the 0545/5545 tests or any other ETS Praxis test, consult the ETS registration bulletin or website. Contact ETS at:

ETS-The Praxis Series
P.O. Box 6051
Princeton, NJ 08541-6051
Phone: (609) 771-7395; (800) 772-9476
Website: *www.ets.org/Praxis*
E-mail: *www.ets.org/Praxis/contact/email_Praxis* and use the online form

Special accommodations are available for candidates who are visually impaired, hearing impaired, physically disabled, or specific learning disabled. For questions concerning disability services, contact:

ETS Disability Services: (609) 771-7780; (866) 387-8602
TTY only: (609) 771-7714

Provisions are also available for examinees whose primary language is not English. The ETS registration bulletin and website include directions for those requesting such accommodations.

You can also consult ETS with regard to available test sites; reporting test scores; requesting changes in tests, centers, and dates of test; purchasing additional score reports; retaking tests; and other basic facts.

Is There a Registration Fee?

To take a Praxis examination, you must pay a registration fee, which is payable by check, money order, or with American Express, Discover, MasterCard, or Visa credit cards. In certain cases, ETS offers fee waivers. The registration bulletin and website give qualifications for receiving this benefit and describe the application process. Cash is not accepted for payment.

Can I Retake the Test?

Some states, institutions, and associations limit the number of times you can retest. Contact your state licensing authority to confirm their retest policies.

HOW TO USE THIS BOOK AND TESTWARE®

What Do I Study First?

To begin your studies, read over REA's subject reviews and follow the Study Schedule found on page 19. Take Practice Test 1 on the enclosed CD to determine your areas of weakness, and then restudy the material focusing on your specific problem areas. Studying the reviews thoroughly will reinforce the basic skills you need to do well on the exam. Make sure to follow up your diagnostic work by taking the practice exams in this book so that you will be familiar with the format and procedures involved with taking the actual test.

When Should I Start Studying?

It is never too early to start studying; the earlier you begin, the more time you will have to sharpen your skills. Do not procrastinate! Cramming is not an effective way to study because it does not allow you the time needed to learn the test material.

FORMAT OF THE TESTS

Computer-Based Testing

The tests numbered 5345, 5543, and 5545 are offered only on computer at flexible times and locations throughout the year. Minimal computer and typing skills are required to complete the computer-based tests. You need to be comfortable with a Windows environment, using a mouse (including clicking, double-clicking, dragging, and scrolling), and typing at a rate (approximately 30 words per minute) that will allow you to complete the assignment in the allotted time. In computer-based testing, examinees complete the tests by selecting answers to multiple-choice questions on-screen.

You may only take a computer-delivered Praxis test once every 30 consecutive days, not including the day of your test. If you wish to retest, you must select a test date that is more than 30 days after your previous test date.

Multiple-Choice Question Formats

The multiple-choice questions assess a beginning teacher's knowledge of certain job-related skills and knowledge. Four choices are available on each multiple-choice question; the options bear the letters A through D. The exam uses four types of multiple-choice questions:

1. The Roman Numeral Multiple-Choice Question

2. The "Which of the Following?" Multiple-Choice Question

3. The "Complete the Statement" Multiple-Choice Question

4. The Multiple-Choice Question with Qualifiers

The following sections describe each type of question and suggested strategies.

Roman Numeral Multiple-Choice Questions

Perhaps the most difficult of the types of multiple-choice questions is the Roman numeral question because it allows for more than one correct answer. **Strategy:** Assess each answer before looking at the Roman numeral choices. Consider the following Roman numeral multiple-choice question designed to test science content knowledge:

The drop in temperature that occurs when sugar is added to coffee is the result of

    I.   sugar passing from a solid to a liquid state
   II.   sugar absorbing calories from the water
  III.   heat becoming latent when it was sensible

    (A) I only
    (B) I and II only
    (C) I, II and III
    (D) I and III only

In reviewing the questions, you should note that you may choose two or three answers by selecting (B), (C), or (D), while it is possible to choose only one answer by choosing answer (A).

The correct answer is (C) because it includes three correct statements. The sugar does pass from a solid to a liquid state (I), the sugar does absorb calories from the water (II), and the heat does become latent when it is sensible (III). Since I, II, and III are all causes of the drop in temperature when sugar is added to coffee, *all three* must be included when choosing an answer.

"Which of the Following?" Multiple-Choice Questions

In a "Which of the Following?" question, one of the answers is correct among the various choices.

Strategy: Form a sentence by replacing the first part of the question with each of the answer choices in turn, and then determine which of the resulting sentences is correct. Consider the following example:

Which of the following is a nondegenerative disorder that affects motor function as a result of brain injury that occurred before, during, or shortly after birth?

    (A) Muliple sclerosis
    (B) Cerebral palsy
    (C) Muscular dystrophy
    (D) Cystic fibrosis

To answer this question you must have the basic information about the cause of each of these disorders, but using the suggested technique would help to identify the answer.

    (A) Muliple sclerosis is a nondegenerative disorder that affects motor function as a result of brain injury that occurred before, during, or shortly after birth.
    (B) Cerebral palsy is a nondegenerative disorder that affects motor function as a result of brain injury that occurred before, during, or shortly after birth.
    (C) Muscular dystrophy is a nondegenerative disorder that affects motor function as a result of brain injury that occurred before, during, or shortly after birth.
    (D) Cystic fibrosis is a nondegenerative disorder that affects motor function as a result of brain injury that occurred before, during, or shortly after birth.

The correct answer is (B). Answer choices (A), (C), and (D) do not result from a brain injury.

Not all "Which of the Following?" multiple-choice questions are as straightforward and simple as the previous example. Consider the following multiple-choice question.

Which of the following should be of most concern to the parents of a third-grader with muscular dystrophy?

(A) Mathematics skills
(B) Mobility
(C) Reading ability
(D) Job training

The answer to the question is (B). But this question requires you to know the basic characteristics and defining factors of muscular dystrophy. Since muscular dystrophy is a congenital impairment characterized by the degeneration and weakness of muscles, the parents should not be concerned about either the mathematics or reading skills of their child, nor would they be worried about job training for a third-grader. Therefore, the answer choice of most concern would be mobility.

Strategy: Underline key information as you read the question. In the question above, two pieces of information are key: (1) the fact that the child is a third-grader, or eight-years-old, and (2) the disability in question, muscular dystrophy.

"Complete the Statement" Multiple-Choice Questions

The "Complete the Statement" multiple-choice question consists of an incomplete statement for which you must select the answer choice that will complete the statement correctly. Here is an example:

Using student classwork to evaluate progress and adapt instruction is known as

(A) guided practice
(B) curriculum-based assessment
(C) standardized achievement testing
(D) summative assessment

The correct answer is (B). Since students' work inherently reflects the curriculum, the assessment is curriculum-based. Guided practice is not an evaluation tool, it is a teaching strategy used to provide instruction. Option (C) is incorrect because standardized tests compare students' scores to their cohort based on age. And summative assessments are used to determine whether students are meeting core requirements, not to direct instruction, so (D) is incorrect.

Multiple-Choice Questions with Qualifiers

Some of the multiple-choice questions may contain qualifiers—words like *most, not, least,* and *except*. These added words make the test questions more difficult because rather than having to choose the best answer, as is usually the case, you now must select by evaluating the conditions set by the qualifiers.

Strategy: Circle the qualifier. It is easy to forget to select the negative; circling the qualifier in the question stem is a flag. This will serve as a reminder as you are reading the question and especially if you must re-read or check the answer at a later time. Now consider this question with a qualifier:

Which of the following statements reflects the **MOST** likely the reason that some culturally diverse school populations are over-represented in special education programs?

   (A) Lack of support for linguistic skills
   (B) Inaccurate assessment process and tools
   (C) Teachers believe they cannot learn as well as their peers.
   (D) Parents with limited skills do not understand the process.

This question asks you to make a judgment about which of the choices is the most reasonable among those choices given. It requires that you know something about the process by which students are identified as needing special interventions. The answer to the question is (B). Some professionals believe that the assessment process and instruments inaccurately identify at-risk youths as learning disabled or mentally retarded.

A good rule of thumb is to budget approximately one minute on each multiple-choice question for each of the practice tests—and on the real exams, of course. The reviews in this book will help you sharpen the basic skills needed to approach the exam and offer you strategies for attacking the questions. By using the reviews in conjunction with the practice tests, you will better prepare yourself for the actual tests.

Integrated Constructed-Response Questions

For the Special Education: Core Knowledge and Mild to Moderate Applications or the Special Education: Core Knowledge and Severe to Profound Applications exams, the test-taker must answer 90 multiple-choice questions and write three essays over the course of two hours. If you spend approximately a minute on each multiple-choice question, that will leave you with approximately 30 minutes for the three constructed-response questions—roughly 10 minutes each. Obviously if you spend less than a minute per multiple-choice question, you will be able to spend more time on your constructed-response questions, which account for 25 percent of the your score. The questions could address any of the following topics:

1. Development and Characteristics of Learners

2. Planning and the Learning Environment

3. Instruction

4. Assessment

5. Foundations and Professional Responsibilities

It is important for anyone preparing for these tests to demonstrate not only knowledge of the content of each subject, but also theoretical reasons and methodological practices that can be used in a classroom setting. This book will provide a review of the basic concepts as well as the theoretical approaches to curriculum, the learning environment, and delivery of services. But, before we examine the subject areas, it is important to consider the task at hand when it comes to answering the test questions.

The constructed-response questions are presented in the form of specific teaching situations in which the writer is asked to discuss an instructional approach, develop an instructional goal, or solve a pedagogical problem by outlining the steps to achieve that goal or solve that problem. In essence, ETS is using a Problem-Based Learning (PBL) approach in this assessment. As Macdonald and Savin-Baden (2004) explain, this type of assessment places the test-taker in the future classroom context in order to assess what the professional will do in practice. This kind of task asks the writer not only to remember the important content he or she has learned, but also to synthesize that information with skills and experiences gleaned from classroom observations, student teaching, and prepared lessons. Thus, it is important for the test-taker to recall these important teacher education experiences when constructing a response. In short, the constructed-response scenarios ask you to activate prior knowledge and then to elaborate on what you would do in a particular pedagogical situation. A problem or a series of problems is presented to the test-taker. While the situation is challenging, it is also a real-life scenario, and the test-taker must reflect on that situation and suggest meaningful ways to address it.

Given the challenges of this type of assessment, how might you write a solid response to this kind of essay question? It helps to first understand the format of these questions. The test question is presented first as a scenario, followed by a series of questions asking you to address that scenario. For example:

In a third grade class, students are preparing to write an Animal Report. Each student has read about his or her animal in books and on the Internet. Each student has been asked to re-read the information and write down important facts about the animal in a chart.

> *List five important steps the students can follow in an effort to help them use the writing process to complete their reports.*

> *Describe two ways the teacher could further assist the students in the classroom. The first example should suggest a way to help the students with written expression. The second example should suggest a way to help them with mechanics.*

How should you approach this question? The following steps will help you break down the scenario.

Read the question.   The most important thing to remember when you are answering an essay question is that you need to read the entire question and answer all parts of the question. In order to read the question very closely, you must recognize key words and phrases in the question. You should be on the lookout for these key words, underline them, and realize what they are asking you to do.

In our example, the writer is being asked to list five steps and describe two ways—one being with written expression and the other with mechanics. Commonly used key words in these types of questions include the following:

DESCRIBE—means examine, analyze, and present your understanding of the situation by including details. Here's a different example that asks the test-taker to describe how s/he would respond in the given classroom situation. The answer models what might be the introductory paragraph to the response.

Example: *Describe* scaffolding and discuss how it can be used when teaching persuasive writing in a 5th grade classroom.

Answer: Scaffolding is the idea that teachers provide temporary assistance to students by demonstrating strategies and then eventually shifting the responsibility of the task onto the student. A fifth grade teacher can provide scaffolding to her students by generating a list of structured questions and eventually encouraging students to generate their own questions of inquiry. This essay will explain how that process can take place.

EXPLAIN—means to analyze the problem and interpret an approach by breaking it into parts and giving examples and details to support your answer.

Example: *Explain* three approaches you would take to support emergent reading in a kindergarten classroom.

Answer: Emergent reading is a theory that in the first five years of life, literacy develops gradually as children emerge from being non-readers to being readers. While there are numerous strategies a kindergarten teacher should employ in a classroom of emergent readers, three important ones are shared reading, partner reading, and using a word wall.

Understand what the question is asking.   Look at it to see how it is broken down into parts. Let's go back to our initial test-taking example:

In a third grade class, students are preparing to write an Animal Report. Each student has read about his or her animal in books and on the Internet. Each student has been asked to re-read the information and write down important facts about the animal in a chart.

List five important steps the students can follow in an effort to help them use the writing process to complete their reports.

Describe two ways the teacher could further assist the students in the classroom. The first example should suggest a way to help the students with written expression. The second example should suggest a way to help them with mechanics.

What is this question really asking you to do? It seems that the question is asking you to envision a research situation and to evaluate where the students are in the process. Then, you are being asked to see that process through by explaining five more steps that would guide the students through to the finish line: the research report. You are also being asked to explain two classroom approaches you would take to help students with the expression and mechanics of writing.

Plan your time.   Say to yourself, "I'm going to brainstorm my ideas and write an outline for the next ten minutes. Then, I'm going to write for fifteen minutes. Finally, I will proofread for the remaining five minutes."

Brainstorm.   Jot down your ideas for the response. Make sure that you provide reasons for your assertions. Underline key words as you brainstorm.

For our sample question, here is an example of a list of ideas from initial brainstorming.

- Give students an outline to follow of specific things I want them to look for in their own animal—this is a kind of scaffolding—I'd want them to ultimately learn this skill and be able to do it on their own later.
- They should include the scientific name of the animal, the group it is from, what it looks like, what it eats, where it lives, and its predators.
- Perhaps with the outline they could go back to their sources and look for additional information to take notes on. I could do this as a concept map.
- Drafting should be at least four paragraphs. I could do the four square method for that.
- I'd like them to peer edit. I could make a page they could follow and pair them up according to strengths and weaknesses each student has.
- For the two classroom activities, I could ask students to read their writing aloud to me, we could edit in a conference situation (this will help with mechanics), I could ask students to type their drafts on the computer and use spell-check and grammar-check. For written expression—I could write comments on drafts and conference with students to tell them where to go further.

Come up with an outline.   Your outline is your best plan of attack. An ideal outline is a well-organized response that collects your thoughts in preparation for writing your actual essay. The outline will flow naturally from the words underlined in your brainstorming notes.

1. Introduction

2. Five Steps:

   a. Give them my outline with specific questions they are all looking to answer.
   b. Concept map
   c. Four Square Method
   d. Drafting
   e. Peer Editing

3. Two classroom approaches:

   a. Conferences about where they can go further and to help them edit—expression
   b. Using the computer in the classroom to type up drafts (spell/grammar check)—mechanics

Structure your response.   You need to have an introduction that briefly and succinctly explains what you will be arguing: this is your central claim. An easy way to do this is to "turn the question around" by making sure that you not only understand what it is asking but also that you have indicated what position you will take regarding it. For example:

> Introduction: There are many approaches a teacher of third grade students can use in showing his or her students how to write a research report about a specific animal. The following five steps and two classroom approaches will demonstrate how the teacher can help students write thorough and balanced reports.

Then, each paragraph you write needs to be guided by a topic sentence that not only refers back to your introduction but also is supported by details, examples, and evidence. Ideas need to be connected to other ideas by using transitional words, phrases, and sentences.

Examples of transitional words: *first, second, third, finally, in addition, furthermore, moreover, therefore, thus, consequently, in short, in summary, overall.*

Finally, you need to include a conclusion that restates the main points that you have made and summarizes where you have taken the reader.

Write your response.   Make sure that you are thoroughly and concisely answering the question by providing details that indicate that you understand content, theory, and practice. Get to the point and express your ideas simply and clearly. Present evidence to back up your claims. Avoid fancy language and over-the-top vocabulary. Also, don't fill your answer with unnecessary information, and avoid repeating yourself. Your reader will recognize if you are padding your response. Don't challenge the premise of the question or try to change it. Stay on topic and demonstrate your knowledge of the field. Write quickly and legibly—you won't have time to re-copy your answer.

This is the final response to the animal report scenario.

While there are many approaches a third grade teacher can use in showing students how to write a detailed research report about a specific animal, the following five steps and two classroom approaches will explain how he or she can help students to write thorough and balanced animal reports.

At this point in the research process, the students have selected an animal, done some reading, and taken notes. Initially, I would give students an outline of specific things I want them to look for as they are researching their own animals. I realize that this is what Lev Vygotsky would refer to as a kind of scaffolding: it's a skill I want to show them now in the hopes that they will be able to do it on their own later. In the outline I'd give them, I would ask students to look for the scientific name of the animal, the group it is from, what it looks like, what it eats, where it lives, and what its predators are. They could use the outline to go back to their sources, look for additional information, and take more notes. Next, I would model for students what the outline would look like as a concept map, and then have them make their own maps of the information. Since I want their drafts to be at least four paragraphs, I would show the students the four square method to give them a graphic organizer prior to drafting. After the drafting process, I'd ask them to peer edit. I could make a page they could follow and pair them up according to the various strengths and weaknesses of each student.

For my two classroom activities, I would write comments on the drafts and conference with them individually, first listening to them read aloud and then showing them what works and also where they could expand. In my conference, I'd use the PQP method whereby I'd encourage them (praise), point out areas for further clarification (question), and show them areas that need more attention (polish). This approach would help them with their written expression. Second, after giving them a mini-lesson on how to cite their sources using a bibliographic entry, I would try to help them with mechanics by asking them to type their drafts and bibliographies on the computer and use spell check and grammar check.

Overall, I believe these approaches would help my third grade students to gain a deeper understanding of the writing process as it relates to research. They will have taken notes on facts, organized those facts into an outline, written a draft, edited it, and composed a final copy, including a bibliography.

Re-read your work to revise sentences and to proofread for sentence-level errors. There may be sentences that need to be refined for greater clarity. You may have accidentally omitted words. Or, there may be mistakes in spelling, grammar, and mechanics that need to be addressed before the thirty minutes are up. Don't forget to plan your time to allow for this final step.

A recap of the steps we've looked at here:

1. *Read the question.* Underline key words.

2. *Understand what the question is asking*.

3. *Plan your time*.

4. *Brainstorm and underline key ideas*.

5. *Come up with an outline*.

6. *Structure your response.* Introduction, body with transitions, and conclusion.

7. *Write your response*.

8. *Re-read your work to revise sentences and to proofread for sentence level errors*.

It's important to note that all of this happens in the ideal scenario, and you may not have enough time for every aspect of the writing process mentioned here. Nevertheless, at the very minimum you should plan your answer (2-4 minutes), answer the question (5 minutes), include an introduction to that answer, write clearly, and proofread (last 1 minute).

You have learned through your course work and your practical experience in schools most of what you need to know to answer the questions on the test. In your education classes, you gained the expertise to make important decisions about situations you will face as a teacher; in your content courses, you should have acquired the knowledge you will need to teach specific content. The reviews in this book will help you fit the information you have acquired into its specific testable category. Reviewing your class notes and textbooks along with systematic use of this book will give you an excellent springboard for passing the Praxis II: Special Education exams.

HOW THE TESTS ARE SCORED

How are the Multiple-Choice Questions Scored?

The number of raw points awarded on the Praxis exams is based on the number of correct answers you tally up. Most Praxis examinations vary by edition, which means that each test has several variations that contain different questions. The different questions are intended to measure the same general types of knowledge or skills. However, there is no way to guarantee that the questions on all editions, or versions of the test will have the same degree of difficulty. To avoid penalizing test-takers who answer more difficult questions, the initial scores are adjusted for difficulty by using a statistical process known as equating. To avoid confusion between the *adjusted* and *unadjusted scores*, ETS reports the *adjusted scores* on a score scale that makes them clearly different from the *unadjusted scores*. *Unadjusted scores* or "raw scores" are simply the number of questions answered correctly. *Adjusted scores*, which are equated to the scale ETS uses for reporting the scores are called "scaled scores." For each edition of a Praxis test, a "raw-to-scale conversion table" is used to translate raw to scaled scores. The easier the questions are on a test edition, the more questions must be answered correctly to earn a given scaled score.

The college or university in which you are enrolled may set passing scores for the completion of your teacher education program and for graduation. Be sure to check the requirements in the catalogues or bulletins. You will also want to talk with your advisor. The passing scores for the Praxis II tests vary from state to state. To find out which of the Praxis II tests your state requires and what your state's set passing score is, contact your state's education department directly.

To gauge how you are doing using the multiple-choice sections of our practice tests, if you get 75% correct, you can be assured that you passed the practice test.

How Will the Constructed-Responses be Scored?

ETS invites seasoned educators to score the constructed responses on examinations based on a three-point, holistic grading rubric. These test evaluations are "normed," which means that the group reads, scores, and discusses some papers together. They engage in a conversation about what kind of an essay merits what kind of a score. By discussing responses and practicing the evaluation process together, an effort towards greater consistency and consensus is made. As a result, evaluators understand how an essay earns a score at each stage of the rubric. Another important measure taken by ETS: essays are read by two evaluators, with the first scorer's decision hidden from the second scorer; each response is awarded points by adding those two scores together. If the evaluators differ from each other by more than one point, a third reader is brought in to evaluate the essay, and the score is determined based on that individual's unbiased input.

Constructed-Response Scoring Rubric

Score	Comment
3	This response not only answers the question clearly, it also shows superior understanding of the subject matter, human growth and development, and pedagogy. The answer is organized and key ideas are developed fully. The examples and details used support the major points being made.
2	This response is adequate, it demonstrates an accurate, although limited understanding of content and pedagogy as they relate to the question at hand. This response answers some parts of the question but not others. It shows some understanding of content and pedagogy, but may have a few factual errors. Only some details and examples are provided.

(continued)

| 1 | This response doesn't answer the question and shows a deficit in knowledge of content and pedagogy. There are problems with organization of ideas and development of them. |
| 0 | This response was left empty, discusses the wrong issue, or can't be read. |

Score Reporting

When Will I Receive My Examinee Score Report and in What Form Will It Be?

ETS mails Praxis II test-score reports six weeks after the test date. Score reports will list your current score and the highest score you have earned on each test you have taken over the last 10 years.

Along with your score report, ETS will provide you with a booklet that offers details on your scores. For each test date, you may request that ETS send a copy of your scores to as many as three score recipients, provided that each institution or agency is eligible to receive the scores.

STUDYING FOR THE TESTS

It is critical to your success that you study effectively. The following are a few tips to help get you going:

- Choose a time and place for studying that works best for you. Some people set aside a certain number of hours every morning to study; others may choose to study at night before retiring. Only you know what is most effective for you.

- Use your time wisely and be consistent. Work out a study routine and stick to it; don't let your personal schedule interfere. Remember, seven weeks of studying is a modest investment to put you on your chosen path.

- Don't cram the night before the test. You may have heard many amazing tales about effective cramming, but don't kid yourself: most of them are false, and the rest are about exceptional people who, by definition, aren't like most of us.

- When you take the practice tests, try to make your testing conditions as much like the actual test as possible. Turn off your television, radio, and phone. Sit down at a quiet table free from distraction, and time yourself.

- As you complete the practice test, score your test and thoroughly review the explanations to the questions you answered incorrectly.

- Keep track of your scores. By doing so, you will be able to gauge your progress and discover your strengths and weaknesses. Carefully study the material relevant to your areas of difficulty. This will build your test-taking skills and your confidence!

- Take notes on material you will want to go over again or research further. Using note cards or flashcards to record facts and information for future review is a good way to study and keep the information at your fingertips in the days to come. You can easily pull out the small note cards and review them at random moments: during a coffee break or meal, on the bus or train as you head home, or just before falling asleep. Using the cards gives you essential information at a glance, keeps you organized, and helps you master the materials.

Study Schedule

The following study schedule on the next page allows for thorough preparation to pass your particular exam(s). This is a suggested seven-week course of study. However, you can condense this schedule if you are in a time crunch or expand it if you have more time. You may decide to use your weekends for study and preparation and go about your other business during the week. You may even want to record information and listen to your mp3 player or tape as you travel in your car. However you decide to study, be sure to adhere to the structured schedule you devise.

WEEK	ACTIVITY
1	After reading the first chapter to understand the format and content of this exam, take your practice test on CD. Our computerized tests are drawn from the tests we present in our book and provide a scored report which includes a progress chart indicating the percentage right in each category. This will pinpoint your strengths and weaknesses. The instantaneous, accurate scoring allows you to customize your review process. Make sure you simulate real exam conditions when you take the test.
2	Review the explanations for the questions you missed, and review the appropriate review sections. Useful study techniques include highlighting key terms and information, taking notes as you review each section, and putting new terms and information on note cards to help retain the information.
3 and 4	Reread all your note cards, refresh your understanding of the exam's subareas and related skills, review your college textbooks, and read over notes you took in your college classes. This is also the time to consider any other supplementary materials suggested by your counselor or your state education agency.

(continued)

WEEK	ACTIVITY
5	Begin to condense your notes and findings. A structured list of important facts and concepts, based on your note cards, college textbook, course notes, and this book's review chapters will help you thoroughly review for the test. Review the answers and explanations for any questions you missed on the practice test.
6	Have someone quiz you using the note cards you created. Take another practice test, this time on CD, adhering to the time limits and simulated test-day conditions.
7	Review your areas of weakness using all your study materials. This is a good time to take the practice tests printed in this book, if time allows.

THE DAY OF THE TEST

Before the Test

- Dress comfortably in layers. You do not want to be distracted by being too hot or too cold while you are taking the test.

- Check your registration ticket to verify your arrival time.

- Plan to arrive at the test center early. This will allow you to collect your thoughts and relax before the test; your early arrival will also spare you the anguish that comes with being late.

- Make sure to bring your admission ticket with you and two forms of identification, one of which must contain a recent photograph, your name, and your signature (e.g., a driver's license). You will not gain entry to the test center without proper identification.

- Bring several sharpened No. 2 pencils with erasers for the multiple-choice section; pens if you are taking another test that might have essay or constructed-response questions. You will not want to waste time searching for a replacement pencil or pen if you break a pencil point or run out of ink when you are trying to complete your test. The proctor will not provide pencils or pens at the test center.

- Wear a watch to the test center so you can apportion your testing time wisely. You may not, however, wear one that makes noise or that will otherwise disturb the other test-takers.

- Leave all dictionaries, textbooks, notebooks, briefcases, and packages at home. You may not take these items into the test center.

- Do not eat or drink too much before the test. The proctor will not allow you to make up time you miss if you have to take a bathroom break. You will not be allowed to take materials with you, and you must secure permission before leaving the room.

During the Test

- Pace yourself. ETS administers the Praxis II test in one sitting with no breaks.

- Follow all of the rules and instructions that the test proctor gives you. Proctors will enforce these procedures to maintain test security. If you do not abide by the regulations, the proctor may dismiss you from the test and notify ETS to cancel your score.

- Listen closely as the test instructor provides the directions for completing the test. Follow the directions carefully.

- Be sure to mark only one answer per multiple-choice question, erase all unwanted answers and marks completely, and fill in the answers darkly and neatly. There is no penalty for guessing at an answer, do not leave any answer ovals blank. Remember: a blank oval is just scored as wrong, but a guessed answer has a chance of being right!

Take the test and do your best! Afterward, make notes about the multiple-choice questions you remember. You may not share this information with others, but you may find that the information proves useful on other exams that you take. Go home and relax!

Understanding Special Education and Exceptional Students

HUMAN DEVELOPMENT AND BEHAVIOR AS RELATED TO STUDENTS WITH DISABILITIES

Everyone is unique, and developmental stages are approached at different times. But as children grow, they usually follow a typical developmental schedule. Children with disabilities may struggle in developing these skills that their typical peers develop so naturally. By understanding the differences between typical students and students with disabilities, special educators will be better equipped to enable students to develop necessary skills.

Social and Emotional Development and Behavior

Students with disabilities often have social difficulties. They may struggle in developing positive relationships with their classmates, parents, and teachers. They may be unable to understand social situations and may not be able to think of themselves and others in an appropriate social manner. They may behave inappropriately in social situations, while missing social behaviors that are typically expected of them by others.

At times these social difficulties are **internalizing**—the students are hurting themselves through this behavior. For instance, students may act shy and be unwilling to interact with others, instead keeping to themselves. They may behave depressed and withdrawn. Or they may display obsessive-compulsive behavior that seems odd to others and causes them to be ostracized.

Other students with disabilities may display **externalizing** behaviors. For example, they may behave hyperactive in class, disturbing other students and creating trouble. Or they may be aggressive toward their classmates, who begin to resent them and begin fighting back. Externalizing behaviors, besides not gaining the student friends, often creates enemies for the students as well.

This is not an either/or—students with disabilities often display both internalizing and externalizing behaviors. A student who tends to be shy and withdrawn when left to himself or herself may become aggressive when the teacher demands participation. A student who often is hyperactive during class time may act depressed when not around others.

At times, a child's social difficulties are inadvertently created by the teacher. Teachers sometimes buy into the idea that the child with learning difficulties is somehow inferior to the other students, and they pass this attitude on to the students. Students who are stigmatized have even greater difficulty succeeding socially, and it always behooves the teacher to take special care in attitudes shown toward every student.

Studies show that students with disabilities interact far more with their general education teacher than with their typical peers. This is not a positive finding, however. Students with disabilities are more likely to approach the teacher when they have a question than they are to approach a classmate. They may ask the teacher inappropriate questions—questions that were just answered or that have no bearing on the topic at hand.

Language Development and Behavior

Students with disabilities often have difficulty expressing what they want to say. They may use incorrect grammar or may not be able to think of the correct word. They may be unable to shift vocabulary for the appropriate social contexts and may use profanity in the classroom. They may not provide enough information, assuming that the listener knows information that was not provided, and they may suddenly change topics without cautioning the listener.

These students also often have difficulty understanding the language of others. They may not be able to follow directions and may not even be able to realize they did not understand what was said. They often have trouble understanding figurative language or confuse multiple meanings of the same word. They very often struggle with understanding more abstract concepts.

Students who struggle with oral communication likely have problems with written communication as well. A poor spoken vocabulary is a good indicator of poor reading vocabulary.

So what exactly is involved in a student's language development? There are several components of language.

- **Semantics.** Semantics refers to the concept or content. It is the idea that is being communicated.

- **Phonology.** Phonology is the sounds produced through speech. A *phoneme* is a unique sound.

- **Morphology.** Morphology focuses on the structure of words. A *morpheme* is the smallest unit of language that still has meaning. There are two kinds of morphemes. A root word is a word that can stand by itself. Affixes, such as prefixes and suffixes, must be added to existing words to be used.

- **Syntax.** Syntax refers to sentence structure. In English, a sentence is structured in a particular way. Usually it is noun, then verb, then object.

- **Pragmatics.** Pragmatics refers to the way we use language to communicate. Once students are more adept in using language, they are able to change their method of communication depending on the context they are in.

Students who miss developing one of these components of language at the appropriate time will require intervention services. Otherwise they will have difficulty learning to read along with the class.

Cognition

Jean Piaget, a Swiss biologist, created the theory of cognition. Piaget's theory suggests that as children develop, their thinking progresses through several stages. Throughout each stage, their minds become more structured and logical.

These stages of cognitive development are not distinct from one another. Instead, each child slowly passes through each stage as his or her thinking process becomes more defined. Children develop at different rates and so will reach each stage at different ages.

- *Sensorimotor stage.* During this first stage, the infant builds and understanding of the environment through exploration. At first the infant focuses only on his or her own body. Slowly they discover the world surrounding them as well and begin interacting with it. Most children operate at this cognitive stage at ages 0 to 24 months.

- *Preoperational stage.* The child develops language skills and is able to think more symbolically. He or she has difficulty seeing things from another's perspective and instead is very self-centered. Further along in this period, the child begins to think more systematically and is able to complete simple operational problems. Children in this stage still find it difficult to understand the idea of **conservation**, that even if something changes its shape the amount will still stay the same. Children usually go through this stage during the ages of 2 to 7.

- *Concrete operational stage.* Children at this age are able to focus on more than one idea at a time. They therefore are able to understand that others may have a different perspective than they do and that people can see things in different ways. These children still think very concretely, based on their immediate environment, and have difficulty thinking abstractly. Models and illustrations are important teaching tools to use with this age. This usually is applicable to ages 7 to 11.

- *Formal operational stage.* Students during this stage no longer depend on concrete representations; instead, they are able to reason abstractly. They also are able to organize calculations systematically in order to solve problems in an organized fashion. Students usually begin developing formal operational thinking during the ages of 11 to 15, and this formulation continues during adulthood. Even adults do not always use formal operational thinking when the situation warrants it.

Students with disabilities may have difficulty progressing from one stage of cognitive thinking to another as easily as their typical peers. Teachers must always take care to reach each student at his or her present level of functioning.

Physical Development, Including Motor and Sensory

Certain disability categories are physical in nature. This includes orthopedic impairments, traumatic brain injury, and other health impairments. Students who do not properly develop physically will have limitations that may affect their ability to access the curriculum.

There are many different kinds of physical disabilities, and students' educational needs will vary greatly. However, students with physical disabilities do not always require an individualized education program (IEP). Many will require only a 504 plan, which states that their physical needs will be met in the classroom. Once those needs are met, the student is able to learn the same way as everyone else. Here's a basic guide to categories you'll need to know:

- Cerebral palsy (CP). Athetoid cerebral palsy causes the student's limbs to stiffen, while spastic cerebral palsy causes the limbs to jerk. CP is often caused by oxygen deprivation in the brain before or during birth.

- Spinal cord injury. The effect of spinal cord injuries depends on which area of the spinal cord was injured. Paraplegia limits movement of the lower half of the body, while quadriplegia affects the upper- and lower-half of the body.

- Spina bifida. Spina bifida is a spinal cord injury the student was born with.

- Muscular dystrophy. People with muscular dystrophy have their muscles attacked and weakened by their own bodies.

- Amputations. An amputation is a missing limb of the body—either because it was removed for some reason, or because the person was born without it.

- Traumatic brain injury (TBI). Traumatic brain injury is a separate category from orthopedic impairments. This includes any injury to the brain caused through trauma. Effects of TBI may include fatigue, sensitivity to light and sound, and difficulty learning new information.

Students with physical disabilities often have impaired motor ability. They may be unable to move their arms and legs the way their typical peers can. They will therefore have difficulty with writing or working with classroom materials. The teacher will need to seek ways to modify the classroom environment, such as by providing a special keyboard with which to write, and the student will likely receive a related service such as physical or occupational therapy to help him or her succeed.

Students may also experience **sensory loss** due to their disability. They may be unable to feel what they touch or may be unable to sense whether it is hot or cold. Often their sense of vision and hearing is also affected. This causes the student to become cut off from what is going on in the classroom, and the teacher must work to address these needs as well.

CHARACTERISTICS OF STUDENTS WITH DISABILITIES

What are the characteristics of students with disabilities? As you will see, it is impossible to provide a blanket answer to this question. A huge range and variety of disabilities exist. Let us take a look at the factors affecting the major disabilities.

Affective and Social-Adaptive Factors

The United States is considered to be a melting pot of different cultures. The American culture is known as a macroculture, or shared culture. Microcultures are cultures within the macroculture that share many aspects of the culture but at the same time are distinct cultures. Often, it is these differences that cause the appearance of a disability—when, in fact, cultural difference rather than a disability cause the academic struggles.

The same is true for students whose first language is not English and who are linguistically diverse instead. Approximately one-fifth of Americans speak a language other than English, and millions of students do not speak English as their first language. These students have difficulty in class due to the language barrier. It is important to differentiate between these students and those who are struggling due to a disability, although there often is an overlap. Students with disabilities whose first language is not English will need these unique needs addressed as well.

Other areas of diversity also may become confused with disability. Gender differences may be wrongly interpreted as being indicative of a disability—the student may be identified as having ADHD, while in fact he is just being a boy. Socioeconomic factors may interfere with the identification process as well; these students may value things other than school, or come from a familial background that did not prepare them as well for the expectations of the classroom, and so they will struggle. It is important that these difficulties not be confused with disability.

Genetic, Medical, Motor, Sensory, or Chronological Age Factors

Many disabilities do in fact have a genetic component to them. Disability, therefore, often runs in families. **Familiality studies** are studies that examine the likelihood of a condition to happen in a family. These studies find that both reading difficulty and speech and language impairment are more likely to run in the family. However, they do not show that these disorders are linked to genetics—other explanations for this phenomenon, such as how the families were brought up, might be possible. Studies that compare the school performance of twins are a better indicator and seem to show that certain disorders are most likely linked to genetics.

Physical disabilities are often caused by defects in one or both parents' genes. Around one-third of those with ADHD have relatives also with ADHD, a strong indicator that this is a disorder with genetic roots. Autism has been strongly linked to genetics, although researchers are still uncertain of how the disorder is transmitted through the generations.

Some disabilities have medical components and many symptoms can therefore be alleviated through medication. ADHD is one example. Ritalin and Adderall can alleviate the symptoms of ADHD, though not of any comorbid disorders. The medication tends to have significant side effects so its use is controversial. Students with emotional disturbance often take psychiatric medication. Students with other health impairments, such as asthma, also take medication for their health conditions. None of these medications works perfectly and so the student is likely to still require services.

Students with autism are affected by **sensory** problems. Their brains map the senses incorrectly so they have trouble with sensory integration. They therefore self-stimulate and indulge in other behaviors that are considered inappropriate. Students with physical disabilities often have motor challenges, as was previously discussed.

At times, a student may be developmentally at a different stage than his or her chronological age. A student who is going through the typical stages of development, but more slowly than usual, should be given the label of **developmental delay** rather than a disability label. A disability can be diagnosed later, if problems persist when the student is older.

BASIC CONCEPTS IN SPECIAL EDUCATION

Definitions of all Major Categories and Specific Disabilities

Who is considered to have a disability? Educators do not decide this on their own. For a child to be diagnosed with a disability that is recognized under the Individuals with Disabilities Education Act (IDEA), he or she must be diagnosed with one of thirteen disability classifications provided by the IDEA.

1. *Autism.* Autism is a developmental disorder that affects the student's communication skills and social skills. Students with autism often respond differently to sensory experiences and struggle with change in their schedules.

2. *Deaf-blindness.* Children who are both deaf and blind experience communication difficulties that cannot be addressed in a program for students who are only deaf, or only blind.

3. *Deafness.* Deafness is a hearing impairment that adversely affects the child's performance in school.

4. *Emotional disturbance.* Emotional disturbance is a term that encompasses many mental and emotional disorders that affect a child's performance in school. Here is IDEA 2004's definition of emotional disturbance:

   (a) *An inability to learn that cannot be explained by intellectual, sensory, or health factors.*

   (b) *An inability to build or maintain satisfactory interpersonal relationships with peers and teachers.*

   (c) *Inappropriate types of behavior or feelings under normal circumstances.*

   (d) *A general pervasive mood of unhappiness or depression.*

   (e) *A tendency to develop physical symptoms or fears associated with personal or school problems.*

   Emotional disturbance includes schizophrenia. The term does not apply to children who are socially maladjusted, unless it is determined that they have an emotional disturbance....

5. *Hearing impairment.* This category includes all hearing impairments that affect the student's performance in school, but are not included in deafness. What is the difference between a hearing impairment and deafness? Deafness is considered to be a very severe hearing impairment. A child who is deaf is unable to respond to most or all sounds, including speech. A child with a hearing impairment has hearing difficulty that impacts his or her school performance, but the student is still able to respond to many sounds.

6. *Mental retardation.* Mental retardation is when a student's IQ and intellectual functioning are significantly below average. As the term "retardation" has come to be used in unflattering ways, many advocate that the term be changed to "intellectual disability."

7. *Multiple disabilities.* Multiple disabilities refers to students whose combination of disabilities does not allow them to benefit from programs serving students

with only one of their disabilities. This term does not include deaf-blindness, which has its own category.

8. *Orthopedic impairment.* This refers to a severe orthopedic impairment that adversely affects the student's educational performance. It may include cerebral palsy, amputations, and bone tuberculosis.

9. *Other health impairment.* This blanket term refers to disabilities other than those covered in IDEA. Here is the IDEA 2004 definition:

> *having limited strength, vitality, or alertness, including a heightened alertness to environmental stimuli, that results in limited alertness with respect to the educational environment, that—*

> *(a) is due to chronic or acute health problems such as asthma, attention deficit disorder or attention deficit hyperactivity disorder, diabetes, epilepsy, a heart condition, hemophilia, lead poisoning, leukemia, nephritis, rheumatic fever, sickle cell anemia, and Tourette syndrome; and*

> *(b) adversely affects a child's educational performance.*

10. *Specific learning disability.* A specific learning disability is a learning difficulty that results from a physiological process—the problem originates from the brain. The term does not include learning difficulties caused by other disability classifications, such as visual impairments, nor does it include learning difficulties caused by cultural differences, low economic status, or environmental differences. Learning disabilities may impact the child's ability to

- listen

- think

- speak

- read

- write

- spell

- do mathematical calculations

11. *Speech or language impairment.* A speech or language impairment is a communication disorder that impacts the child's ability to communicate in class, and thereby benefit from classroom instruction.

12. *Traumatic brain injury.* This is an injury to the brain caused by an external force. This is not a disability someone is born with. Many adverse conditions may

result from an injury to the brain that adversely affects the child's ability to benefit from school. Students may have difficulty with memory, attention, problem solving, and sensory, perceptual, and motor abilities, among other difficulties.

13. *Visual impairment including blindness.* This category encompasses students with all levels of vision impairment that adversely affects their school performance.

Note that to receive special education services, the student must not only be diagnosed with a disability, but that disability must be adversely impacting the student's school performance.

The Incidence and Prevalence of Various Types of Disabilities

As you can see, students with disabilities are not all the same—many disability categories exist under which each student's needs may be classified. And even within each disability classification students may have a wide range of needs. The latest report on this subject from the U.S. Department of Education, published in 2007, identifies 11.61 percent of students in grades PreK–12 as having an identified disability and receiving services under IDEA. How prevalent is student disability, and how prevalent is each kind of disability?

Less severe disabilities, including specific learning disabilities, ADHD, and speech or language impairments, are also called **high-incidence disabilities**. This is because they are far more common among students with disabilities; students with these mild disabilities account for over 90 percent of public school students who have been identified with a disability.

Specific learning disabilities (SLD) are the most common disability classification. Nearly half of students with an identified disability have been identified with a specific learning disability, and they account for 5.25 percent of the student population. Students with SLD are usually able to remain in the general education classroom and benefit when provided with the proper supports.

Around 18 percent of students served under IDEA, or 2.31 percent of all students, have speech and language impairments. Most students classified under speech or language impairment (SLI) are in preschool or elementary school. By the time students reach middle school, they have benefited enough from the interventions that they no longer require services.

Students classified under mental retardation (MR) make up around 0.94 percent of students. Often students are diagnosed with MR later in their school career. Often a less stigmatizing diagnosis is given when the child is younger, and further testing is done throughout the years. Therefore, middle schools and secondary schools generally have a greater percentage of students with MR than do elementary schools.

Around 0.90 percent of students are classified under emotional disturbance. These students sometimes are in prison or other disciplinary settings and receive their educational services there.

Nearly 84 percent of all students with disabilities make up four disability categories—specific learning disabilities, speech and language impairments, mental retardation, and emotional disturbance. Students with low-incidence disabilities make up the remaining 16 percent.

Hearing impairment is one low-incidence disability. Around 0.14 percent of students are diagnosed as hearing impaired. Visual impairments and blindness are even more uncommon; they apply to only 0.05 percent of students.

Around 0.37 percent of students have autism. Students with autism usually are unable to be included in general education classroom, even with supports. On the other hand, nearly half of students with orthopedic impairments are serviced within general education classrooms. Students with traumatic brain injury are also often accommodated appropriately in the general education setting. Students with orthopedic impairments account for 0.12 percent of all students, while students with traumatic brain injury make up 0.04 percent of students in grades PreK–12.

The category of other health impairments (OHI) includes many different disabilities. The fastest-growing condition included in this category is ADHD. Students with OHI make up 1.09 percent of students. Students placed in the deaf-blindness category, on the other hand, were calculated as being less than 0.001 percent of all students; as deafness or blindness on their own are comparatively rare, it makes sense that deaf-blindness as a condition is exceedingly rare. More students were categorized as having multiple disabilities, at 0.23 percent of the population.

The Causation and Prevention of Disability

While efforts are always underway to better serve students with special needs in the classroom, we also should be seeking to decrease incidences of disability as well. By understanding the causes of disability, one can better find ways to try and prevent more incidences of disability among students.

Statistics show that most disabilities are due to genetic factors. Genetic counseling has been shown to decrease the incidence of certain severe disabilities. Couples who undergo genetic counseling better understand the risks that may be involved and are better able to arrive at an informed decision.

During pregnancy, screening should be done to check for possible developmental disorders. If a problem is caught at this early stage, medical intervention can often be done to take care of the problem. Expectant mothers should also be offered nutritional advice so they can better care for the developing child.

Immunization is also very important. When children are immunized, certain diseases that may cause severe disability are curtailed. The practice of educating parents about the importance of immunizations and ensuring that everyone has access to immunizations is far more economically sound than providing all those services the child will require if a disability develops.

The Nature of Behaviors

Often, a student's disability causes behaviors that adversely impact his or her performance in school. These behaviors may include getting out of the seat during inappropriate times, inattention, talking, and working off-task. Adverse behaviors are especially common among students with emotional disturbance.

A special educator's job therefore cannot only be to teach the student academic material. An effective special educator will also coach the student to develop effective behaviors and decrease adverse behaviors. How is this done?

The first step is to track the occurrence of the desired or undesired behavior. To address a problem, we must first have solid data that inform us what the problem is.

Frequency

To track the frequency of a behavior, the data collector tracks how many times this behavior occurred within a certain amount of time. This is especially useful for short-lived behaviors, such as nail biting. The teacher may use tally marks to mark off each time the student bites his or her nails.

Duration

The duration is how long the behavior lasts. This is useful for behaviors that take longer periods of time. An example would be if a student gets out of his or her seat, or talks to a neighbor during inappropriate times. A teacher may use a stopwatch to track the duration of the behavior.

Intensity

The intensity of the behavior refers to the severity of the behavior. The teacher or other professional gathering data tracks how severe the behavior was at each given time.

Degrees of Severity

The frequency, duration, and intensity of the behavior will determine the severity of the behavior. Later, when the classroom professionals go back to analyze the data, this information will prove very useful. The data will show whether this behavior occurs more frequently during certain times of day. Perhaps the intensity of the behavior increases during certain events, such as when the student is given directions or is expected to transition to another activity. The duration of the behavior will also vary according to different factors, and after data collection a pattern should emerge.

The Classification of Students with Disabilities

To receive special education services under IDEA, a child must be diagnosed with a disability—and given a specific disability category. Classification is easy when the subject of the classification is a variety of cakes in a bakery. But when it is children who are being classified, it becomes more complicated. What are some of the issues with disability classifications?

Labeling of Students

By assigning a disability classification, we are essentially labeling the student as a child with a particular disability. How does labeling affect the student?

Labels often are found to stigmatize students. When others hear that the student has been identified with a particular disability, they may make assumptions about the student before having met or worked with him or her. In addition, people unfamiliar with the terminology of special education may misconstrue labels and disability categories. Parents and paraprofessionals may wind up believing something about the student that is untrue and potentially harmful.

So should we work to get rid of labels? Not necessarily. Labels allow us to differentiate between who should qualify for services under IDEA. Labels also allow special education professionals to communicate with other professionals more easily and meaningfully.

The solution is to take care to recognize the limitations of disability categories. A child should never be viewed by his or her label. Instead, special education teachers and those working with them should remember that every child is different. Within each disability category are students with very varied needs. Each child has the right to an education particularly suited to his or her needs, and it is those particulars that should be noted.

ADHD   Attention deficit hyperactivity disorder (ADHD) is quite common in schools. Although ADHD is not a disability classification under IDEA, students with ADHD often require special services in order to benefit from classroom instruction. To enable these students with ADHD to be serviced, students are either classified as OHI—other health impairments—or under Section 504 of the Rehabilitation Act. Section 504 will be further discussed in Chapter 6.

The symptoms of ADHD can be divided into three categories. The first is inattentiveness, or lack of attention; students have difficulty paying attention to what is going on in class, and instead focus elsewhere. They make careless mistakes in their work and have difficulty following instructions and finishing their work. They have difficulty with organization and often lose their belongings. They are easily distracted and even when spoken to directly may not seem to listen.

The next is hyperactivity. Students with ADHD who have symptoms of hyperactivity have difficulty sitting still. They leave their seats at inappropriate times and run or climb. They talk excessively and are constantly on the move.

The last category of ADHD symptoms is impulsivity. Students with ADHD often have difficulty waiting for their turn. They shout out the answers to questions and interrupt private conversations.

These symptoms will all interfere with student performance in the classroom. Although ADHD is not specifically addressed in IDEA, it is important to ensure that students with ADHD receive the supports they require in order to succeed.

The Implications of the Classification Process for the Persons Classified

What does it mean when a student is assigned to a disability classification? Simply that this child has one of the thirteen disability categories under IDEA, and this disability affects his or her ability to benefit from class instruction. The disability classification allows the child to benefit from services under IDEA.

The Influence of Level of Severity and Presence of Multiple Exceptionalities on Students with Disabilities

Until 1997, special education law differentiated between levels of severity of disabilities. Severe disabilities included severe emotional disturbance, including schizophrenia; autism; severe and profound mental retardation; and those with severe multiple disabilities. Students with severe disabilities often have severe communication difficulties; they may even be nonverbal. They may exhibit severe abnormal behaviors such as self-mutilation, temper tantrums, and self-stimulation. They may also have very fragile physical conditions.

This definition of levels of severity disappeared with the passage of IDEA in 1997. It was deemed unhelpful, as it took portions of students from across several disability categories and lumped them together into a new category. This only confused teachers trying to create a personalized education plan for the student.

Advocacy organizations over the years have suggested new definitions for levels of severity. According to TASH (TASH.org) emphasis should be placed on the amount and types of support the student requires, rather than on characteristics the student exhibits. A student who requires long-term support in major life activities, such as feeding, would be considered as having a severe disability.

Multiple exceptionalities is another label that is often confused. Multiple exceptionalities is a category that is still in use today—under IDEA—the Multiple Disabilities category. Multiple disabilities does not include deaf-blindness, which has been given its own category, as discussed earlier.

There is tremendous variety within the multiple disability classification. School districts often use the terms to classify students who require many related services, as well as students who have severe mental retardation along with a physical disability.

CO-OCCURRING (DUAL DIAGNOSIS) CONDITIONS

Co-occurring, or comorbid, disabilities are disabilities that often occur together. The IEP team will identify the student under the student's primary disability classification. So if a student has both ADHD and a specific learning disability, the IEP team will likely classify that student under SLD. At other times, the second condition is severe enough that the student can no longer be serviced with students identified with their primary disability classification. It is then that the student is identified as having multiple disabilities, as discussed above.

So what are some common co-occurring conditions? ADHD and learning disabilities is one. Around one-third of students with ADHD also have a specific learning disability. SLD also co-occurs often with speech and language impairments.

In fact, speech and language impairments co-occur with a variety of disabilities. Mental retardation is one. Cerebral palsy, an orthopedic impairment, is another. Students who are deaf or have hearing impairments also will have speech and language impairments.

Children with mental retardation often have a host of co-occurring conditions. Depending on the cause of the intellectual impairment, they may have hearing loss, vision loss, and cardiac conditions. Other conditions that cause MR also lead to learning disabilities or ADHD. Emotional, behavioral, and psychiatric conditions are also very common among those with MR.

Students with emotional disturbance often have specific learning disabilities or ADHD. In these cases, IEP teams tend to at first classify students with the less severe disorder, in an attempt to avoid stigmatizing the student at a young age. Teachers should, however, recognize the severity of the students' needs and work to accommodate them in order that the student's school experience can be successful.

Autism may often co-occur with mental retardation. Severe and multiple disabilities, as well as deaf-blindness, also co-occur with mental retardation.

In each case, the school district and the IEP team classify the student under the primary disability, and note the presence of the secondary, co-occurring disability. When servicing these students, teachers should be sure to take all conditions into account and tailor the instructional plan especially for the student's needs.

HOW FAMILY SYSTEMS CONTRIBUTE TO THE DEVELOPMENT OF INDIVIDUALS WITH DISABILITIES

All students benefit when their parents are involved in their education. Parental participation ensures that homework is completed—essential in order that skills be reinforced. Problematic behaviors are more easily addressed when the parents are fully involved. The student gets the message that learning and schoolwork matter.

But parental involvement is especially important when the student is one with a disability. In fact, parental involvement is a legal requirement. An IEP cannot be implemented without parental consent. Parents are entitled by law to receive written notice of each meeting thirty days before it is scheduled. The notice must be written in the family's native language.

So how can special education teachers work to communicate and collaborate effectively with the families of students with disabilities? The first thing to remember is to be sensitive to cultural differences. All parents care about their children's progress and want their children to succeed. But some parents may have cultural beliefs that limit them from accepting some of the suggestions offered, while others are struggling to feed their families and do not have the time required to meet with the teachers. This should not be interpreted on the special education teacher's part as a lack of interest—instead, education professionals must work to meet the family where they are.

At times, parents or family members are in denial over the child's disability label. They may take actions that are harmful for the student because they are feeling hurt and overwhelmed. Other families may seek special education services that are in their own interests rather than the child's—for instance, placing the child in a local school when the child would greatly benefit from a school that is farther away. It is at these times that education professionals must ensure that the IEP is written with the student's needs in mind. At times the school will need to file due process and legally contest the parents' requests. This legal process will be further discussed in a later chapter. Care must be taken that even during legal proceedings, the child is always looked out for and serviced in the best possible manner.

When speaking with the child's parents, be sure to use appropriate language. Don't speak in terminology that the parents will not understand and that may make them feel nervous. Be sure they are fully included in the conversation.

Teachers should also seek to keep parents updated on their children's progress in school. Parents have the right to know how their child is performing, and they should know. They are an integral part of the child's life. By spending the time to keep parents in the loop, everyone wins.

ENVIRONMENTAL AND SOCIETAL INFLUENCES ON STUDENT DEVELOPMENT AND ACHIEVEMENT

Students from lower income homes and backgrounds often achieve less academically than students from differing backgrounds. Why would this be so? These students often are raised in environments with risk factors that include abuse, neglect, illness, rejection from family members, and lack of community. All this contributes to difficulties later in life, especially mental health problems.

Some psychologists and researchers suggest that students from these disadvantaged backgrounds do not receive the intellectual stimulation that is needed for them to develop appropriately. Students do not gain adequate vocabulary and do not gain adequate socialization skills. This is known as the **deficit model**, because it focuses on the deficits that students may be experiencing in these homes.

Another model, the **difference model**, focuses on the idea that schools are geared toward guaranteeing the success of the middle-class white student. Students from different backgrounds therefore are at a disadvantage when in school. Advocates of this model suggest that educators be trained to understand the values and behaviors of these students and be welcoming toward these differences in the classroom.

Researchers also point to the differences in services available to students in differing living environments. Living conditions today have improved dramatically from what they once were for those with less money, but services for children with psychological difficulties are not always available for them. These students therefore may not receive the help necessary when it is required.

So how can we help students to succeed? The first way is through the prevention of problems. We can find ways to ensure that students do receive the appropriate instruction so they don't later fall behind in school. This can be done by creating community programs and support programs that encourage healthy families. Families that have supportive relationships, who participate in a variety of activities, who have healthy personal attributes, and who belong to a larger community are better equipped to raise well-developed children. Programs encouraging and supporting this familial growth will go a long way toward preventing gaps in student achievement later on.

Another way is through early intervention programs that allow students access to instruction they may not be receiving at home. These programs provide young children with instruction that encourages them to develop appropriately. Students from disadvantaged backgrounds may not be receiving the parental input that would allow this to happen at home.

Intervention is another way to help students succeed. Once a problem has developed with the student, treatment is provided to try and correct the student's issues. If that is not possible, then every effort is made to ensure that the student's condition is at least stabilized.

After this comes social prevention. Work is done to ensure that those who have externalizing difficulties do not negatively impact others in the community.

Research strongly indicates that environmental factors in the home affect student development and achievement in school. Societal influences, such as the presence of a supportive community, play a strong role as well. It is for this reason that teachers should not contain their efforts only to instruction within the classroom. A social worker or other support person within the school should be consulted when risk factors are discovered, in order to allow students the best possible chance for success.

IMPACT OF DISABILITIES ON INDIVIDUALS, FAMILIES, AND SOCIETY ACROSS THE LIFE SPAN

A child's disability does not affect only that child. Each person is part of a family and part of a greater society, and the disability has a ripple effect on everyone in the child's life. Every family reacts to disability in a different way; there is no one right way to react to a disability. The severity and type of disability also will influence familial reaction.

The mother of the student is often the one most impacted by the disability. This is because the mother is very often the one responsible for raising the child, and so she is especially stressed by the additional duties a child with a disability engenders. The presence of a disability changes the rules and routines the family requires, and the family dynamics may shift dramatically. The presence of support systems such as a supportive husband or family can be tremendously useful for the parents of those with disabilities. Respite care, which allows the family of the student to get a break, is also valuable.

While the effect these students have on their fathers may have been ignored in the past, today we realize that fathers also play a tremendous role in the lives of students with disabilities. Studies show that fathers and mothers react to disability differently. While mothers worry about the factors that need to be taken care of from day to day, fathers instead worry about more long-term issues. Fathers tend to be less emotional in responding to disability. Often the father sets the tone for how the others in the family react to the disability.

What effect does a child with a disability have on the parents' marital relationships? Studies show that the effect varies. While mothers and fathers both appear more stressed when these students are part of their families, they do not seem to divorce at a rate greater than parents of typical peers. Many factors go into marital relationships and it is difficult to draw generalizations.

Siblings also are tremendously affected by the presence of the student with a disability in the family. The student with a disability is also affected by the siblings. Siblings have been shown to withdraw socially and to have lower self-esteem. They also may feel anger over being asked to help with the care of their sibling with special needs, or may worry that they will "catch" the disability as well. Being such a sibling has tremendous benefit as well. Siblings tend to develop greater compassion toward others as a result of what they experienced growing up.

Finally, the grandparents may be affected by the disability. Grandparents worry about not only the outcome of their grandchild, but also their own child when a diagnosis is first made. Often, grandparents make a difference in the situation—if they are supportive, they can hold the family together through the difficult periods. Grandparents can find different responsibilities to take on that are tremendously helpful to the parents and the rest of the family, or they can take on more of a cheerleading role. Either way, they can truly make a difference in the family dynamics.

IMPACT OF LANGUAGE, CULTURAL, AND GENDER DIFFERENCES ON THE IDENTIFICATION PROCESS

The **identification process** is the process of identifying children who are eligible for disability services. IDEA requires that schools work to identify students who would benefit. Child Find is the government program that works with schools, hospitals, social services, and families to identify students with disabilities who require special services. Students are also identified through early intervention programs, parents, and teachers.

Certain factors may interfere with the identification process. One factor is cultural differences. Students from diverse backgrounds are often identified as having a disability when in fact their difficulties in school stem from their cultural differences. Teachers and school administrators should be trained to be culturally sensitive and attuned to any biases they may have against a particular culture. They also should be trained to be culturally competent, enabling them to interact appropriately with other cultures. In this way teachers will be able to teach effectively for students from all kinds of backgrounds.

The way in which racial and cultural differences figure in the definition of good behavior, along with miscommunications, can lead to the inequitable punishment of students of color by school personnel who do not recognize and respect legitimately different styles of classroom participation. Arbitrary and excessive consequences for minor transgressions can lead to a sense of powerlessness and anger in the students which can either lead to further misbehavior or shutting down.

Gender is another issue; special education has an overabundance of male students, suggesting that male students are overidentified as having disabilities. Some observers suggest that this is related to most teachers being female and therefore unfamiliar with male learning differences.

Students from low socioeconomic status (SES) backgrounds are also overrepresented in special education programs. In fact, overidentification of students from diverse backgrounds usually happens when those students come from households that also are low SES.

Why does low SES impact the child's school performance—and disability identification—in this manner? These students often come from single-parent homes, which means that the parent is stressed and has less time to participate in the child's education, including homework. The parents of these students are also likely to have a lesser education. This means they may value education less and so the child has less motivation to work hard and succeed in the school environment.

Care should always be taken that language differences do not interfere with the identification process. Testing should be done in the student's native language to ensure that the student is not mistakenly identified with a disability. A language barrier should not get in the way of the child receiving an appropriate education; instead, the teacher must work with the child to ensure that he or she is educated along with the class, and not receiving an inappropriate placement.

INFLUENCE OF EXCEPTIONAL CONDITIONS THROUGHOUT AN INDIVIDUAL'S LIFE SPAN

While IDEA provides services only for students ages 3 to 21, a disability affects the person's life throughout his or her life span. By knowing the challenges that will crop up in the student's life, teachers are better prepared to prepare their students for what is to come.

From birth to age 5, the child is considered to be in the early childhood stage. At this point the primary concern is that the child receive a correct diagnosis and find the appropriate services. The family also must struggle to make peace with the diagnosis—after all, no one expects a child to have a disability. They must find positive aspects to the situation and decide how to deal with the hardships that will follow. They also need to deal with the stigma that comes with having a child with a disability as part of the family.

Children ages 5 to 12 are school age. The family has developed a routine to work with the variety of services the child requires. Now they must begin to worry about the child's educational placement. They attend IEP conferences and try to determine what the best setting would be—what are the issues involved and how should they decide? A relaxing outlet should be found for the child outside of school, which is often stressful for students with disabilities—extracurricular activities can be useful. This is also the time when the student seeks to gain access to community resources that can help.

Adolescence is from ages 12 to 21. This is the time when the student begins to take over his or her own educational and personal needs. The student must be prepared for the possibility of an entire life with a disability. As students become more socially aware and seek friends, they must also be prepared for the possibility of social rejection. Leisure time must also be structured with the student's help. The student must begin with transition plans for career development or post-secondary education. Puberty and emerging sexuality also occur at this time and the student will need to be supported through the process.

After age 21 is adulthood—the student has aged out of the educational system. At this time students are usually enrolled in a career program. They may have socialization opportunities there, or if they are not able to socialize independently, the family may need to find ways for them to socialize, perhaps with others with disabilities. The family must prepare for the possibility that the child will require guardianship or be dependent on others, and will likely require supports to work through the process.

Each of these stages of the student's life comes with its own challenges. Transitioning from one stage to another is especially challenging for the student, parents, siblings, and others who are involved in the life of a child with disabilities.

REFERENCES

29th Annual Report to Congress on the Implementation of the Individuals with Disabilities Education Act, 2007. Vol. 2. Washington, D.C.: U.S. Department of Education, 2010. http://www2.ed.gov/about/reports/annual/osep/2007/parts-b-c/29th-vol-2.pdf

Alberto, Paul A., and Anne C. Troutman. *Applied Behavior Analysis for Teachers,* 7th ed. New Jersey: Pearson Education, 2006.

"Assistive Technology Continuum of Low to High Tech Tools." *Boston Public Schools.* Accessed October 18, 2011. http://blog.vcu.edu/ttac/AT_Continuum_Generic10_06.pdf.

"Attention deficit hyperactivity disorder (ADHD)." *PubMed Health.* Last modified April 11, 2011. http://www.ncbi.nlm.nih.gov/pubmedhealth/PMH0002518/.

Bowe, Frank. Making Inclusion Work. New Jersey: Pearson Education, 2005.

"Categories of Disability under IDEA." *National Dissemination Center for Children with Disabilities.* Last modified April 2009. http://nichcy.org/disability/categories.

"Deafness and Hearing Loss." *National Dissemination Center for Children with Disabilities.* Last modified June 2010. http://nichcy.org/disability/specific/hearingloss.

Gargiulo, Richard M. *Special Education in Contemporary Society,* 3rd ed. California: SAGE Publications, 2009.

"Indicator 13." *National Dissemination Center for Children with Disabilities.* Last modified December 2010.

Pierangelo, Roger. *The Special Educator's Survival Guide,* 2nd ed. California: Jossey-Bass, 2004.

Wright, Pam, and Pete Wright. *Wrightslaw: From Emotions to Advocacy,* 2nd ed. Virginia: Harbor House Law Press, 2007.

Planning and the Learning Environment

CHARACTERISTICS OF GOOD LESSON PLANS

As a special education teacher, you will need to know how to create a good lesson plan. If you are in a special education classroom, you will be required to write your own lesson plans for your students. If you are in an inclusive environment you will need to collaborate with a general education teacher to write the lesson plans. Although as special educators you will work to individualize instructions for students with disabilities, your first step before providing individualization is to find a way to create lesson plans most of your students will benefit from.

Work to decrease transition times between lessons so time-on-task increases. That time your students spend finding their books and settling in their seats is time you are losing from what was allocated to your lesson. There is never enough time in the classroom as it is, so create routines that will enable you to take full advantage of the time you have.

Also exercise care in **time management**. You want to be able to complete your lesson with all its components before it is time to move on to the next part of your day. Without the opportunity to wrap up your lesson, students will not learn as effectively. Learn to pace your lessons and always keep an eye on the clock.

When creating your lesson plan, be careful with what materials you choose to use. Be sure that they are appropriate for your students. Reading material may need to be provided at a variety of levels as students may not all be able to benefit from the same level. Some students may benefit from guided notes while others are able to take their own. Also obtain manipulatives for student use when possible; many students learn best when they are able to learn through manipulation.

Be thoughtful about the topics you choose to teach. Not only should they be intrinsically tied to your instructional goals, but students must be ready for them. Pay attention to the sequencing of your lessons so that they are arranged in a way that students will learn well.

Find ways to engage students during your lesson. The person doing the work is the person doing the learning—and you already learned this material. So don't work harder than your students!

- Response cards give everyone the opportunity to participate—for instance, have students write the answer on a whiteboard rather than raising their hands.

- Draw cards or sticks with the students' names written on them to randomly choose students for participation.

- Have students respond chorally to the question.

- Ask for choral responses, but with a twist: "If the answer is *Yes*, make this animal sound!" "If the answer is *No*, say *Boo*!"

Build constant review into your lessons. This will ensure that your students do not only master the material at the end of the lesson but that they store it in their long-term memory. Good times to review are at the end of the week, at the end of the month, and at the end of the unit.

Basic Elements of Effective Lesson Plans

During your teacher preparation program and during administrative observations, you will likely be required to complete detailed lesson plans before your lesson. On a day-to-day basis your lesson plans will not be quite as detailed. Still, you will need to ensure that all elements of a lesson plan are included as you prepare to set the stage for effective instruction.

The first step to be done is to create a clear objective, or goal, for the lesson. More information on creating objectives is below. Once this has been done, you are ready to decide on a plan of instruction to bring students to reach these goals. But don't launch into your instruction just yet! Instead, you must first create an **anticipatory set** for the lesson.

The anticipatory set is where you first catch your students' attention. Students have a lot on their minds—what will make them sit up and pay attention? How is this applicable to them, or to their interests? Be sure to identify for students what the goal of the lesson is, so they also know what to work toward. You may wish to post the objective on the board. Students who know what to expect are students who are more attuned to what is being taught.

The anticipatory set also should work to activate students' prior knowledge. The teacher explains to students how this lesson fits into the overall unit and the overarching instructional goal. To help students understand this continuity, use the same vocabulary and ideas that were used previously during the unit. Also work during this time to gain some understanding of how much students already know about the instructional topic so you can better tailor your instruction to your students' needs.

Once the anticipatory set has been planned, you are ready to get into the mainstay of your lesson plan—**direct instruction**. Think about how best to present the new material to your students so they all can achieve proficiency. To reach instructional goals, what ideas will they need to learn? What vocabulary will they need to master? What can you add to promote student engagement? How can you increase student participation and discussion during the instructional delivery—you don't want to be the only one talking! For students to learn, they must be actively engaged in the instruction; you are not teaching for yourself but for your students.

Be sure during direct instruction to model the skill you desire students to attain. Provide both verbal and visual prompts when modeling. Before students are able to perform the skill on their own, they must be able to understand exactly how to do it and exactly what is expected; otherwise, you will be stuck providing much student correction that could have otherwise been avoided.

After you have checked for student understanding, you can move on to the **guided practice** portion of your lesson plan. Decide on an activity that will allow students to practice the new skill—a worksheet, discussion, experiment, poster, or another project. If possible, think of ways to provide students with a variety of options to practice the skill; this will allow students to tap into their strengths and practice the skill in a way that is best for them. You also can decide how students should practice—whether to create opportunities for individual practice or to allow them to work cooperatively in groups. As students practice, your role is to guide—walk around the room to listen in or watch student performance and coach them through areas of weakness.

Students with disabilities may need extra assistance during guided practice, while other students may be able to perform more independently. Be sure to observe all students and ensure that they all receive the coaching they need. You may wish to create peer supports, empowering students who have mastered the material to support students who need additional help. Students who have completed the practice and are not needed for support should not sit idly and waste time; instead, create classroom procedures that ensure students always know what to do when extra time becomes available. There are always learning opportunities that students will benefit from.

Finally, you are ready to formulate a **closure**. The closure wraps up the lesson plan by providing students with a brief overview of what they have learned. This allows the students to effectively categorize the new information in their minds. The teacher can create closure through asking guided review questions of students, promoting student discussion of the new information, or asking students to compare and contrast the new information.

Now is the time to find ways for students to perform **independent practice**. Be sure this is practice that students are ready to perform independently; you may need to adapt the assignment if you see students are struggling during guided practice. Here also, you should seek to allow for some student independence when choosing assignments. Instead of simply creating worksheets, think of different ways to allow for student differences.

Independent practice is a solid guide toward whether students have mastered the material. Based on the performance you see in students' completed work, you will be able to provide interventions necessary. However, independent practice should not be used as a grade; instead, once independent practice has been completed, you are ready to formulate an *assessment*.

The assessment checks whether the lesson's objectives have been achieved. It therefore should be directly connected to the learning objectives. Student learning can be assessed through tests and quizzes, of course, but feel free to think out of the box. Student projects can also be used to measure student learning and also build skills such as socialization, cooperation, and student leadership. Class discussions can also be used, and students can be assessed graphically through creating posters or storyboards.

LEARNING OBJECTIVES THAT ARE MEASURABLE AND APPROPRIATELY CHALLENGING

When writing learning objectives for the lesson, a teacher must ensure that the objectives are clear and precise. They should be written in **behavioral terms**—what the child will do, rather than what the teacher will teach. In this way we can tell what the student is accomplishing. After all, the goal of instruction is not that the teacher teach the lesson—it is that the student benefit from the lesson and master the skills that are taught. To ensure that you are coaching the objective in appropriate terms, you may want to begin by stating, "The students will be able to . . ." or "Tom will . . ."

A good rule of thumb is to create SMART learning goals.

- **S**pecific

- **M**easurable

- **A**ttainable with the time and resources allotted

- **R**elevant to the learner

- **T**argeted to the learner's level of learning

The learning objective should first state what the child will do. This should be as specific as possible. For instance, the learning goal should not be that the student will eat on his or her own; a better goal would be that the student use a fork correctly when eating lunch. Instead of stating that the student will learn to recognize letters, write that the student will identify each letter correctly when it is pointed to.

Next, the learning objective should state how students will demonstrate what they know. Again, the key is specificity. Will students complete a worksheet? Be assessed orally? Will this method be an accurate demonstration of the student's knowledge?

Now specify the required level of accuracy. How many mistakes can the student make and still be considered proficient? Rather than saying the student "will show improvement," determine how much improvement is adequate at this time. Should it be 8 out of 10 opportunities? Or will the opportunities given vary, and the goal be met 70 percent of the time?

Here are a few examples of measurable learning objectives:

- The students will complete a graphic organizer comparing and contrasting different varieties of leaves with at least five observations with 90 percent accuracy.

- John will put on his backpack before going home at least 75 percent of the time.

- Mary will correctly answer 9 out of 10 single-digit multiplication math problems.

- Kay will remain on task, looking in her book and writing the answers, at least 80 percent of the time.

Learning objectives should always be determined through the assessment information that has been collected. You may wish to provide a pretest to determine current student knowledge, or to ask student questions. You may be surprised by what students know and don't know! Being aware of students' present levels of mastery ensures that you do not waste instructional time by teaching above or below them. Limit your objectives to the main skills you would like students to master. This ensures that your lessons are properly focused.

To ensure you create learning objectives targeted to your students' present levels of functioning, you will want to pay close attention to **Bloom's Revised Taxonomy**. This is a multitiered classification system for thinking. Students must progress through lower levels of thinking before they can reach higher levels of cognitive thinking about their new skill.

- *Remembering*. This is the first level students reach when material is first taught. Students recall information by rote. This also can be described as retrieving, recognizing, or recalling. For example, the students may describe where Rumplestiltskin lived.

- *Understanding*. Students are able to interpret what they have learned. Exemplifying, classifying, summarizing, inferring, comparing, and explaining are examples of understanding. Students can summarize what happened to Rumplestiltskin.

- *Applying*. Using the new skill. Students can solve problems, demonstrate skills, or construct tables and graphs. Students theorize why the Princess promised Rumplestiltskin her baby.

- *Analyzing*. Breaking it down to understand how the parts relate to one another and to an overall structure. Students can distinguish between facts and inferences or determine the relevance of information. They may differentiate between the Princess's actions and how they would act in a similar situation.

- *Evaluating.* Judging the value of ideas based on standards. Determine the value of the work or whether there are adequate data to support conclusions. They can determine whether *Rumplestiltskin* is a realistic story.

- *Creating.* Putting the elements together to create a whole. Organizing the different parts to create a new structure. Students create their own version of the story of Rumplestiltskin.

Teachers who use Bloom's Revised Taxonomy as a guide to their instructional objectives will find that their students are ready for the objectives when they are taught. When cognitive processes are not needed, students may not be ready for instruction and may not benefit.

MEANS OF PROVIDING ACCESS TO THE CURRICULUM

All students learn differently and require different methods of instruction and different materials in the classroom. Yet teachers are often reluctant to adapt materials for students with disabilities or other students that require them. They argue that it is unfair to other students who do not receive adapted materials, as they will need to work harder during class.

Actually the idea is not how hard students are working. Rather, it is about allowing all students access to the content that is being taught. While most students are able to learn with the materials as they are provided, there are some students who are unable to do so due to their disability. The materials therefore need to be modified—not to make it easier for them, but simply so they can learn.

Studies find that contrary to what may be assumed, other students do not resent the teacher when modified materials are provided to students that would benefit. Rather, the students appreciate the teacher's effort to reach all students at their level. Students especially appreciate when teachers create flexible groupings and vary their instructional styles to meet all students' needs.

The best way to allow all students access to curriculum is by creating a **universal design for learning**, or UDL. Universal design is when the design of something is created from the outset to be available for use universally, by people with every level of ability. Without universal design those with disabilities are discriminated against, as they do not have the same opportunity to access the curriculum. With universal design, everyone ends up benefiting.

Universal design is now the norm when it comes to architecture. Curb cuts along our roadways are an example of universal design—they allow those using wheelchairs and canes to access the sidewalks, and also benefit those with small children and strollers. Automatic doors are another example; they allow those with disabilities easy access, and are more convenient for everyone. Today, when most students with disabilities are being included in the general education classroom, universal design must come into the picture as well.

In UDL, the teacher first creates an overview of the unit. What are the learning goals students should be mastering? Then the teacher works to **differentiate instruction** or individualize the teaching to student needs. Since each student learns differently, how can he reach each student where their strengths are? Are there different instructional methods he can use? Can she assess students in a variety of ways, so they all have a chance to show off what they know?

How can we know the best way to instruct each student? Howard Gardner created the theory of multiple intelligences to explain how people learn. Everyone is stronger in one or two areas and if instruction is geared toward those areas of intelligence, that student will learn far more. While Gardner suggested that there are eight forms of intelligence, some of these forms commonly go together.

- *Verbal/linguistic*. These students think in words. They are best at reading, writing, and telling stories. They benefit from creating writing projects, preparing speeches and playing with words.

- *Logical/mathematical*. These students solve problems through logic and reasoning. They understand numbers and patterns. These students benefit from creating graphs and time lines and playing games of strategy.

- *Visual/spatial*. These students think three-dimensionally, perceive the visual world accurately and are strong directionally. They benefit from looking at maps and showing off their knowledge through drawing or painting.

- *Bodily/kinesthetic*. These students use their bodies to communicate, through body language or mime. Hands-on activities are very useful for these students. They also enjoy role playing and work better when they are able to move around.

- *Musical/rhythmic*. These students are musical. Teachers can find creative ways to incorporate music into their lessons by rewriting song lyrics to reflect what they have learned or learning the music of different cultures.

- *Interpersonal*. These students understand the feelings of others and are able to interact effectively. They benefit from group projects and cooperative learning.

- *Intrapersonal*. These students know their strengths and weaknesses and are able to use that knowledge to set their own goals. They do well with individual projects and benefit from journal writing, which enables them to reflect on their work. Teachers can provide students with opportunities to reflect on each other's work as well.

- *Naturalist*. This is a more recent addition to Gardner's theory. These students recognize the different aspects of nature and appreciate natural knowledge. Often teachers can incorporate field trips or find other ways to bring nature into the classroom.

The teacher first plans activities to implement throughout the unit that will reach each type of intelligence. Only then the teacher plans each individual lesson. In this way she is assured that each student's strengths will be tapped into throughout the unit.

But not every activity will be geared toward each student's strengths. What are some ways to ensure that your classroom is universally accessible?

- Find ways to offer classroom materials electronically by posting them online or placing them on a USB drive. This helps students with reading difficulties or vision difficulty, as they can use computer software to help them read; it also helps students with organization difficulty, as they may lose the sheets they need.

- Read aloud anything you write on the board or on a sheet. This allows students both auditory and visual input. It also slows down the lesson so everyone is able to follow.

- Teach students how to use headings and find ways to write notes clearly, so they are easily followed.

Teaching with the concepts of UDL in mind is a lot of work to begin with. But soon enough it will pay off. When teachers teach using the tenets of UDL, they ensure that all students receive supports they need, not only those with disabilities. And once teachers create accessible lessons for one year, students who struggle the following year are sure to benefit as well.

ORGANIZING THE LEARNING ENVIRONMENT

Many of us are accustomed to the old way of setting up the classroom—the students' desks are lined up and face the classroom. The teacher's desk is at the front of the classroom, right in front of the board.

But research shows that this is not an effective way to set up a classroom for teaching. It is an efficient setup for the maintenance crew to clean the room—but that is not who we have in mind when we are organizing the learning environment!

In a classroom containing students with disabilities, it is especially important that the layout provide a variety of available seating options. Student grouping will vary—students may be working independently, in pairs, in small groups, or as a class, as part of their flexible groupings.

When possible, the classroom should contain both desks and tables. Tables are useful for cooperative learning and small-group instruction, when groups of students are seated together. Desks are useful for whole class instruction and can be moved when necessary for paired work or independent work. Also in the classroom should be dividers to separate groups of students from each other. This will enable students with attention difficulties to focus on their group or their work.

While it is important to display student work on the walls, care should be taken that not everything is posted. A busy-looking classroom is detrimental to students with focusing difficulty. Instead, ensure that there is a special display space reserved on the walls. Also ensure that everyone's work is represented, including those of students who may not perform as well.

Be sure to accommodate students with low-incidence disabilities that may be placed in your classroom. Students in wheelchairs or who are blind will require that there be large, obstacle-free aisles throughout the room so they can move around easily. Students who are deaf will need to be placed away from a light source so they can see easily.

Allow comfortable time-out areas for students. Try placing a comfortable chair in the library section of the classroom. When students become overstimulated and need a break they will be able to use this place to relax themselves.

Creating a room that is comfortable for all students takes a lot of planning on the teacher's part and is an investment. But it is worthwhile in the difference it will make for many of your students.

THEORY AND PRACTICE OF POSITIVE BEHAVIOR SUPPORTS

Over the past decade, schools have been struggling with creating a school environment that is safe and supportive for all students. While students are coming to school with more behavioral difficulties and greater tendencies for violence, schools are being pressured to accomplish more academically and behaviorally with all students. How can schools keep up?

In the past, many schools have used the theory of **zero tolerance** to try and create an appropriate school environment. Zero tolerance is what it sounds like—there is no tolerance for serious misbehavior. Students who violate serious school rules about drugs and weapons automatically receive consequences up to and including expulsion.

But studies show zero-tolerance policies to be ineffective. Instead, they may even have the opposite effect of creating a school climate of intolerance. Zero-tolerance also discriminates against those students who come into school not knowing the appropriate way to behave. These students are not given the opportunity to learn appropriate behavior. Often students with disabilities violate school rules out of ignorance, and so expulsion means they are being discriminated against on the basis of their disability.

Positive behavior supports, or PBS, is an alternate discipline theory. This system seeks to reinforce students when they are behaving appropriately rather than punishing them when they misbehave. Teachers are expected to catch the students being good and to offer them rewards. PBS works best when the entire school participates and the rules for reward are consistent throughout the school.

PBS is therefore not a response for when misbehavior occurs. Instead, schools who use this theory seek to prevent misbehavior from occurring in the first place. Aside from offering student rewards, they work to create a school culture where everyone is welcome and supported. Misbehavior in this sort of school is less and the consequences for misbehavior are expected. Students know they gain more from behaving appropriately than they will if they violate school rules.

During PBS, students are also taught appropriate classroom behaviors and their practice of these behaviors is reinforced. Students may be misbehaving simply because they do not know appropriate classroom behavior, and this behavioral instruction enables them to be successful.

So what does PBS look like once implemented? It is a tiered approach that looks like a pyramid when illustrated. Most students receive the first and bottom layer of interventions, while the few students who require it receive the top peak of interventions.

- *Primary prevention.* This level of prevention is intended for all students. It is provided at the classroom level and is intended to create an overall positive school culture. Basic instruction and reinforcement is provided at this level.

- *Secondary prevention.* This is the middle of the pyramid. It is intended for students who are considered at-risk for inappropriate behavior and so need additional intervention than what is provided to most students at the primary level. These students are served as a small group and may receive more frequent reinforcements and more intense behavior interventions.

- *Tertiary prevention.* This level is intended only for those students who do not succeed with the other levels and are considered to have chronic and intense behavioral difficulties. It is the most intense level of behavioral intervention. These interventions are designed especially for those students who require them.

When implementing PBS, data should be collected continuously. In this way teachers and school officials can tell which interventions are effective and which are not. The goals of PBS should always be clearly defined, preferably with student input. To assure the best possible intervention for the student, only a limited number of goals should be created.

But even the best behavior plans are not always successful. What happens if a student with a disability commits a serious behavioral infraction?

IDEA states that if a student with a disability is expelled from school, the state is still required to provide him or her with a free and appropriate public education. However, a **manifestation determination** should be made by the school—is this misbehavior a manifestation of the student's disability? If the misbehavior is not due to disability, the student can be removed from school for up to 10 days. A student cannot be removed or placed in an alternate educational setting for more than 10 days, as that constitutes a change of placement in the student's academic instruction and so requires the approval of the IEP team.

If the school does decide to remove the child for more than 10 days, the IEP team must convene. They need to determine whether this misbehavior is occurring because of the student's disability or because the IEP was not implemented properly. The school cannot simply change the student's academic placement. The parents have the right to dispute the decision after it is made and in the interim, the student "stays put" —he or she remains in the current class environment.

At this point the IEP is revised to contain information and instructional goals specifically for behavior. If a **functional behavior analysis**, or FBA, was not yet completed, the teachers complete one now.

What is a functional behavior assessment? The FBA is a document that looks to explain the function of the student's misbehavior. What does the student feel he or she gains by misbehaving in this manner? Teachers try to understand the misbehavior by looking at when the student misbehaves and when the misbehavior occurs less. The FBA therefore documents:

- *Antecedent.* What happened right before the behavior occurred? The teacher should think: How might this be impacting the student's behavior? Can we change it?

- *Behavior.* What exactly is the behavior the student is doing? If we're not sure what we're dealing with, we won't be able to correct the wrongdoing.

- *Consequence.* What consequence did the student receive once he or she misbehaved? Did it make sense? Was it effective? What other consequences should be administered instead that may be more effective?

The answers to these questions and more will prove useful when the IEP team sits down to write the BIP, or **behavioral intervention plan**. To write the BIP, the IEP team takes a look at the FBA and translates that information into strategies to use to change behavior. The focus is on the student's need for the undesired behavior and how the need can otherwise be met. Curricular modifications and positive strategies are agreed upon and written.

THEORY AND PRACTICE OF EFFECTIVE CLASSROOM MANAGEMENT

Classroom management refers to the process of managing the classroom and the students belonging to the classroom. It does not refer to discipline, which happens after a student misbehaves. Rather, it refers to the rules and procedures that have been put into place proactively to ensure that an appropriate learning environment is created.

Many teachers allow student misbehavior to occur, and then punish the student for the misbehavior, in the hopes that another incident will not occur. These punishments are often administered inconsistently and students may not understand why they are being punished or that what they did was inappropriate. A teacher who understands the concepts of classroom management will instead start out the year with a set of specific procedures in place. Rather than teaching content that first day, students will learn how they are expected to perform in the classroom.

These teachers enable students to take charge of the classroom as well. At the beginning of the school year, they discuss the classroom rules with the student and even accept input on what the rules should be. Students understand the reason why the procedures are in place—it is for their benefit, to allow them to best learn in a supportive classroom environment. Students, therefore, are more likely to follow the procedures and to encourage their classmates to follow them as well.

The golden rule for good classroom management is prevention. It is far easier to prevent misbehavior from occurring than it is to work with the misbehavior after it has happened. To this end, work to increase student engagement during the lessons. Engaged students are far less likely than bored students to try and disrupt the class.

Constantly move around the room while you are teaching. Your proximity to students will make them sit up and pay attention. Scan the room to ensure that all your students are following the lesson and no one has been left behind.

Teachers need to ensure that their classroom is a positive place rather than a negative place. The positive interactions with each student should far outweigh negative interactions. To nip misbehavior in the bud and prevent the need for negative interactions, the teacher should keep an eye out for slight behavioral errors and redirect the student as necessary. When the teacher knows that the student has a tendency to behave incorrectly, she should precorrect—anticipate the misbehavior and remind the student of the appropriate behavior.

When a student does misbehave, those teachers with a good classroom management style have it much easier. The student knows exactly what the consequence will be and knows it is fair—after all, anyone else who performs that misbehavior will receive the same consequence. Teachers also may want to create class rewards that are contingent on the whole class's performance, as this encourages the class to come together and be certain that everyone participates in the learning process.

DESIGN AND MAINTENANCE OF A SAFE AND SUPPORTIVE CLASSROOM ENVIRONMENT

Students in an inclusive classroom are all at different academic levels and have differing educational needs. And yet there are ways to make every student feel safe and supported. Certain teaching methods will not only enhance teacher instruction but will also serve to create a positive environment for everyone in the class.

Encouraging cooperative learning is one strong way to create a supportive classroom environment. Cooperative learning shifts the roles of the students and teachers; the students become active participants in their learning, while the teachers act as facilitators. This method of learning creates a sense of unity in the class, as they work together to gain skills.

For cooperative learning to be successful, the teacher works to promote interdependence among the groups of students through working together for a common goal. The teacher also must hold each individual student accountable for the material by demonstrating his or her mastery of the goal. The teacher should provide students with social skills instruction so they are capable of working together to achieve.

There are a few different methods that can be used for cooperative learning.

- *Round robin.* The students go around the classroom sharing ideas with each other.

- *Think-pair-share.* The students think to themselves an answer to the topic provided, they pair up with another classmate to talk about it, and they then share with the class or the group.

- *Jigsaw.* The students work together in groups to research a topic. New groups are then created containing one student from each of the old groups. Each student teaches the others about his or her expert topic.

- *Corners.* Students divide into four groups and discuss the topic. The groups are then shuffled and each student presents ideas from the other groups.

- *Co-op.* The students work together to create a group project to share with the class.

Peer tutoring is another way to create an atmosphere of cooperation among students. In peer tutoring, a student without disabilities tutors a student with disabilities. This allows the student with special needs to interact with and befriend typical peers. The typical peer can serve as a role model for social skills for the student in addition to providing a strong way to differentiate academic instruction.

Students with disabilities also benefit from the opportunity to become tutors themselves. They can tutor a younger student and thereby learn through teaching. This enables the student to feel that he or she is also able to give help and take on important responsibilities.

Through peer tutoring and cooperative learning, the classroom becomes desegregated. Students are not left feeling that they are in the "stupid group" or the "smart group." Instead, they are able to focus on each other's strengths and see what each student can contribute to the class. Students learn to listen to each other and depend on each other to succeed.

When necessary, teachers should also work directly with students with disabilities to allow them to see the important role they play in the classroom. Students with disabilities know they do not learn as easily as many of their classmates. Often they are left to feel badly about themselves and do not feel like an integral part of the class. There are certain steps that teachers can take to ensure that students do not develop harmful attitudes toward school and lose motivation altogether.

One important process teachers can enforce is **demystification**. Teachers and parents speak openly with the student about the nature of her disability. Students learn why they feel the way they do during class and why they do not always understand instruction and are unable to follow. Most importantly, they learn the vocabulary for the struggles they are facing. This way, when they find themselves the only one unable to follow instructions, they are able to think "There goes my spatial processing problem" rather than "I'm just stupid."

How can parents and teachers teach the child this shift in attitude?

- *Understanding.* Tell the student the importance of understanding yourself and the way you think. Everyone has parts of them that don't work perfectly and need intervention.

- *Strengths.* Tell the student about the areas where he or she shines. Don't make it up—students will know when you're not being truthful. But every student has one area where he or she is stronger than the rest of his or her peers. Be sure to point it out.

- *Weaknesses.* Tell students about the areas that need to be improved using language they can understand. Ask the students if they agree with what you are sharing. Ask them to share times when this weakness became an issue for them. Then ask the students to repeat what their weaknesses are so they understand them. When students know exactly what is going on they feel less overwhelmed and more in control.

- *Optimism.* Tell students that these weaknesses can be overcome. There are interventions available to help. No one is to blame for what is going on, and yet they are being asked to do things they are not yet capable of. This does not mean they won't be able to do these things in the future—with help they will.

- *Alliance.* Tell the student you look forward to working with them in the future. Everyone needs help in certain areas, even you. Show the student that you truly believe in them and that they can work through both their strengths and weaknesses.

Demystification should be a continuing and looping process. Students are not going to internalize all this information right away; they may not even understand it all immediately. They will need the opportunity to discuss what you have shared again, whenever necessary.

REFERENCES

"Assistive Technology Continuum of Low to High Tech Tools." *Boston Public Schools*. Accessed October 18, 2011. http://blog.vcu.edu/ttac/AT_Continuum_ Generic10_06.pdf.

Bos, Candace S., and Sharon Vaughn. *Strategies for Teaching Students with Learning and Behavior Problems,* 5th ed. Massachusetts: Allyn & Bacon, 2002.

Bowe, Frank. Making Inclusion Work. New Jersey: Pearson Education, 2005.

"Building the Legacy: IDEA 2004." *U.S. Department of Education.* Retrieved November 1, 2011. http://idea.ed.gov/explore/view/p/,root,regs,300,A,300% 252E8,c,.

"Developing the Lesson Plan." *Air University.* Retrieved November 11, 2011. http://www.au.af.mil/au/awc/awcgate/af/af_safety_ctr-dev_lesn_plans.doc.

"Effective Use of Performance Objectives for Learning and Assessment." *University of New Mexico School of Medicine.* Last modified 2005. http://ccoe.umdnj.edu/ forms/EffectiveUseofLearningObjectives.pdf.

Forehand, Mary. "Bloom's Taxonomy: Original and revised." *Emerging perspectives on learning, teaching, and technology.* Retrieved November 13, 2011. http://projects.coe.uga.edu/epltt/index.php?title=Bloom%27s_Taxonomy.

Levine, Mel. *Educational Care,* 2nd ed. Massachusetts: Educators Publishing Service, 2002.

Lewis, Beth. "Top 8 Components of a Well-Written Lesson Plan." *About.com.* Retrieved November 11, 2011. http://k6educators.about.com/od/lessonplanheadquarters/ tp/8_steps_lp.htm.

Lipsky, Dorothy Kerzner, and Alan Gartner. *Inclusion: A Service, Not a Place*. New York: National Professional Resources, 2008.

Pierangelo, Roger. *The Special Educator's Survival Guide,* 2nd ed. California: Jossey-Bass, 2004.

Reynolds, Cecil R., and Elaine Fletcher-Janzen, eds. "Classroom Management." *Encyclopedia of Special Education*. 3rd ed. New Jersey: John Wiley & Sons, 2007. PDF e-book.

"What is the difference between accommodation and modification for a student with a disability?" *AccessSTEM*. Last modified November 2, 2007. http://www.washington .edu/doit/Stem/articles?83.

Delivery of Services to Students: Instruction and Assessment

4

BACKGROUND KNOWLEDGE

Conceptual Approaches Underlying Service Delivery to Students With Disabilities

Educators, like psychologists and social workers, seek to understand why people behave as they do. By understanding why certain behaviors develop in students, teachers are able to find the way to teach those students. A teacher's job is to change student behavior—to teach him or her to start doing certain behaviors and stop doing others.

Over the years, many different explanations for human behavior have been suggested. How do we know whether an explanation will prove useful when applied to the classroom? A useful explanation will meet four requirements.

- *It is inclusive.* Most behaviors are understandable when this explanation is used. An explanation that does not allow teachers to understand much of human behavior will not prove useful when teachers try to change student behaviors.

- *It is verifiable.* Teachers should be able to test and see whether this explanation accounts for behaviors.

- *It has predictive utility.* It is able to predict what student behavior is likely to be when certain conditions are met.

- *It is parsimonious.* It is the simplest way to account for the observed behavior.

The following are several conceptual approaches toward understanding and changing student behavior.

Cognitive

The cognitive theory of education emphasizes the student's inner thought patterns and how those patterns affect behavior. For behavior to be changed, cognitive theorists believe, the teacher must find a way to change the student's thought patterns. The teacher's role is to rearrange the student's environment to allow the student to discover new ideas and change his or her thoughts, and thereby his or her behavior.

Constructivist

Constructivists believe in experiential learning. According to the constructivist model of learning, student behavior is caused by his or her experiences. To cause behavior change, the student must be provided with a variety of experiences.

Psychodynamic

The psychodynamic model views the student as possessing dynamic forces within him or her. These forces interact to create the student's personality, and the resulting personality is what causes particular student behavior. Behavior can be changed when the student is led to understand the causes of his or her behavior.

Sociological

Educators who follow the sociological approach view the school as being part of a larger society. These educators look at the role society plays in individual student behavior, and whether social forces within society are serving to increase or decrease a particular behavior. When creating interventions, teachers focus on how students' interactions influence them.

Ecological

The ecological model views the behavior within a larger context. What is in the vicinity of the student that may have caused this behavior? For instance, the teacher's being nearby may cause certain speaking behavior, or a nearby chair may cause sitting behavior.

Medical

The medical approach to service delivery, also known as the biophysical explanation of learning, understands behavior as being caused by the body. Some behaviors are attributed to genetics and heredity. If the parents behave in a certain manner, it is likely that the student will have that same behavior. Other behaviors are attributed to excesses or deficiencies of chemicals found in the body. Behavior can be changed through changes in diet and through prescription medications.

Therapeutic (Speech/Language, Physical, Occupational)

In addition to the teacher's role in changing student behavior, many students also receive services from therapists such as speech and language pathologists, physical therapists, and occupational therapists.

- Speech-language pathologists focus on remediation of speech problems and language difficulties.

- Physical therapists focus on gross-motor skills. They work to prevent muscle atrophy and strengthen students' muscles.

- Occupational therapists focus on fine-motor skills. They work on practical skills such as feeding, dressing, and writing.

Behavioral

The behavioral approach focuses on how behavior impacts student learning. Did the student increase or decrease the behavior as a result of the teacher's response? Educators following the behavioral approach in their classrooms view the teacher and other students in the role of providing consequences to students. Learning is controlled through different consequences.

The behavioral approach is the one most commonly used by special educators. This is because behaviorism has been shown to be the most useful explanation of behavior—it is inclusive, verifiable, predictive, and parsimonious.

Recall that according to behaviorists, educators change student behavior by administering consequences. The consequence administered will change depending on the behavior the teacher desires. There are a few behavioral concepts you should know.

Positive reinforcement causes the behavior to increase. The student does the behavior, the teacher delivers the consequence, and the student does the behavior again. For instance, a teacher who wants the student to identify letters correctly may give the student a sticker for each correct answer. The student will in turn give more correct answers. Sometimes teachers inadvertently provide students with positive reinforcement—for example, they will give more attention to students who misbehave. If the student was looking for attention, the teacher has reinforced this undesired behavior and the student is likely to continue misbehaving.

Negative reinforcement also causes the behavior to increase. This time, the increase is caused because a condition is taken away or reduced. An example would be if a fire alarm went off and was bothering the student. If the student leaves the room, the noise will go away. The student therefore will leave the room next time.

Punishment causes behavior to decrease, and so it is used for undesired behaviors. A consequence is considered a punishment only if it causes a change in the student's behavior.

PLACEMENT AND PROGRAM ISSUES

Inclusion

Inclusion is a popular topic among special educators, but there is some disagreement over what qualifies as inclusion. Most educators believe that inclusion is when students with disabilities are educated within the general education population for most of the school day. Others advocate full inclusion, which means that all students are educated in the general education classroom, together with their typical peers, for the entire day.

Why should students with disabilities be included in general education classrooms? Having students with exceptional needs attend school together with students with typical needs ensures that these students learn the same content. It also forces local school officials to take responsibility for the continued growth of these students, rather than dismissing them as being someone else's problem.

Inclusion also provides students with disabilities with models for appropriate behavior; rather than imitating the sometimes inappropriate behavior of peers with disabilities, they are shown every day what typical behavior looks like. Inclusion also benefits typical students by exposing them to diverse people and giving them the opportunity to give to others. Including students with disabilities in the general classroom can prompt teachers to use creative teaching methods such as cooperative learning and differential instruction.

But when inclusion is inappropriate for the student, it can be detrimental. Students with more severe disabilities may have needs that the school cannot meet in the general education classroom—and placing students in that environment will prevent them from receiving the education they deserve. It is for this reason that IDEA, the Individuals with Disabilities Education Act, does not guarantee inclusion for students with disabilities.

Least Restrictive Environment

So if inclusion is not guaranteed, then what does IDEA guarantee students with disabilities? Least restrictive environment, or LRE, is a major component of IDEA—and it has been called the single most controversial provision in the law. LRE guarantees that students with disabilities will be educated together with their typical peers *to the maximum extent appropriate*. In other words, these students must receive educational placements that fulfill their educational needs. If they can be educated within the general education classroom together with their peers, then the appropriate aids and services must be provided to enable them to succeed. If, however, the IEP team determines that they won't be successful in the general education classroom, the students will be placed in an alternative educational placement.

LRE, therefore, will change according to what the student's needs are at that time. A student may start out in a general education classroom, receiving support from a special education teacher. If his or her needs become more intense and can no longer be met in that setting, the IEP team can determine that LRE is no longer being met in that classroom; instead, they may decide to place the student in a self-contained classroom with more support.

Continuum of Educational and Related Services

When it comes to least restrictive environment, individualization is key. Inclusion cannot be the only placement that is suggested. What are the different educational placements available to students with disabilities? We can view the educational placements as being on a continuum, ranging from least restrictive to most restrictive.

The least restrictive environment is the general education classroom, of course. Students remain in the classroom and receive instruction together with their typical peers. If necessary, they will receive extra services to help them succeed; this may include adapted or modified tests, and/or having a special education teacher available for extra instruction for part or all of the day.

Students who need more support will be sent to a resource room for part of the day. Students still receive most of their instruction in the general education classroom. However, the students leave the general education classroom for part of the day in order to receive specialized instruction.

A more restrictive environment is the self-contained classroom. Self-contained classrooms are located within the same school building as general education classrooms, but the student receives instruction only with other students with disabilities. Often students placed in self-contained classrooms attend special activities, such as gym, art, and music, together with their typical peers.

Students whose needs cannot be met in self-contained classrooms will be instructed in special day schools. These day schools are only for students with severe disabilities whose needs cannot be met in general education schools. Even more restrictive are residential schools, where students spend their time in a residential setting rather than returning home each night.

Homebound services are educational services for students who are unable to attend school due to their disability. Students who receive homebound instruction often have medical conditions that limit their ability to sit in a classroom with others. Homebound services are not necessarily restrictive; their use depends on student need.

When determining a student's educational placement, the first placement suggested should be inclusion. Only if inclusion is not a viable placement should the other placements be considered.

Categorical, Noncategorical, and Cross-Categorical Programs

Under IDEA, a student must be identified with a disability in order to receive special education services. Schools at times use that disability label in order to place the student in a categorical classroom, or a classroom containing other students with that disability. For instance, a student with autism may be placed in a classroom servicing other students with autism. School districts reason that these students likely have similar needs and so will be better serviced together with other students with that same disability.

There are times, however, when the school district chooses to place students from a variety of disability categories within the same program. Such programs are often known as cross-categorical or noncategorical programs, as they group students identified with different disability categories. In any case, schools must ensure that they are paying attention to the student's needs, not the disability category the student was placed in, when determining program placement.

Related Services and Their Integration into the Classroom

Recall that least restrictive environment, or LRE, ensures that students receive aids, services, and other supports to enable them to be educated as much as possible with children without disabilities. Related services are any services that the student with a disability requires in order to benefit from special education. As you can imagine, there is a huge list of related services that may be provided—it all depends on the need of the student.

Students with disabilities are sometimes unable to take regular school transportation; they instead have a special bus that picks them up and drops them off at their homes. Students may require physical or occupational therapy to strengthen their bodies so they can benefit from the lessons. Interpreters may be required for those who are deaf, and school health services for students with medical conditions. Speech therapy is a common related service that is provided, as is social work, counseling, and psychological services. Assistive technology is often required in the classroom.

Schools are required to provide related services when necessary, and they are not allowed to excuse themselves by pointing to the lack of available funding. However, there are certain related services that schools are not required to provide. Schools do not pay for surgically implanted medical devices, such as cochlear implants. Medical services provided off school grounds are not funded by the school district.

Accommodations, Including Access to Assistive Technology

Accommodations are necessary for students with disabilities to be successful in the classroom. An accommodation is anything that alters the environment, curriculum format, or equipment to allow students with disabilities to access the lesson. Since an accommodation does not alter the material being taught, the student can still be graded the same way as his or her typical peers. Examples of accommodations may include larger print on tests and worksheets for students with visual impairments, a sign-language interpreter for students who are deaf, and extended time on tests for students with motor difficulties or learning disabilities.

A modification, on the other hand, is a change in the classroom that modifies the way the student is graded. A teacher may choose to simplify the material the student is required to master or make the student responsible for less material. It is usually preferable to try and accommodate the student so he or she can access the same material as the other students before modifications are made.

Assistive technology is a good way to provide accommodations for students. Assistive technology is any kind of technology that helps children with disabilities to do what those without disabilities can do without support.

There is a huge variety of technology that can be used in a classroom setting. Many computer programs are available to enhance the instruction of students with disabilities. Computer software reads aloud information on the computer screen for those with visual impairments or language disorders. Speech recognition software is also available that transcribes the student's voice onto the computer, for those unable to write on their own. Word-prediction software guesses what the student is trying to write, which decreases the amount of typing necessary. Students with low vision can use text-enlarging software.

Remember that assistive technology does not need to be sophisticated. With some imagination, all forms of technology can be used in the classroom to aid students with disabilities.

- Pencil grips and special paper help students with motor difficulties.

- Electronic recorders are useful for students who cannot write the answers to test questions.

- Highlighters help students with attention deficits to focus on key areas.

- Timers aid students with anxieties in transitioning smoothly.

Other forms of assistive technology have been developed specifically for individuals with exceptional needs. For instance, augmentative communication devices are computers that speak for students who cannot verbalize words on their own. Students with physical disabilities may require special walkers or seats.

If assistive technology is required for the student's success, the IEP team should include someone qualified to conduct assistive technology assessments. Often the IEP states that the assistive technology be available to the student at home as well as in school, because in that way the student will have more time to gain mastery of the technology and truly benefit.

Role of Individualized Education Program (IEP) Team

Each year, the student's individualized education program, or IEP, is reviewed. The IEP is the legal document that states the special education and related services the student will receive. The IEP is revised based on the student's current needs.

As you can see, the IEP is a very important document for the child's education. Who decides what is written in the IEP?

IDEA requires that an IEP team be formed in order for an IEP to be written. The IEP team includes:

- The student's parents.

- The general education teacher, if the student will be included in the general education classroom at least part of the day.

- The special education teacher.

- Someone who can explain the evaluation (this may be the special education teacher or a psychologist).

- A representative from the school district (local education agency, or LEA).

- Others as requested by the IEP participants.

The IEP team begins by looking at assessment data that have been collected on the student. The data provide a picture of the student's present academic levels and functional performance. The IEP team members then work together to develop an individualized educational program. The team determines a method of progress monitoring to track whether the IEP is effective for the student.

What exactly is written in the IEP? While IDEA tries to limit the burden placed on special educators by lessening the amount of paperwork required, many aspects of the IEP are crucial for the student's needs to be met. Each IEP states:

- The child's present levels of educational performance. This includes an explanation of how the child's disability affects his or her involvement in the general education curriculum.

- Measurable annual goals, including short-term objectives.

- Related services and supplementary aids.

- An explanation of the extent, if any, to which the child will *not* participate with nondisabled children.

- Modifications required during standardized state assessments. If the IEP team decides that the student is unable to take the standard test, an explanation must be provided as well as an alternate way of assessing the student.

- The projected date when services will begin. The IEP should also provide the anticipated frequency, location, and duration of services.

- Starting from age 16, or younger if necessary, the IEP team should identify needed transition services.

- How progress toward annual goals will be measured, and how the child's parents will be regularly informed of the child's progress.

IDEA emphasizes the important role families have in their child's education. An IEP cannot be implemented without the approval of the child's family members. If the family members feel that the child's educational needs are not being met, and they are unable to resolve their disagreements with the IEP team, then they have the right to challenge the school district through due process.

Due Process Guidelines

In a perfect world, parents, teachers, and school district officials would be able to always work together to create a program where the student can best succeed. Sometimes, however, a parent is unhappy with what the school and teachers are willing to provide. IDEA provides them with procedural safeguards known as due process.

The first step usually is mediation, where a go-between attempts to create a compromise between the family and the school officials. If the family refuses mediation, or if mediation fails, the case goes to an independent hearing officer (IHO). The IHO decides between the school and the family. The losing party is entitled to appeal to a state review officer; if the losing party decides to appeal that decision, the case then goes to the federal courts. From there, the case may work its way through the federal court system. On rare occasions cases have reached the U.S. Supreme Court.

Due process can take a long time until the case is decided. The student is entitled to receive free appropriate public education during this time. The student may continue to receive the same educational services he or she was receiving before due process was begun; or the school and family may agree that the student receive other services until the case is decided.

Early Intervention

Research shows that the earlier the student's disability is identified and addressed, the better the student's outcome will be. One state found that of the children who received services before age 3, fewer than half required special education upon beginning public school.

Early intervention centers, which provide services to students from birth to age 3, are funded by state and county governments rather than by the public school district. Early intervention services are often delivered in the home rather than in school. Individualized family services plans (IFSPs) are written and followed, rather than IEPs. This is because a key role of early intervention services is assisting the family in finding services for the child.

While an IEP focuses on the student, and how he or she can best be served educationally, the IFSP focuses on the child's role in the family and how other family members are affected. Parents and siblings may receive services through the child's IFSP. Counseling services may be provided to teach coping skills, and respite services may be offered to allow family members some downtime.

When providing services to very young children, an instructional method known as embedding has been found especially helpful. Embedding takes advantage of what is commonly called "teachable moments." The student with exceptional needs participates in the same activities as his or her peers while receiving additional instruction and therapy. Embedding draws on the child's natural interests and the student is thereby motivated to continue learning.

Transition of Students into and within Special Education Placements

IDEA requires early intervention teachers to implement a transition plan when the child turns 2.5 years-old. The early intervention teacher talks with the family about what their plans are for preschool—do they want to enroll their child in a program such as Head Start? Should the Early Intervention records be transferred to the school? A meeting is then arranged between Early Intervention staff and preschool staff to ensure a smooth transition.

Normally, a student over age 3 has an IEP rather than an IFSP. The family can, however, choose to keep the IFSP, though certain services are limited for children over the age of 3.

Other transitions during the school years are also complex—for instance, moving from preschool to elementary school, elementary school to middle school, and middle school to high school. IDEA does not provide specifics on how these transitions should be planned. Special education teachers should do what they deem necessary to ensure that students transition smoothly to their new settings. Usually it is helpful for the former teachers and new teachers to meet and decide on what skills to teach the student in order for him or her to succeed.

Community-Based Training

Students with intellectual disabilities and other severe disabilities often have difficulty generalizing their learning. For instance, they may learn how to count money using plastic coins, but be unable to transfer that knowledge when it is time to pay a grocery clerk. It is for this reason that many schools institute community-based training.

During community-based training, students work with their instructors to learn in real-life settings. These may include stores, restaurants, and banks. The instructor will model the desired behavior for the student and work toward teaching the student to perform the behavior independently.

Community-based training is particularly useful once students reach middle school and high school; it is then that students begin thinking about life after school. Community-based training can be used to expose students to a variety of job settings and train them in a particular job.

Postschool Transitions

Indicator 13 of IDEA requires that schools work with students over the age of 16 to transition to life outside of school. Communication among the IEP team is especially important, as the transitions necessary will vary depending on the student's plans following high school.

Students who plan to go on to college must learn self-advocacy skills first and foremost. When a student is in public school, the IEP team advocates for him and makes decisions about his education; but once in college, it is his or her job to decide and request any necessary services. Studies show that very low percentages of students with disabilities end up graduating college. Transition plans addressing both functional living skills and academic skills are imperative for students to succeed.

Other students with disabilities choose to enter the workforce directly after secondary school. To best ensure student success, much thought should be put into matching student skills and interests with appropriate employment.

Studies find that these students often falter more in nonvocational skills rather than in vocational skills. That is, they are successful in fulfilling their employment duties, but struggle in becoming part of a work team and, for example, following appropriate dress code. These skills can—and should—be taught through community-based training during the secondary school years.

Still other students will be unable to begin working or begin college upon graduation. The focus for these students, who have very severe disabilities, is to prepare them for independent life as much as possible. Special education teachers help these students prepare for life outside of high school by aiding them to master functional skills such as cooking, shopping, and taking public transportation. Students also are put in touch with those support services that will be available to them upon graduation, such as counselors and advocates.

INTEGRATING BEST PRACTICES FROM MULTIDISCIPLINARY RESEARCH AND PROFESSIONAL LITERATURE INTO THE EDUCATIONAL SETTING

For a new special education teacher—and even an experienced one—choosing an educational intervention for one's students can be confusing. New programs are developed each year, each one promising terrific benefits. How does an educator know which interventions are appropriate?

It is tempting for teachers to use interventions with which they were previously successful. A teacher who has had a student benefit from using whole-language instruction, for instance, is likely to want to use whole-language instruction when working with other students. This is not necessarily what is best for the student, however; the purpose of an IEP is for instruction to be tailored to that particular student.

The No Child Left Behind Act of 2001, which is the reauthorization of the Elementary and Secondary Education Act, requires teachers to use science-based research when making decisions about interventions. The National Institute for Literacy, a federal agency, explains that just as a doctor is expected to use his or her scientific knowledge when treating a patient, teachers must also take advantage of their professional scientific backgrounds to teach. Of course, the comparison is not exact—sciences such as biology, chemistry, and physics, which doctors must study, are sometimes known as "hard sciences" because the phenomena being studied can easily be observed. Educational research, on the other hand, is the study of many inner processes that cannot easily be observed. How can a teacher know whether interventions are backed by science-based research?

Truly effective teachers are first and foremost lifelong learners, always seeking to improve their educational practices. Too often, however, materials are published that offer claims not backed by solid research.

The National Institute for Literacy explains that science-backed research uses systematic, empirical methods. Empiricism is the practice of relying on observation. Systematic research is when the observed data are structured in a way that the material conveys meaning to the researcher. Simple observation will not prove helpful, as the teacher will be unable to understand the meaning behind what he or she sees.

Good research also involves rigorous data analysis. The researcher must be able to test the hypothesis and determine whether it is correct through the data collected.

Another area that holds science-based research apart is its reliance on measurements or observational methods that hold true across multiple evaluators, measurements, and observations. The findings must be able to be duplicated, or replicable, by other researchers.

An easy way to differentiate between science-based research and shoddy research centers on whether the research was accepted by a peer-reviewed journal, or approved by a panel of independent experts. This is not to say that everything published in a peer-reviewed journal is correct; but if an intervention was not included in a peer-reviewed journal, one has special reason to be suspicious.

Carefully reviewing the data behind available interventions takes time, and a busy special educator may be tempted to simply reach for a popular intervention. But careful consideration of available options is imperative to ensure that students receive the best possible instruction.

REFERENCES

29th Annual Report to Congress on the Implementation of the Individuals with Disabilities Education Act, 2007. Vol. 2. Washington, D.C.: U.S. Department of Education, 2010. www2.ed.gov/about/reports/annual/osep/2007/parts-b-c/29th-vol-2.pdf

Alberto, Paul A., and Anne C. Troutman. *Applied Behavior Analysis for Teachers,* 7th ed. New Jersey: Pearson Education, 2006.

"Assistive Technology Continuum of Low to High Tech Tools." *Boston Public Schools*. Accessed October 18, 2011. http://blog.vcu.edu/ttac/AT_Continuum_Generic10_06.pdf.

"Attention deficit hyperactivity disorder (ADHD)." *PubMed Health*. Last modified April 11, 2011. www.ncbi.nlm.nih.gov/pubmedhealth/PMH0002518/.

Bowe, Frank. Making Inclusion Work. New Jersey: Pearson Education, 2005.

"Building the Legacy: IDEA 2004." *U.S. Department of Education*. Retrieved November 1, 2011. http://idea.ed.gov/explore/view/p/,root,regs,300,A,300%252E8,c,

"Categories of Disability under IDEA." *National Dissemination Center for Children with Disabilities*. Last modified April 2009. http://nichcy.org/disability/categories.

"Deafness and Hearing Loss." *National Dissemination Center for Children with Disabilities*. Last modified June 2010. http://nichcy.org/disability/specific/hearingloss.

Frost, Pamela. "Soft science and hard news." *Columbia.edu*. Retrieved October 19, 2011. www.columbia.edu/cu/21stC/issue-1.1/soft.htm.

"Indicator 13." *National Dissemination Center for Children with Disabilities*. Last modified December 2010.

"NEA IDEA Brief #6." *National Education Association*., Accessed October 17, 2011. www.nea.org/home/18719.htm.

"No Child Left Behind." *Education Week*. Last modified September 19, 2011. www.edweek.org/ew/issues/no-child-left-behind/.

Rumrill, Phillip D. Jr., and Bryan G. Cook. *Research in Special Education: Designs, Methods, and Applications*. Illinois: Charles C. Thomas, 2001.

Stanovich, Paula J., and Keith E. Stanovich. *Using Research and Reason in Education*. New Hampshire: RMC Research Corporation, 2003.

"What is the difference between accommodation and modification for a student with a disability?" *AccessSTEM*. Last modified November 2, 2007.www.washington.edu/doit/Stem/articles?83.

CHAPTER 5

Instruction and Assessment

APPROPRIATE INSTRUCTIONAL STRATEGIES AND TECHNIQUES

Students with disabilities have so much to learn. How can a teacher find the best way to instruct each student? It is important that the special educator be aware of the variety of instructional techniques available in order to be able to choose an appropriate strategy.

The human brain is very complex, and many theories have been developed to explain how students learn. These theories were discussed in the last chapter. Psychologists have used these learning theories to create instructional strategies that are effective and research-based.

One method of instruction is **cognitive strategy instruction**. This method has been shown to be useful when instruction is intended to change the student's way of thinking. The teacher identifies the thought processes involved in the skill being taught. He then works to teach these thought processes to the students so they will be able to use them when working.

How can students be taught thought processes, when they occur internally? One good way is through **modeling**. While demonstrating the new skill for the students, the teacher discusses aloud why he or she is choosing to acquire the skill in this way. Students then are able to grasp both the behavior being observed and the internal thinking processes.

Modeling is useful when it comes to problem solving, reading comprehension, and social skills. It does not always need to be the teacher providing the model; a proficient classmate can verbalize thought processes for others as well. Videos and puppets have even been used to model thought processes for students, especially when teaching social skills.

Cognitive strategy instruction also stresses **self-regulation**. Self-regulation enables students to become responsible for their own learning through self-talk. Students learn to self-monitor their work by talking it through. This enables them to recognize when a strategy is no longer working and to use an alternate strategy instead. It also allows them to evaluate their completion of the task and decide whether correction is necessary. Students also are able to learn to self-reinforce, which enables them to become self-motivated. With practice, this self-regulation becomes ingrained and students no longer need to specifically self-monitor.

Sociocultural theory of cognitive development is another group of instructional strategies that have been drawn from learning theories. Sociocultural theory views learning as a social activity and works to instruct students in a more social manner.

Scaffolded instruction is a major instructional strategy within sociocultural theory. A scaffold is a temporary support used in construction; when the structure is strong enough to stand on its own, the scaffold is removed. So too, the teacher provides temporary support to students as they begin to master new skills. Once students are competent enough to practice the skill on their own, the teacher removes their scaffold.

Lev Vygotsky, a key psychologist in sociocultural theory, views the point where learning occurs as the **zone of proximal development**. This is the area between what the student already knows and what he or she can do with teacher or classmate support. The teacher slowly fades out support by continually asking for student involvement, and by slowly allowing students to take over the learning process for themselves.

Another instructional strategy often used is derived from the theory of informational processing. This theory views learning as changing the structure of the brain. For an instructional skill to be mastered, those cognitive changes must be made permanent.

What are some ways to impact the student's information processing?

- Cue students to important information. Provide them with an outline of the class, or help them to write notes that contain the important parts of the material.

- Chunk the material into smaller pieces that students will be able to remember. Be sure when chunking that the information makes sense the way it is divided.

- Aid students in organizing information effectively, so it enters their long-term memory.

- Relate learning to prior experiences; this will aid in student recall later on.

As you can see, there are many instructional techniques available to teachers. Teachers should take advantage of what is understood about the human brain to aid in student learning.

INSTRUCTIONAL STRATEGIES FOR ENSURING INDIVIDUAL ACADEMIC SUCCESS

Students with disabilities often benefit from a variety of instructional settings. On the one hand, these students are often behind their typical peers in many areas and require individualized instruction. They will need some extra instruction in areas their peers have already learned and mastered—for instance, a student with a disability may require further practice in simple multiplication, while his or her typical peers have mastered that and are ready for more complex multiplication problems.

Students with disabilities also may need more practice when learning new skills. While typical peers may be ready to move on to more complex skills, these students will require further time to reinforce the skill that was introduced earlier. This extra instruction cannot be provided to the whole class without the risk of boring and alienating classmates.

Yet students with disabilities benefit from being serviced in the general education classroom, and have the right to do so. How does the educational team—both the special and general educator—work together to accomplish this goal?

A key method of delivering the best possible instruction to all students is flexible grouping. Through flexible grouping, students are continuously grouped in a variety of ways, based on their educational needs at that particular time. Students are not grouped according to their disability; as we discussed, a student's disability label does not dictate what his or her educational needs are. Rather, students are grouped based on their strengths and deficiencies within this particular skill.

Here are some possible ways of flexible grouping:

- *One-to-one instruction.* At times, a student with special needs will have educational needs that differ greatly from those of his or her classmates. It is then that he or she is best serviced with one-on-one instruction. This instruction should be scheduled in a manner that does not cause the student to miss important whole-class or small-group instruction.

- *Small-group instruction.* Teachers may create small groups that are **heterogeneous**, or made up of students with differing ability levels; or **homogeneous**, made up of students with similar ability levels in that curriculum area.

- *Large-group instruction.* There are certain activities best done as a class. During these activities, teachers should be cautious that all students are following and understanding the lesson.

How do the special education teacher and general education teacher decide which arrangement to use when?

Students with learning and behavior problems should receive one-to-one instruction each day. This allows the teacher to gather data on the student's present skill levels and to provide specially individualized instruction. One-to-one instruction allows the student to clarify any questions or misunderstandings he or she may have on the material. Preferably a special education teacher, tutor, paraprofessional, or volunteer would be available to meet with the student. Although general education teachers may also find time to work individually with these students by assigning the other students collaborative learning or independent learning.

Small-group instruction is useful when the teacher wants to work with more than one student at a time while still providing highly individualized instruction. Teachers may instruct these small groups within the general education classroom or within a resource room. This form of instruction is often used for core subjects, such as reading and math. Students with disabilities often struggle with these subjects and require a more individualized program of instruction.

Heterogeneous groups, or mixed-ability groups, which group students with a variety of ability levels, allow stronger students to aid weaker students in the activity. Mixed-ability groups also ensure bonding among all students, without stigmatizing some students as weaker and some as more capable. The teacher is able to provide a lesson on social skills to small heterogeneous groups who are having difficulty getting along.

Homogeneous groups, or same-ability groups, are gatherings of students with similar ability levels. These groups allow the teacher to assign work particular to that group's educational needs. Care should be taken when using same-ability groups that the groups smoothly shift according to what each student's needs are for that particular skill. The same students should not be consistently placed within the same groups, as this risks stigmatizing weaker students and students with disabilities.

Large-group instruction refers to instruction provided to groups of six or more students. This method of instruction is used often for content-area subjects such as social studies and science; students with disabilities often receive the same instruction in these areas as do their typical peers, rather than instruction being individualized. Students receive less corrective feedback when in this environment and often have fewer opportunities to contribute to the class.

Large-group instruction is especially common when students are in middle school and secondary school, as elementary teachers often choose to teach by grouping students. Students who are transitioning from elementary school to middle school, or who are transitioning from a special education environment to an environment that is primarily large-group instruction, should receive supervised experience in large groups in order to prepare for success.

There are other ways for teachers to shift students in order to enable everyone to receive the best possible instruction. Some other methods commonly used:

- *Independent learning.* Once a student has become somewhat proficient in the skill being taught, independent practice will help him or her toward mastery. How can the student practice the skill without input from teachers or peers?

Working on computer activities, listening to a recorded book, or creating a related art project are all activities that the student can do independently while reinforcing skills.

- *Cooperative learning.* In cooperative learning, students are placed in small groups and asked to cooperate to learn the material. In order for this method of instruction to work effectively, each student must be held responsible to both master the material and to contribute to the learning process. Students may create a group project together or may each be assigned a part of a project, without which the project cannot be completed.

- *Peer tutoring.* Teachers may pair students to work together to practice material. Students are usually paired according to varied ability levels, as in this way one student to helps the other with when needed. This method is especially useful when it comes to reading practice. Another reason to utilize peer tutoring is to bolster the self-confidence of students with disabilities by allowing them to tutor a younger peer and thereby gain authority.

INSTRUCTIONAL STRATEGIES THAT FACILITATE MAINTENANCE AND GENERALIZATION OF CONCEPTS

Psychologists agree that learning is acquired through stages. The student begins not being able to use the skill at all, and the goal is that the student be able to use the skill during everyday life. In the interim, the student works to strengthen and extend his or her grasp of the skill.

Learning begins through **acquisition**. This is the instructional stage, when the student performs the different parts of the skill with assistance. When the student has grasped the different components of the new skill, he/she is ready to move on to **proficiency**. The student works to increase accuracy and fluency when performing the skill.

Once proficiency is attained, the next stage is **maintenance**. The student works to maintain accuracy and fluency without frequent reinforcement and instruction. Next is **generalization**, when the student works to generalize the behavior to other settings, people, and objects. Students with disabilities often struggle to generalize new skills, and so this stage may require further instruction from the teacher.

The final stage is **application**. During this stage, the student is able to figure out ways to use the new skill in different situations.

As mentioned before, students with disabilities have difficulty with generalization. These students often view the skill as being something that happens in the classroom, with their own teacher providing guidance and support. However, the goal of instruction is not for the student to put on a good show when being instructed but to be able to use the new skill in real-life situations as well. How can we aid students to take their new skills outside of their teaching situation to use when needed?

The Council for Exceptional Children (CEC), the accrediting agency for special education, offers a few suggestions:

- *Change reinforcement.* Students often grow accustomed to the method of reinforcement being offered in the classroom, and will not perform the skill when not offered that reinforcement. In order that they not be as dependent on one type of reinforcement, change the types or the amount of reinforcers.

- *Change cues.* Students may grow accustomed to performing the skill only when cued in a particular way. Try changing the way you instruct the student to perform the skill. Instead of consistently instructing students in the same way, change it so they get used to varied wordings. Provide more complex written directions so they will be able to follow instructions in general education classrooms.

- *Change materials.* Use different kinds of paper, different writing instruments, and computers. This will show the student that the skill being taught is not dependent on the materials being used.

- *Change response set.* Change the way the student responds—writing the answers, supplying them orally, circling them. Lessen the amount of time given for the answer as you go along.

- *Change settings.* Instead of one-to-one teaching, allow the student to work within a small or large group. Work in different areas of the classroom. Allow independent work.

- *Change teachers.* Assign the student to work with a variety of instructors, rather than only with you.

SELECTION AND IMPLEMENTATION OF RESEARCH-BASED INTERVENTIONS

Students with disabilities who are behind in a particular skill subject will require intense interventions so they can benefit from instruction. Teachers need to make sure that interventions used are research-based, to ensure that students are receiving the best possible method of instruction.

Students who struggle with reading may be struggling in a number of different areas. They may be unable to read the words, they may be unable to read accurately and fluently, and they may be unable to comprehend what it is they are reading. The interventions provided will vary based on what the student is struggling with.

Some students have poor phonological awareness—they don't understand how letters relate to the sounds. Phonological awareness also allows students to blend and manipulate sounds, and to segment words according to syllable or sentences according to words.

What are some interventions for students who need to improve phonological awareness?

- Reading Dr. Seuss books and noticing the alliteration contained within them

- Generating rhyming words

- Chanting a word and clapping for each syllable

- Listening for words that begin or end with the same sound

Students also may struggle with identifying or decoding words. Sight words are words that students have seen many times and recognize automatically. Words that are not sight words need to be decoded and require decoding skills. Students without a large sight-word vocabulary will need to decode most words, causing reading to become burdensome. Students who do not have the skills to decode words will be stuck when they need to read an unfamiliar word.

- Flashcards are useful in aiding students in mastering sight words. Certain high-frequency words are constantly used in written work, and these are the words that should be taught first to struggling readers.

- Activities that ask students to blend letter sounds together to form words will aid them in decoding. **Synthesizing** is when sounds are combined to create a word.

- Students can learn to segment words into smaller parts that are easier to read, so they can better decode unfamiliar large words.

- Students should learn the common syllable types in order to familiarize themselves with the types of words they may come across. For instance, closed syllables are also called CVC—consonant/vowel/consonant—and refer to a word that begins and ends with consonants, with a short vowel in between. Examples include *rag* and *branch*. An open syllable, also known as CV, ends in one long vowel. Examples include *me* and *glue*.

- Students can be taught to use syntax to monitor their decoding of unfamiliar words. They should decide whether their interpretation of the word makes sense within the larger sentence.

Students who lack fluency in reading take too long in identifying and decoding words. While they are able to eventually decode each sentence, so much effort is invested in decoding that they miss the content of the sentence. These students are able to comprehend much more when a story is read to them. How can we help students to read fluently?

- *Previewing*. The teacher first reads the book to the students, and then the students then read independently. This provides students with a model for fluent reading. It also provides students with background knowledge, so they will have an easier time reading the book independently.

- *Repeated reading.* The students reread the passage until fluency is reached. Rereading the passage helps the students to decode unfamiliar words, as their memory of the story assists them in identifying words.

- *Choral reading.* In choral reading, the teacher and student read the book together. The teacher is able to help the student to identify words and to comprehend the story without interrupting the flow of the story.

- *Assisted reading.* The child reads the book while the teacher provides unfamiliar words without stopping to teach a skill. Students can also be paired up and read to each other, helping each other if they get stuck.

- *Performance.* Students practice the passage until they are fluent, and then perform the passage. They may perform a play or read to younger students. This intervention is not as intense, but it is a good motivator and confidence booster for students with disabilities.

Students with disabilities also frequently struggle with reading comprehension. They read the passage correctly, but they don't understand what they are reading.

- *KWL charts* activate students' background knowledge before they begin to read the passage. Students write what they *Know* about the topic, what they want to know, and after they have read, they *Write* about what they have *Learned*. This helps students to both think beforehand about what they will be reading, and reflect on their reading after.

- *ReQuest.* ReQuest stands for reciprocal questioning. The goal is that students learn to ask comprehension questions of themselves while they are reading. During ReQuest, the teacher models by asking comprehension questions of the student. The student reciprocates by asking questions as well. A variety of questions should be used—questions that are right in the book, questions that require the student to put together different parts of the story to answer, questions that the student must use prior experiences to answer along with using the text, and questions students must answer on his or her own using prior knowledge.

- *Story mapping.* Story mapping allows students a visual guide to retell the story that was read. This helps students to remember and comprehend what they have read. Students will also benefit from paraphrasing and summarizing stories.

Writing is another important aspect of school curriculum, and is frequently a struggle for students with disabilities. Special educators should work to allow students to feel pride in their written work and to understand that writing is a means to a goal—having a written piece to share with the world.

Poor spelling often affects a student's ability to write well. Conventional methods of teaching spelling are not research-based, and so they will not help students with disabilities to become proficient. Here are some tried-and-true approaches to try:

- Teach fewer words at a time. Try teaching three words each day, rather than twenty at the beginning of the week.

- Teach spelling patterns. Use words that are connected to each other in some way and students are more likely to remember how to spell them.

- Review previous words. To maintain words, continually review those words that were previously taught.

- Test, then study, then test. Test students on the spelling words first and then instruct them to practice words they don't already know. Students then are able to practice just those words they have not already mastered.

Aside from language arts, students with disabilities often struggle with mathematical concepts. There are many aspects to mathematical instruction and a variety of evidence-based interventions are thankfully available for students who require them.

Mathematical instruction begins with prenumber skills, which includes matching one object with another, classifying objects by sizes and shapes, and ordering objects according to different attributes. Students who require interventions to learn prenumber skills are often young and so games are especially useful with this crowd of learners. Here are some tips:

- Give students a number card and ask them to place that number of blocks on top of the card. Switch things up by putting out a specific number of blocks and asking them to put out a number card.

- Ask students to group an assortment of objects. Other students need to guess how they classified their groups of objects.

- Stack rings on a peg in order from largest to smallest.

Many students struggle with the concept of numerals and place value. These concepts are necessary in order to estimate computations, to regroup, and to apply mathematical concepts to everyday problems. Here are some tips:

- Use manipulatives to create groups of ones and tens. Mark the groups and their totals on a chart.

- Give students a pile of Popsicle sticks. Ask them to bundle the sticks in a way that they will be easier to count.

Addition, subtraction, multiplication, and division are simple computation skills; but they are absolutely required for students to progress any further in math, so mastery is imperative. It is here that many students with disabilities fall behind their peers and are lost. Here are some things to try:

- When provided with a computation problem, have students use words to explain exactly what the problem is asking.

- Have students count on to add. For example, to add three to four, they would count—five, six, seven.

- Peer-assisted strategies are useful as motivators and to help students memorize and reinforce these important facts.

Measurements such as distance, length, weight, and time can be taught through real-life problems. Manipulatives such as money and clocks can be used. Teachers should start with concrete examples with manipulatives, move to representational examples with pictures, and only then provide abstract problems that are usually seen in class. This way the student will understand how to think of the abstract problem in a concrete manner.

SELECTION AND IMPLEMENTATION OF SUPPLEMENTARY AND/OR FUNCTIONAL CURRICULUM

Students with disabilities need to master the same skills as their typical peers—and yet they often require instruction in additional skills their peers master without instruction. Therefore a functional curriculum is often created, or what is commonly termed as *life skills*. Learning life skills is especially important during times of transition; before moving on to a new, more independent setting, students will need to be competent in those life skills commonly expected from them at his their age or stage.

What skills are imperative for these students with severe disabilities? There never is enough time in the school day, and yet there is always so much to be mastered. Reading is always important; students will need to read bills, follow directions on a job application, or read the instructions on a bottle of medicine. Writing is also valuable, as students may need to write checks or send thank-you notes, not to mention as an outlet for developing their identities and a sense of the broader world. Math is vital when it comes to personal finances; once they gain more independence, students will need to compare the cost of different food items and decide whether to do their laundry at the self-service laundry or at home. Math also is important when it comes to telling time or reading the thermometer.

When teaching reading, writing, and math to these students who will be transitioning to life after school, life skills should be integrated into each lesson. Students with severe disabilities are far more motivated to learn when they can easily see the benefit of the knowledge. Including real-life situations in the lessons also allows these students to more easily generalize their knowledge.

Some skills that other students pick up naturally may need to be taught to students with disabilities. Listening skills are very valuable during transitions—students will need to follow oral directions during employment, they will need to listen to a weather forecast to dress appropriately, and they will need to attend lectures or meetings. Effective speaking is also important, as students may need to negotiate salary with their boss, describe medical symptoms to a doctor, or call a store to find out if groceries are available. During class instruction, care should be taken that along with the math and reading these skills are also acquired.

Students may also need social skills instruction. These skills are imperative for students to succeed in interacting with others outside of the classroom, and students may not be able to master these skills without direct instruction. Problem-solving skills may also need to be taught—students need to know how to choose a health provider or create a budget.

Finding time to teach this functional curriculum can be a challenge. Schools today strongly emphasize learning standards and teaching to the general education curriculum. While this is in many ways a positive thing—we do not want any student denied access to an appropriate education—for many students, it would be more appropriate to prepare them for independent living rather than for college. Students with severe disabilities have needs that are not addressed within state academic standards, but it is vital that these nonacademic skills be taught.

This is not to say that students with severe disabilities should not receive academic instruction. Often students with these particular needs are able to benefit from training in academic skills. But teachers also need to ensure that students are receiving the skills they will require to succeed in the lives they will live after school is over.

How can all these skills be included in the curriculum? One way is to create specific life skills courses for students who require them. These courses may teach about hygiene, finance, or communication. Schools with more freedom to change curriculum may even create a series of courses to be taken in sequence, so students get a better grasp of these important skills.

However, not all schools are able to create these unique courses for their students. In this case, schools will need to integrate the life skills instruction into already existing classes the students will be taking, such as math, science, language arts, and social studies.

There are a few ways to integrate the life skills material into class instruction. One way is **augmentation**. Augmentation is when additional class time is devoted to life skills. For instance, after teaching a consumer math class, the teacher provides an additional lesson on how to decide where to shop. This requires that the teacher have some flexibility with the curricular schedule and is able to fit in these additional instructions.

The other method of teaching life skills is **infusion**. Infusion is when life skills are taught as part of existing course content. For example, during language arts the teacher may use a social story on getting along with friends. This instructional method helps instructional courses become more relevant for students as well as providing a way of teaching life skills without using additional instruction time.

OPTIONS FOR ASSISTIVE TECHNOLOGY

Sometimes the path toward allowing students better access to the general education curriculum is a simple one. With the technology available today, students with varied needs can more easily be serviced in the general classroom and teachers can more easily differentiate instruction to meet all students' needs.

Assistive technology refers to technology that allows students with disabilities to access the general curriculum. Students who require assistive technology are entitled to receive it under IDEA free of cost. This includes the cost of training to use the technology and coordinating the technology with the other interventions that are in place for the students.

When choosing assistive technology, the IEP team should look for ways to increase student independence in the classroom. Assistive technology should also be provided to allow students to participate more and perform better in the classroom.

Computers are always useful to have in the classroom. Many software programs are available today that allow students with disabilities to complete the same assignments as their typical peers. Software programs aid in allowing for easier vision, provide auditory input or auditory output, and offer spelling prediction and spell check. Computer software also is available to allow students more specialized instruction, so they can work on the skills they need to reinforce even while there may not be a teacher available.

Voice recorders are also tremendously helpful. Teachers can record books for students to read along with and build up reading fluency. Textbooks can be recorded to allow for greater student access. Students can take tests verbally if they are unable to complete the answers by writing. Teachers can create small groups or allow students to work independently by prerecording instructions.

Document cameras have an important presence in many classrooms as well. Document cameras such as the Elmo allow teachers to project worksheets onto a wall of the classroom. This allows teachers to better model instruction for them. The teacher can highlight, write, or point and it will all display on the wall. Students can be encouraged to come up to the document camera to demonstrate work, this increases student involvement and motivation.

Response cards that allow students to answer teacher questions visually rather than verbally are very successful with students with special needs. They allow the students to each respond individually in their own time to teacher questions. Each student is able to think about and answer each question, providing greater reinforcement. Whiteboards can be used as response cards.

Another necessity in the classroom is a stopwatch, to encourage students which can gain automaticity in skills such as mathematical calculations. Calculators are also useful for these students when they are completing routine assessments, as they allow students to show off their academic knowledge without calculation weaknesses getting in the way.

INSTRUCTIONAL STRATEGIES/TECHNIQUES THAT SUPPORT TRANSITION GOALS

Transitions are always difficult, and they are especially difficult for students with disabilities. Planning ahead, collaborating, and communicating will all help to allow students a successful transition.

The special educator begins transition planning by completing a transition assessment with the student. The teacher collects data on the setting the student will be transitioning to by speaking with the student, the parents, and researching the program into which the student will transition. In this way the teacher will know what the student needs in order to be successful and what accommodations will be available to the student once he or she has moved.

There are a variety of assessments available to teachers who work with students facing transitions. **Needs assessments** measure what competencies the student will require against skills the student has already acquired. Assessments measuring **life skills** inventory functional skills the student has mastered to find any gaps that will need to be addressed.

Also assessed during transition planning is a student's **self-determination**. This refers to students making their own decisions about their lives. Along with self-determination is **self-advocacy**, being able to stand up for one's rights and demand what one is entitled to. To succeed in the larger world, students must be able to be assertive without being aggressive.

Quality of life is also measured during this time. The educational team must work to determine what factors go into deciding the student's quality of life. Freedoms and privileges the teacher appreciates may not be what is important to the student. For instance, the student may prize having the freedom to be out late but may not necessarily value the independence of making his or her own meals. The team must ensure that it is the student's own wants and needs that are the focal point throughout the transition process,

Work-related behavior and **social skills** are both assessed by the teacher or transition specialist. Social skills are tremendously important once the student has transitioned to life outside of school.

Once the assessments are completed, the teacher can then evaluate the student's current competencies to decide what skills need work. A list of transition goals is created based on the student's needs.

There are two types of goals students at the transition stage will need to work on: instructional goals and linkage goals. **Instructional goals** are academic and social goals. Examples of instructional goals important to transitioning students may be improving time management skills, improving confrontation skills, and developing a variety of writing skills. These goals are not particular to transition, but should be met in the student's instructional environment.

Linkage goals are directly related to the transition and deal with connecting the student to programs and services he or she will need post-transition. For instance, a student's goal may be to identify resources needed to self-disclose a disability to the college in order to gain required services. Another possible goal would be to connect the student with someone at the college whom he or she can go to when issues crop up. These goals are particular to the transition process.

Academic goals are written as usual in the IEP, while linkage goals are written in a separate section of the IEP. Certain states require that a separate document be written for students who will be transitioning—an **individualized transition plan**, or ITP. In other states, an extra section is included in the IEP that is devoted to transition plans. The important thing is that these linkage goals be included somewhere in the IEP and that the educational team work toward the goals.

Care should be taken to include the student as much as possible in the decision-making process. This will aid the student in developing important self-determination skills. Students may need to be taught how to be constructively involved in educational planning, and there are many curricula available today to aid in this process. Some class time should be dedicated to giving the students familiarity with the changes that will be taking place and how they can get involved in making those changes happen smoothly.

Next the teacher must implement the plan of action. Attention must be paid to the transition goals—they were not created for the fun of it! Communication with the agencies that will be involved in the transition is key having everything work smoothly.

PREVENTIVE STRATEGIES AND INTERVENTION STRATEGIES FOR AT-RISK LEARNERS

Anyone who has entered a classroom knows that students are performing at a variety of different levels. There are those students who are gaining from instruction and are becoming proficient at their goals. And then there are those students who are struggling through class and are at risk of failing to meet the instructional goals. How can teachers intervene and help these students before they become a failing statistic?

Thankfully, today we have a process known as **response to intervention**, or RTI. RTI is a three-tiered pyramid model that provides students with instruction and interventions before they are failing. This allows them to receive the help they need earlier, before the problem turns serious and it is difficult for them to catch up to the rest of the class.

To implement RTI, schools provide research-based interventions and collect data on how well the students are performing through that intervention. Data is carefully tracked and students who are succeeding continue to receive their instruction. Students who are not succeeding receive a higher level of support.

The three tiers of the RTI pyramid can be viewed as follows:

- Tier I is the universal program that all students receive. Between 80% and 90% of students should be able to succeed at Tier I, if the instruction provided in the classroom is high quality and well-differentiated.

- Tier II is targeted interventions. Students who are unsuccessful in Tier I receive interventions that are targeted to their particular deficits, as determined by the data. These interventions can be provided to groups of students as long as their academic needs are similar. Students usually remain in Tier II for several weeks, until the data show that they have made sufficient progress and can return to Tier I instruction. Five percent to 10% of students will require Tier II.

- Students who have not progressed appropriately in Tier II may instead receive Tier III instruction. Only by a small percentage of students receive Tier III. Usually these students are students with disabilities. Data collected during the previous two tiers are useful when referring students for special education services.

RTI is having a major impact on special education today. It better integrates special and general education, allowing all students who require it to benefit from interventions. It allows students to receive interventions before being labeled with a disability, and at times students do improve through these interventions and are found not to have a disability after all. This means that fewer students are referred to special education, and instead their academic needs can be successfully met in the general education setting.

RTI is also being used today instead of the IQ discrepancy model to identify students with learning disabilities. The practice of identifying students as learning disabled only if there is a large gap between their tested IQ and their scholastic achievement is a controversial one and is not necessarily effective. IDEA allows the RTI process to be used as identification instead, and many districts are now adopting this model.

EFFECTIVE AND APPROPRIATE EVIDENCE-BASED ASSESSMENTS

When providing interventions for the student with learning or behavior problems, assessments are key. Assessments should be completed to determine what interventions the student requires. Later, after intervention has begun, assessments must be performed to check whether the intervention is effective and how it should be adjusted.

Progress graphs are one way to chart student growth. Progress graphs are useful when data are easily measured in numbers. For example, the teacher can compute a student's fluency reading rate of words per minute, the number or percent of test questions answered correctly, or the number of times the student got out of his or her seat inappropriately.

The unit of measurement will be along the vertical axis, such as time elapsed or percentage. The number is along the horizontal axis—the date or session number. Data points are then plotted and the data depicted through either a bar graph or a line graph.

Progress graphs are helpful because they allow the data to be seen through a quick glance. The number of occurrences over time is visually clear and easily seen. Another way to depict data is through a progress chart, which tallies the data rather than creating a graph. This is more difficult to see visually.

Another way to collect data is through a performance record. The teacher evaluates the student's performance of goals that are listed on the IEP and checks off whether the goals have been mastered and to what extent. Often teachers also write comments that document student progress during instruction.

Portfolios are another way that teachers assess. A portfolio is a collection of student work samples collected over the school year. The portfolio should contain not only finished products, but it also should have samples of student notes and brainstorming processes. Photographs of projects not easily included in a portfolio can also be collected. This allows a visual snapshot of student work over the year.

DEFINING AND USING VARIOUS ASSESSMENTS

To arrange appropriate instruction for the student, assessments must first be completed. An assessment enables the teacher to know what the student is able to do and what he or she still needs to learn. Different kinds of assessments are useful within different situations.

Assessments can be divided into formative and summative assessments. A **formative assessment** assesses the student's knowledge while the subject is being taught. Pretests, homework, quizzes, and oral questioning are all examples of formative assessments. These allow the teacher to evaluate throughout each unit and see whether instruction is successful or if the instructional plan must be changed.

Summative assessments occur at the end of instruction, such as at the end of a unit. Rather than using the results of these assessments to change current instruction, teachers use the results to communicate student achievement and teacher proficiency.

Observation is a good way of doing formative assessments for behavior. By collecting data on teacher observations, more can be learned about the behavior—when it usually occurs, for how often, what factors interplay with the behavior. The best method of observation is systematic observation, when one instrument of measurement is consistently used to record observations.

We can further divide summative assessments into criterion-referenced and norm-referenced assessments. **Criterion-referenced assessments**, also known as **curriculum-based assessments**, are teacher-created assessments that follow the curriculum being taught. These assessments are especially useful because they assess exactly what is being used in the classroom.

Curriculum-based instruction can occur naturally in the classroom, through instructional activities that would be used regardless. This is useful because it allows the teacher to assess students without losing instructional time. The score on this assessment is determined by how well the student has learned the material taught.

Norm-referenced assessments are assessments that compare the student's performance on the assessment to the norm. The norm has been determined by testing a large group of students, then statistically concluding how an average child at that particular age or stage whould perform on the test. The student's score will therefore report not how many questions he or she answered correctly, but rather how the student has performed compared to others in that age or grade.

What tests are commonly administered to students to assess their knowledge? There are many, but certain tests tend to be more popular in school systems. The following is a list of reading tests that you are likely to encounter during your career.

- *The Woodcock Reading Mastery Test – Revised (WRMT-R)*. The test includes letter identification, word identification, and nonsense words, to test for the student's ability to decode words. Also on the test are word comprehension and passage comprehension to measure the student's ability to comprehend what he or she has read.

- *The Gray Oral Reading Test, Fourth Edition (GORT-4)*. The student reads several passages aloud while the examiner scores the reading for rate and accuracy. The student is then asked comprehension questions and the answers to those are scored as well.

- *The Kaufman Test of Educational Achievement, Second Edition (KTEA-2)*. This test evaluates letter and word recognition and nonsense word decoding. Reading comprehension is tested as well. Also on the test is a fluency check— decoding fluency of nonsense words as well as word recognition fluency, where the child is asked to read real words and timed.

While the above tests measure only reading ability, other tests measure student ability in multiple subjects. Examiners can choose which sections of these tests they wish to use.

- *Wechsler Individual Achievement Test, Second Edition (WIAT-II)*. This test measures word reading, pseudoword decoding, reading comprehension, numerical operations, math reasoning, spelling, written expression, listening comprehension, and oral expression. It is therefore useful not only to measure reading ability, but mathematical ability and listening and oral ability as well.

- *Peabody Individual Achievement Test, Revised (PIAT-R)*. This measures general information, word recognition, reading comprehension, mathematics, spelling, and written expression. Students answer by pointing rather than by oral responses or writing. This is therefore very useful for students with limited oral and written ability.

- *Woodcock-Johnson III Tests of Achievement (WJ-III ACH).* This test includes letter–word identification, reading fluency, passage comprehension, story recall, understanding directions, calculation, math fluency, applied problems, spelling, writing fluency, and writing samples. *WJ-III* subtests are shorter than most tests and the argument has been made that it is therefore unable to provide strong data on the child's performance.

Other tests measure students' intellectual or cognitive abilities. When evaluating the results for these tests, teachers should keep in mind that they are not always accurate; the student may have had difficulty focusing that day or may be unfamiliar with some concepts that were tested.

- *Wechsler Intelligence Scale for Children, Fourth Edition (WISC-IV).* This test assesses problem-solving skills for students ages 6–16. It measures verbal comprehension, perceptual reasoning, working memory, and processing speed. The resulting overall score is presented as the full scale IQ score.

- *Differential Ability Scales (DAS).* This test measures IQ and includes twelve core subtests, five diagnostic subtests, and three achievement tests. It includes a Special Nonverbal Composite, which measures IQ for students with language-based disabilities or hearing impairments.

- *Stanford-Binet, Fifth Edition (SB:V).* This test provides a full-scale IQ, verbal IQ, and nonverbal IQ.

- *Woodcock-Johnson III Tests of Cognitive Abilities (WJ III COG).* This test measures general intellectual ability. The subtests also provide scores for verbal ability, thinking ability, and cognitive efficiency. This test was normed on the same population as the *WJ III Tests of Achievement.* Using these two tests to compare cognitive ability and achievement will therefore achieve a more accurate result.

- *Leiter International Performance Scale, Revised (Leiter-R).* Included in the full-scale IQ score are three composite scores: fluid reasoning, fundamental visualization, and spatial visualization. Nonverbal attention and memory are also measured. This test is intended for those with severe disabilities and so it is administered through pointing rather than speaking.

INTERPRETING ASSESSMENT RESULTS

Interpreting assessment data can be complex. It is sometimes overwhelming to look at a test booklet and see all those numbers penciled in. How do you know what it all means? Normed-reference tests rely on statistical calculations to determine where the student falls within the norm. With some basic knowledge of statistics, you can manipulate the numbers to gain a better understanding of assessment results.

The **frequency distribution** is a table of how often a score occurs within a set of data. This allows you to see what score is most common. The **range**, on the other hand, is the difference between the high score and low score. The trouble with calculating the range is that one extreme score will throw off the calculation.

Knowing the **variance** of data is often helpful. This refers to the spread of scores within the distribution. For instance, you can have two sets of scores, each with a mean of 30. Recall that the **mean** is the average of all the numbers. Yet the range of the scores may be very different—one group has scores that are far more spread out. The group with a greater spread of scores has a greater variance.

Standard deviation is also important to know. This is the spread of scores around the mean. It is calculated by finding the square root of the variance.

The **bell curve** is considered to be the typical curve. This is the distribution of scores that would be found if every student in that age or grade level took the test. The bell curve never changes. We can find this distribution useful many times during special education, particularly when it comes to understanding IQ. On most IQ tests, the mean score is 100 with a standard deviation of 15. We therefore can figure out that students who are gifted, with IQ scores that are two standard deviations above the mean, have an IQ score of 130. Students who are classified with mental retardation and are two standard deviations below the mean have an IQ score of 70 or below.

At times, instead of a curve being symmetrical the way the bell curve is shaped, it has a skewed distribution. This is when one side of the bell is larger because more scores fall at the high or the low end, rather than right in the middle. A **positively skewed distribution** has most scores falling above the mean. A **negatively skewed distribution** has more scores falling below the mean.

A **correlation** is a relationship between two variables. A positive correlation is when both factors increase together. For instance, IQ and academic achievement are positively correlated. This would look like a positive line on a graph. Negative correlations are when one factor goes up and the other goes down. For instance, increasing anxiety usually decreases student performance. This looks like a negative graph. A zero correlation, when plotted, is just a bunch of dots with no particular pattern. In this case there is no relationship between the two variables at all.

UNDERSTANDING AND USING THE RESULTS OF ASSESSMENTS

Once the assessment has been administered and interpreted, it is time to write a comprehensive report. This report explains the assessment results and puts forth some recommendations for the student's instruction. The report must be clear and easily understood in order to be useful.

There are certain rules of thumb that should be followed to ensure the report is as professional as possible. One is never to write in first person, using "I." The report should always be written in the third person. This is a legal document, not a school project. Another is to use the past tense when possible. The assessment was already completed and it should be referred to as having already occurred.

There are some formatting suggestions that are also useful to keep in mind. One is to format the report single-spaced, rather than double-spaced. This way the parent will not be scared off by a report that appears to be dozens of pages long. Another suggestion is to center and bold headings so they are easy to find.

There is certain information that each report should contain. The following is a suggestion for an outline of an assessment report, taken from the book *Assessment in Special Education* by Pierangelo and Giulani (2009):

- *Identifying data.* This information will also be found in school records, but it is easier to access when it is written on the report. The student's chronological age at time of testing should be included. Often reports are only read months after the assessment is administered, and if the age is not clear the report will be misleading.

- *Reason for referral.* This section should be only a few sentences long. Why was the decision made to assess this student?

- *Background history.* This is a thorough history of the student that shows why a disability is suspected. Included should be family history—what the family background is at home. Developmental history is whether the student developed at a normal pace and what might have happened that is out of the ordinary. Academic history is the student's performance in school and on standardized tests. Social history provides a snapshot of the student's social life and activities.

- *Behavioral observations.* This is a description of how the student behaved when completing the assessment. Along with the assessment results, it may shed light on reasons for the student's struggles.

- *Tests and procedures administered.* This is a list of assessments that were administered, as well as procedures that were performed, such as classroom observations and parent or student interviews.

- *Test results.* This section states the test results and also explains what they indicate. It should explain whether this test should be considered a valid measure of the student's capabilities.

- *Conclusions.* This is a summary of the student's overall performance. What is the bottom line? This section should include brief information about the student, the student's strengths and weaknesses, and some information on student behavior.

- *Recommendations*. This contains practical suggestions for how to strengthen the student's areas of weakness. Suggestions should be included for the school, the teacher, and the parent.

When an assessment report is written well, it can be a tremendously valuable tool for helping the student. Not only does it give a clear snapshot of student performance, but it also provides suggestions that can immediately be implemented.

REFERENCES

Alberto, Paul A., and Anne C. Troutman. *Applied Behavior Analysis for Teachers,* 7th ed. New Jersey: Pearson Education, 2006.

"Assistive Technology Continuum of Low to High Tech Tools." *Boston Public Schools.* Accessed October 18, 2011. http://blog.vcu.edu/ttac/AT_Continuum_ Generic10_06.pdf.

Bos, Candace S., and Sharon Vaughn. *Strategies for Teaching Students with Learning and Behavior Problems,* 5th ed. Massachusetts: Allyn & Bacon, 2002.

Bowe, Frank. Making Inclusion Work. New Jersey: Pearson Education, 2005.

"Developing the Lesson Plan." *Air University.* Retrieved November 11, 2011. www. au.af.mil/au/awc/awcgate/af/af_safety_ctr-dev_lesn_plans.doc.

"Effective Use of Performance Objectives for Learning and Assessment." *University of New Mexico School of Medicine.* Last modified 2005. http://ccoe.umdnj.edu/ forms/EffectiveUseofLearningObjectives.pdf.

El-Hazmi, Mohsen A.F."Early Recognition and Intervention of Prevention of Dis-ability and its Complications." *Eastern Mediterranean Health Journal* 3, no. 1 (1997): 154–161. www.emro.who.int/publications/emhj/0301/22.htm.

Forehand, Mary. "Bloom's Taxonomy: Original and revised." *Emerging perspectives on learning, teaching, and technology.* Retrieved November 13, 2011. http:// projects.coe.uga.edu/epltt/index.php?title=Bloom%27s_Taxonomy.

Levine, Mel. *Educational Care,* 2nd ed. Massachusetts: Educators Publishing Service, 2002.

Lewis, Beth. "Top 8 Components of a Well-Written Lesson Plan." *About.com.* Retrieved November 11, 2011. http://k6educators.about.com/od/lessonplanheadquarters/ tp/8_steps_lp.htm.

Lipsky, Dorothy Kerzner, and Alan Gartner. *Inclusion: A Service, Not a Place.* New York: National Professional Resources, 2008.

Lipson, Marjorie Y., and Karen K. Wixson. *Assessment & Instruction of Reading and Writing Difficulty: An Interactive Approach,* 3rd ed. Massachusetts: Allyn & Bacon, 2003.

Pierangelo, Roger, and George A. Giuliani. *Assessment in Special Education: A Practical Approach,* 3rd ed. New Jersey: Pearson Education, 2009.

Pierangelo, Roger. *The Special Educator's Survival Guide,* 2nd ed. California: Jossey-Bass, 2004.

Reynolds, Cecil R., and Elaine Fletcher-Janzen, eds. "Classroom Management." *Encyclopedia of Special Education.* 3rd ed. New Jersey: John Wiley & Sons, 2007. PDF e-book.

Smith, Peter K., Helen Cowie, and Mark Blades. *Understanding Children's Develop-ment,* 4th ed. Massachusetts: Blackwell Publishing, 2003.

CHAPTER 6

Foundations and Professional Responsibilities

HISTORICAL MOVEMENT AND TRENDS

There was a time when people with disabilities were hidden from the general public and received few, if any, services. Today these students are often included in the general education classroom together with their typical peers. How did society reach this place?

Deinstitutionalization and Community-Based Placements

During the 1800s, concerned people began to open facilities, often known as asylums or institutions, for those with disabilities. These institutions were intended to manage people rather than to treat and educate. Once institutions became a movement, states began to open institutions as well.

While these institutions were initially created to care for those with disabilities, they began to deteriorate during the 1900s. These facilities became overcrowded and their residents suffered from poor care and isolation. Instead of these buildings being places of care for those with disabilities, they became warehouses to store those who had been forgotten.

In the mid-1900s, the movement to place students with disabilities within public schools began. These classrooms were self-contained and segregated, but they were still in a school with their typical peers. The students with exceptionalities did not interact with their schoolmates, however, but instead spent their time with their own classmates and teacher.

Inclusion

In 1954, the Supreme Court reached its landmark ruling in *Brown v. Board of Education*. This ruling, which was passed with students of color in mind, declared that separate was not equal and that it was illegal to segregate students into separate classes. The consequence was that segregating students with disabilities also became illegal. This was not decided, however, until the 1970s. Two separate cases went to court; one concerned students with mental retardation, and the other students with physical and emotional disabilities. These cases led to the Education for All Handicapped Children Act and slowly schools moved to include these students in the general education classrooms.

Application of Technology

Technology has vastly changed the lives of many people with disabilities. In fact, schools today are required to provide students with free access to assistive technology if it is necessary for the student to gain from instruction.

Transition

Transition services refer to the process of facilitating the child's moving from school to post-school life. Whether the students intend to move on to college, vocational education, supported or integrated employment, or independent living, the special educator is there to coach them through the transition process.

Advocacy

Advocates are those who work to improve the lives of students with disabilities. **Lay advocates** use their knowledge of educational law to attend meetings or write public letters. They may represent parents at due process hearings. **Educational advocates** evaluate the academic achievements of students with disabilities and make recommendations. They often attend IEP meetings with the parents or guardians. Teachers and other educational professionals often advocate for students with disabilities, as do parents.

Accountability and Meeting Educational Standards

A student cannot receive special education services if the child is academically behind due to lack of appropriate instruction. This includes math instruction, reading instruction, or English as a second language. Many students who are identified with learning disabilities in fact are not gaining the academic skills because the teachers are not properly prepared to teach.

This aspect of special education law was added after NCLB, the No Child Left Behind Act, was passed. NCLB seeks to ensure that all students have the opportunity to reach proficiency on state academic assessments, among other goals.

Another change in the law that was directly influenced by NCLB is the requirement that special education teachers be highly qualified. NCLB requires that all teachers who teach core academic subjects, such as language arts and math, must be highly qualified to teach those subjects. This includes special education teachers who are teaching core subjects to students with disabilities. Those teachers must now demonstrate their competence in those subjects.

FEDERAL DEFINITIONS

IDEA uses many terms throughout the law that at first glance seem self-evident. However, as with all legal documents, things are a bit more complicated. IDEA therefore takes the time to provide definitions for much of its terminology. What follows are the main definitions provided by IDEA. Other definitions can be found by searching for the text of IDEA Section 1401; there are 36 definitions in all.

- *Child with a disability*. Students with disabilities are not automatically eligible for services under IDEA. The child's disability must also affect educational performance so the child requires special education and related services.

- *Special education*. Special education includes a variety of services and is not limited to specialized instruction in a resource room. Students may receive tutoring, ABA programs, and services in the general education classroom with a teacher or paraprofessional. The term refers to all educational interventions that are appropriate for the student.

- *Supplementary aids and services*. These are services provided in the general education classroom. They enable students to participate together with their typical classmates.

- *Related services*. These include transportation to school if required. Also included may be therapies, nursing, or counseling if required for the child to benefit from special education. A surgically implanted medical device is not considered a related service.

- *Parent*. This includes natural parents, adoptive or foster parents, legal guardians, and those acting in the place of the parents.

FEDERAL REQUIREMENTS FOR THE PREREFERRAL, REFERRAL, AND IDENTIFICATION

How do students become qualified for services under IDEA? Back when the special education law was first passed in 1975, many students were identified through Child Find—the outreach program required by IDEA. Schools worked together with hospitals, agencies, and parents to search for students that may have required services. Today, Child Find has much less relevance.

Instead, most identification today occurs through the teacher. When the teacher first notices the student is having a problem in the classroom, the teacher will observe the student for a few weeks. He or she takes notes on student academic performance and behavior, recording any apparent patterns observed. The teachers will also look through student records to see whether there is a possible explanation of the issues. He or she will also interview past teachers and the child's parents for more information.

The special education process begins with the **prereferral**. Or rather, the prereferral is what happens before the process is set into motion. When a student is struggling in school, the first step is to provide interventions within the classroom. The hope is that these interventions will be effective and the student will not need to be referred to special education.

Prereferral interventions can be effective without overwhelming the teacher with extra work. A student who is unable to sit still may be given small jobs to do that will allow him or her to move around. A student who is often off-task may benefit from the teacher using his or her name in a word problem or finding ways to relate the material being taught to the student's interests. A student who has difficulty following the lesson may be provided with an advance organizer, which can be a graphic organizer, study guide, chapter outline, or perhaps a word bank.

If the teacher concludes that the child should be formally evaluated, a **referral** is made to the IEP team. Thorough documentation must be included with the referral. The teacher must note what the child is struggling with, why the teacher thinks the child would qualify under IDEA, what prereferral interventions were provided, and what the consequences were.

The next step is **evaluation**. The family must first be notified that the school thinks it necessary to evaluate their child. This notice also contains a request for the parents' (or guardians') permission to administer the evaluation of their child. This request must be made in the family's native language and in simple terminology. Once the school receives parental consent, the initial evaluation must be completed within 60 calendar days (rather than school days).

The school may need to reassure parents of the importance of the evaluation and that it is safe to acquiesce. If the family refuses, the school may choose to dispute through mediation and due process to assure that all students who require it are receiving services under IDEA. However, if the family consents to the evaluation but refuses to allow special education services to be provided, the school may not dispute the family decision. In this case, the school does not violate IDEA by not providing services to the student.

The parent may also request that an evaluation be conducted. Requests for evaluations of students should be sent in writing.

Finally, the **initial evaluation** may be administered. The IEP team brings in the specialists necessary to determine whether there is a disability—this may include psychologists or auditory specialists. The team then determines whether the child has a disability as defined under IDEA and is therefore eligible for special education services.

Reevaluations occur a minimum of every three years. If the parent and school agree that the reevaluation is unnecessary, as the child clearly still manifests the disability, then the reevaluation can be skipped. If the student's educational needs change, then a reevaluation is necessary. It is also necessary that the student be reevaluated if the parent or teacher requests it.

The school cannot determine with a single test whether the child has a disability. Rather, a variety of tools must be used to determine the level of student functioning. This information is used to determine what interventions should be included in the IEP. The evaluation must be administered in the language and form that will provide the most accurate information on the child's capabilities.

FEDERAL SAFEGUARDS OF THE RIGHTS OF STAKEHOLDERS

Parents and all those with a stake in the child's education have many rights under IDEA. Section 1415 of IDEA enumerates those rights and explains what recourse parents have if they are unhappy with the education and services being provided to their child.

The state government and local school district create most of the educational procedures that the parents and educational staff must follow. Federal law requires that these procedures build in parental rights; these are known as **procedural safeguards**. What rights must these procedures allow? Parents must have access to all student records, including test data. They should request data in writing. Parents have the right to participate in all meetings throughout the IEP process, from identification to evaluation to placement determination.

Parents can choose to have their child receive an independent educational evaluation. This is often done in cases where the school decides an assessment is unnecessary or parents disagree with the result of the school assessment. In such cases, the school cannot dictate which professionals they will accept assessment data from; parents have the right to see the assessor they choose.

In the event that parents disagree with a school decision and choose to go to court via due process, they must first provide the school with a written due process complaint notice. The due process hearing cannot begin until a notice has been filed. States are required to create forms that assist parents in filing this notice. Parents also are entitled to receive notice in the case that the school district chooses to enter due process against them, and again written notice must be provided, this time from the school.

The school district is required to provide the parents with **written prior notice** each time they suggest a change in identification, evaluation, or placement, or if they refuse to make a change that a parent has requested. This written notice must include a description of what action the school has proposed or refused and an explanation for their decision. They must describe the data that was looked at to make this decision and describe those other options that were looked into.

Also in this written notice, the parents are informed that they have procedural safeguards to which they are entitled. Depending on whether this is their first time receiving a written notice, parents are either told where a copy of these safeguards can be obtained or are provided with a copy. This **procedural safeguards notice** is provided to the parents upon initial referral to special education, the first time a complaint is filed, when the parent requests it, and at least once a year.

The procedural safeguards notice must be written in the parents' native language whenever possible. It must also be written in language that is easy to understand. This notice includes a summary of all those procedural safeguards discussed here.

When parents and the school district disagree over how to educate the child, the first step is mediation. A mediator is someone approved by the state who has strong knowledge of the laws relating to special education. The state takes on the cost of mediation.

When mediation is used, discussions are always confidential. Information shared during this process cannot be used later if there is a due process hearing. The meetings must be scheduled at a time and place convenient for everyone. If a resolution is reached, a written agreement is created and is signed by the parent and a school representative.

A preliminary meeting is scheduled within 15 days of the school receiving the parents' complaint. IEP team members knowledgeable about the area of the complaint must attend, as well as a local educational agency (LEA) representative with the power to make a decision. At this meeting, the parents and school officials attempt to reach an agreement.

If both sides reach an agreement, a legally binding document is written to that effect. If the complaint was not resolved within 30 days then there may be a due process hearing. Evaluations, recommendations, and all documents that will be used as evidence during the hearing must be disclosed at least five days before the hearing.

If the disagreement is not solved through mediation, the next step is due process. There is a two-year statute of limitations; if the event in question occurred over two years ago, the parents no longer have the option of a due process hearing. This limitation does not apply if the school withheld required information or misrepresented what was happening in the school.

If the parents prevail at the due process hearing, they receive their attorney fees from the school districts. The school districts also has the right to recover attorney fees from the parents, but only if the parents' or attorney's complaint was frivolous or ruled to be harassment of the school district.

During this process and all disputes with the school, the student is to *stay put*—remain in the current educational setting until a new decision is made. If this setting is not workable for the school, another setting may usually be used as long as the nature of the educational program remains the same.

COMPONENTS OF A LEGALLY DEFENSIBLE INDIVIDUALIZED EDUCATION PROGRAM

The IEP is a legal document and must be completed in the prescribed manner. IDEA outlines the mandatory components of the IEP. They are:

- The student's *present levels* of educational performance. This is a list of the student's strengths, needs, and achievements in the classroom. Here is where the IEP team writes how the disability is hindering the student from accessing the curriculum. If they think being in the general education classroom is hindering student achievement, they must include why they believe that would be. Care should be taken to enumerate the student's needs in this section, not the parents' or teacher's.

- *Measurable annual goals.* Aside from the annual goals, **benchmarks**, or short-term objectives for the student, also should be included in this section. These allow the IEP team to see whether the student is making progress toward the overall annual goal. The goals must be measurable—in other words, the educational team must be able to determine through data collection whether the goal has been mastered. When creating goals, the IEP team needs to think about whether the student can realistically master this goal in a school year, and whether instruction toward this goal can be provided within the general education classroom.

- Special education, **related services**, and **supplementary aids and services** to be provided to the student. This section enumerates how the student will reach the annual goals that were determined. Parents and teachers may disagree over what services should be provided to the student—the parent may feel the child will benefit from a certain service, but the teacher feels the cost would be unreasonably high or performing the intervention would be impractical for the teacher. A local educational agency official must therefore be present at the IEP meeting, to determine what funds are available for servicing. Frequency and duration of services must also be decided and specified in the IEP.

- The extent, if any, to which the student will not participate in general education classes. This is required because of the requirement of LRE—least restrictive environment. If student needs require that the student not participate in general education curricula for all of the time, then that is considered LRE, but it must be included and explained in the IEP. This is only a general statement of intent, however; the actual placement decisions are made after the completion of the IEP.

- An explanation of whether the student will participate in state and district assessments and, if so, what modifications and accommodations would be required. If the student will not participate, an alternate method of assessment must be specified. If modifications and accommodations are provided to the student on high-stakes tests, they also should be provided in the classroom throughout the year.

- The start date and duration of services. The start date would be after the IEP is completed, and the duration is usually over a school year. Some students will require ESY, or extended school year, in order that they not regress over the summer, and so these students' IEPs will have a longer duration.

- How progress toward annual goals will be measured and parents informed. Measuring progress is simpler if the student's IEP goals are mainly academic; the student's progress is measured through assignments and classroom assessments, and progress reports and report cards are sent home to the parents. Students who have behavioral goals or functional goals will need an alternate method of assessment to demonstrate progress toward these goals.

- Transition services. This is an important component for students aged 14 and older. The IEP team must determine what services the student requires to succeed post high school. If applicable, they may want to invite the student to the IEP meeting to provide input as well.

- A list of the IEP team members and their signatures.

The IEP must be reviewed annually to determine whether the student is progressing and if changes are required.

MAJOR LEGISLATION

IDEA

The law that declared the appropriate education of students with disabilities to be a legal requirement, the Education of All Handicapped Children Act, was first passed in 1975. This law was last revised in 2004 and renamed the Individuals with Disabilities Education Improvement Act of 2004, or IDEA. IDEA 2004 is also known as Public Law 108–446.

IDEA states that its purpose is to ensure that all students with disabilities receive a free and appropriate public education. This education must meet the student's unique needs. It should prepare him or her for further education, employment, and independent living.

Before the original law was created in 1975, fewer than half of children with disabilities received the education to which they were entitled to. Many students with disabilities were excluded from educational institutions entirely. The focus of the law back then was to ensure that these students gained access to educational programs. Today, much progress has been made. The focus of IDEA 2004 is instead on accountability and improved educational outcomes for students with disabilities.

Section 504

Section 504 of the Rehabilitation Act was passed in 1973, shortly before the passage of IDEA. Section 504 states that those with disabilities cannot be discriminated against on the basis of their disability. This provision applies anywhere that federal funding is used—it is not specific to schools.

Section 504 is a civil rights declaration. Unlike IDEA, federal funding is not offered to help schools comply with this provision. Still, Section 504 is vital to reach all students with disabilities.

Recall that to receive services under IDEA, students must be categorized under a limited list of disabilities. Students must also have their access to education impacted and so require special education services. Without these conditions being met, a student with a disability cannot receive services under IDEA. However, they are still protected under Section 504. Students receiving services under IDEA automatically are protected under Section 504.

An evaluation must be performed for a student to be eligible for protection under Section 504. To qualify, the student must have a significant physical or psychological disability that significantly affects a major life activity.

Students protected under Section 504 are protected from discrimination. They may receive accommodations and modifications if those are required for them to access classroom instruction together with their typical peers. However, these students do not receive the individualized instruction that is provided to those receiving services under IDEA.

ADA

The Americans with Disabilities Act, or ADA, granted additional civil rights to those with disabilities. It was passed in 1990.

ADA, like Section 504, does not enumerate specifically who is covered by the law. Instead, it refers to all people with disabilities. Someone with a disability has physical or mental impairments that substantially limit at least one major life activity. Someone may also be considered to have a disability if there is a history of a major impairment or if there is a perception of this impairment by others. ADA prohibits discrimination due to disability in certain areas.

Employers with 15 or more employees are required to adhere to the act. They may not ask questions specifically about disability when conducting interviews, as this would point to discrimination. They may not make hiring decisions based solely on disability. They must make a reasonable effort to accommodate employees' disabilities unless doing so would result in undue hardship.

All governments, no matter whether they receive federal funds, must adhere to ADA. Government buildings must be accessible to everyone, including the wheelchair bound. They must find ways to provide access in older buildings, or move programs out of those buildings if necessary. Public transportation also must be accessible. If the transportation is on a fixed route, then para-transit services must be offered door-to-door to those who require them, unless this would cause undue hardship.

Businesses and nonprofits that contain services for the public must also be accessible. Private corporations that offer certain courses or exams, or transportation, must conform to ADA as well. New buildings must be built accessible, and existing buildings changed where possible. Policies and procedures need to be user-friendly for those with disabilities. Care must be taken to communicate effectively with those with hearing, speech, and vision difficulty.

Finally, ADA assures those with disabilities access to telecommunications. TTY, and that tele-typewriters are available for those with hearing or speech difficulty. Third-party assistants must be available for those who are unable to speak directly with the other person.

MAJOR LEGAL CASES

Many court cases have been filed since the Education of All Handicapped Children Act was passed into law. Parents and schools attempted to clarify exactly what was required from school districts according to the law. A few major legal cases are discussed below.

Hendrick Hudson Board of Education v. Rowley, 458 U.S. 176 (1982)

Amy Rowley, a deaf child attending a public school in New York, was denied a sign-language interpreter. The board of education pointed out that Amy was performing well in class without the assistance of a sign-language interpreter and it was an unnecessary expense for the school. Amy's parents felt that her not receiving an interpreter was a violation of FAPE, Amy's right to a free and appropriate public education. The Rowleys fought the decision in court, and when they lost the initial court decision, they appealed to the U.S. District Court.

In *Hendrick Hudson Board of Education v. Rowley*, the U.S. District Court found that Amy indeed was performing better than most of her class both academically and socially. However, the court also felt that Amy would understand far more of her class instruction if she were not deaf, and so her disability was causing a disparity between her achievement and her potential. They therefore ruled that she was entitled to receive an interpreter so that she would be able to achieve her full potential in the same way other students can.

The school district then appealed, and when the court of appeals affirmed the district court's ruling, they appealed again. Now the case went before the Supreme Court.

In 1982, the Supreme Court ruled that Amy Rowley was not entitled to an interpreter. IDEA does *not* mean that students with disabilities are entitled to the best possible education. It only guarantees students access to an educational curriculum from which they can benefit. Amy was able to benefit from her classes without an interpreter, and so the district was not required to pay for one.

Irving Independent School District v. Tatro, 468 U.S. 883 (1984)

Amber Tatro, a student with spina bifida, required that a catheter be inserted every few hours. The school agreed to educate Amber but refused to take on the responsibility of catheterization. Although the process required only that someone in the school take a short training course and then spend a few minutes each time it was required, the school felt that catheterization was a medical service. Remember that medical services are not included under related services on the IEP, and students are not entitled to medical services in school.

The U.S. District Court found that CIC, clean intermittent catheterization, was not a related service. The U.S. Court of Appeals declared that it was. *Irving School District v. Tatro* then was decided by the Supreme Court.

In 1984, the Supreme Court found that the school district was responsible to provide CIC for Amber. It explained that Amber was unable to benefit from special education without this service, as she would be unable to attend school. CIC is therefore considered a related service.

Oberti v. Board of Education of the Borough of Clementon School District 995 F.2d 1204 (1993)

Rafael Oberti, a student with Down's syndrome, was evaluated before entering kindergarten. The district recommended that Rafael be placed in a segregated classroom for students with intellectual disabilities. Rafael's parents visited all the local specialized classrooms but did not feel any would be appropriate for Rafael, and the district reached an agreement that in the morning Rafael instead attend a kindergarten for the developmentally delayed. Rafael attended a specialized kindergarten in the afternoon as per the original plan.

During that year, Rafael made academic, social, and behavioral progress during both the morning and afternoon class. However, Rafael displayed aggressive behaviors during the morning class that did not abate even after an aide was provided. These behaviors did not manifest themselves in the afternoon. The district therefore decided that for the following year, Rafael could no longer be included in the general education classroom at his home school. Instead, he would need to travel to a neighboring school each day to be educated in a specialized classroom.

The Obertis then filed for due process, arguing that Rafael was entitled to be included in his home school. A compromise was reached wherein Rafael attended a class for students with disabilities in a nearby school, with the provision that efforts would be made to include him with typical peers. However, the Obertis found that Rafael was not included with typical peers and they again filed for due process in *Oberti v. Board of Education of the Borough of Clementon School District*.

Expert witnesses testified on both sides. In 1992, the court determined that many of the supplementary aids and services that had been provided to Rafael in the special education classroom could in fact be provided in the general education classroom as well. The district therefore neglected to provide appropriate supplementary aids and services to Rafael, and so was in violation of least restrictive environment.

ROLES AND RESPONSIBILITIES OF THE SPECIAL EDUCATION TEACHER

All teachers must wear many different career hats. It is not enough to instruct students in their learning—the teacher must also meet student needs to enable them to benefit from instruction. This is especially important for the special education teacher, who services students with exceptional needs. The Council for Exceptional Children, the accrediting agency for special educators, identifies certain professional standards that special educators must meet: they must manage behavior, connect students with necessary support services, create relationships with parents, and advocate for their students.

When instructing students with disabilities, special educators must ensure that the instructional methods used are appropriate for the student's needs. Grading students and moving them in and out of the program should be according to whether the student has mastered his or her individual goals. Teachers must keep accurate data to provide to other professionals, and maintain student confidentiality.

Students with disabilities often have adverse behaviors that must be managed. Special educators are required to choose behavioral interventions that do not undermine the student's dignity. All behavioral procedures must be allowable according to state law.

Special educators must be especially careful when it comes to the use of *aversives*. This refers to the controversial practice of reinforcing appropriate behavior through an unpleasant sensation such as a spray of water on the face or a bitter substance in the mouth. Use of aversives has been severely restricted legally and it has been questioned whether they are a violation of students' basic rights. They should be used only if other methods have failed and parents and support staff have been first consulted.

Special educators must exercise caution when they are asked to do something for which they may not have appropriate training. Due to the nature of students' disabilities, schools may ask them to administer medication or a feeding tube when the nurse is unavailable. The special educator may also be in a situation where he or she needs to restrain a student who is displaying aggressive behavior. Teachers are responsible to ensure that what they are doing is legally appropriate and that they receive any required training.

As was previously discussed, special educators have responsibilities toward their students' parents as well. They are required to reach out to the parents to involve them in their child's education. When communicating with parents, they must use terms the parents can understand. They must be respectful at all times and be aware of possible cultural differences. They also should seek opportunities to educate the parents in ways to get involved in student education and success.

Finally, special educators have the responsibility to advocate for students with exceptionalities. Through speaking up and writing letters and articles, they can work to improve the rights of their students. They can work to influence government laws toward persons with disabilities. Care should be taken that they do not appear to speak for their school or agency, however; they must make it clear that they are speaking as individuals. Other professionals can be encouraged to work to improve the special services that are provided. They also must take care that students do not receive inappropriate placements in special education; teacher have the obligation to intervene when necessary.

ROLES AND RESPONSIBILITIES OF OTHER PROFESSIONALS

Aside from the special educator and the parents or guardians, many other professionals are involved in the schooling of students with disabilities. This is especially so among students with severe disabilities. Each of these professionals will have necessary input in the student's education, and it can be challenging for the teacher to communicate with all professionals and ensure that the educational team is running smoothly.

Many students with disabilities require that aside from receiving special education services, they receive other related services as well such as those listed below. Remember that these students are entitled to related services under IDEA.

- *Speech-language pathology* is provided to remediate speech problems and work with language difficulties. ASHA, the American Speech-Language-Hearing Association, represents pathologists.

- *Counseling.* Students with ADHD, emotional and behavior disorders, and traumatic brain injury (TBI) will benefit from counseling. Students who are in the transition process also benefit from counseling services. Counselors are represented by the American School Counselor Association.

- *Physical therapy* is delivered to improve gross-motor activity and prevent muscle atrophy. Physical therapists belong to the American Physical Therapy Association.

- *Occupational therapy* is intended to improve fine-motor activity and teach practical occupational skills. For children, occupational skills would include getting dressed and eating food independently. Their organization is the American Occupational Therapy Association.

- *Interpreters* are useful for the deaf or hard of hearing. They interpret the teacher's or classmates' words into American Sign Language. They are represented by the Registry of Interpreters for the Deaf.

It is important that all professionals communicate with each other so that they enhance each other's work. Teachers and professionals often struggle to find time to communicate with each other. They may also run into communication difficulties, with each having expectations that do not align with the other professionals' ideas. The administration should work to create time for everyone to meet, and teachers and professionals should make the effort to try and communicate with each other during the school day.

Another difficulty teachers and professionals run into is when to schedule the student's related services. Often professionals try to schedule these services during specials, such as art and gym, or during lunch or recess. The student is pulled out according to a schedule and receives services in a separate room. But this means the student misses out on these activities and on opportunities for socialization. On the other hand, if a student is removed during a core academic subject, he or she will miss important instruction.

Many schools therefore try and work within the push-in model instead, in which the therapist or other professional comes into the classroom to work with the child. This reduces the number of transitions the child requires, which is important because students with disabilities often struggle with transitions. The student also does not have to move to another room, which saves valuable time. The therapist being in the classroom also allows the therapy to be an extension of what is happening inside the classroom.

Still, push-in has its disadvantages. Students may not focus as well within the classroom as they would within a one-on-one situation. Therapists would not be able to see many students at once, which may be financially unviable for the school. It is for this reason that some schools continue to use the pull-out model, but use block scheduling—that is, they find ways to schedule related services back to back. This way the student is out for a set time during the week and is free during the rest of the week to work within the classroom.

Aside from coordinating students' related services, educators may need to work with representatives for other agencies. Many students receiving services under IDEA, particularly students with emotional disturbance, require services from social agencies such as mental health agencies. If a teacher refers a student to an agency, the teacher must always follow up. Often the parents do not take care of what needs to be done and the student is in danger of falling through the cracks.

STRENGTHS AND LIMITATIONS OF COLLABORATIVE APPROACHES

In an inclusive environment, the general and special education teachers must work together to assure that student needs are being met. There are a few different collaborative approaches available for teachers, and each one allows the teachers to work together in ways that will best allow them to serve their students. Teachers should choose methods, or mix and match methods, depending on classroom need.

The **consultation** approach is one in which the special educator serves as a consultant for the general educator. The special educator listens to the general educator's description of classroom needs, or visits the classroom to decide the best possible way to serve the students.

In the **collaboration** approach, the special educator and general educator interact as equal partners in the decision-making process. They work together to brainstorm ways to serve the students. Most teachers vastly prefer collaboration as it allows both teachers to have input and often causes great ideas.

Coteaching is another way to serve student needs. In coteaching, the special educator and general educator provide instruction together. There are a few different ways to coteach.

- One leading, one assisting. While one teacher teaches the whole class, the other teacher goes around to check that each student is following the lesson. The assisting teacher provides some individual interventions to students who are struggling to follow.

- Parallel teaching. Students are divided into groups to be taught the content by one teacher. These groups may be mixed-ability level, and the advantage is that smaller groups allow for greater student participation and interaction. Same-ability groups allow the teachers to customize instruction for the ability of those students.

- Station teaching. Students are divided into groups and the teachers take turns teaching each group. An alternative is to divide students into student-led centers, and the teachers go around to monitor the centers.

- Team teaching. The teachers teach the whole class together. Since each teacher has differing teaching styles, students benefit from each teacher's strengths.

Another way special and general educators may interact is through the consultant teaching process. The special education teacher assesses students and helps to adapt materials and instruction, but does not actually instruct in the classroom. Yet another method of collaboration is through paraprofessionals—the special education teacher coordinates the paraprofessionals and instructs them on how to work with the students in the classroom.

In order for special and general education teachers to collaborate effectively, they must have a common meeting time to plan. Without this planning time teachers are unable to communicate effectively and plan to meet student needs. This therefore needs to be a priority for both teachers and administrators.

Another issue teachers need to pay attention to is the concept of "student ownership." General education teachers have traditionally had the view that the students with disabilities are in the jurisdiction of the special education teacher. Now that all students are included in the classroom as much as possible, teachers should take the view of "shared ownership." They both have a stake in the success of these students and the input of both is required for them to succeed.

Teachers should realize that they are all specialists in the classroom. The general education teacher is the content specialist, while the special education teacher is the specialist able to adapt and modify instruction. It is when they come together to work and collaborate that the needs of all students can be solidly met.

COMMUNICATION WITH STAKEHOLDERS

Effective communication is tremendously important for special educators. There are many educational professionals involved in working with students with disabilities—parents, general education teachers, administrators, psychologists, therapists, and advocates, among others. It is therefore important for special educators to learn how to communicate with others effectively.

- Build respect and trust. Parents and other educational professionals need to feel that they have a working relationship that will allow them to best serve the child. When parents feel that the teacher is advocating for their child they will be able to trust the teacher and work with him or her.

- Actively listen. Echo what the parents are saying to show that you understand. This gives them the opportunity to correct you if necessary. Ask open-ended questions that give the opportunity to answer with a variety of information.

- Use layperson's terms. Don't pepper your speech with special-education jargon that parents won't be able to understand or that makes them uncomfortable.

- Offer encouragement. Find something positive to say about what the students are doing and offer positive feedback about parental interventions with the student.

Teachers should communicate with parents and other stakeholders as often as possible. In-person meetings are useful and include parent-teacher conferences, spontaneous meetings in the hallway, or informational meetings. Phone calls can be used in cases when teachers don't often meet parents or to follow up after a parent-teacher conference. Teachers also can call home if there is a sudden problem in school. Written communication also can be sent home in the form of journals or progress reports.

POTENTIAL BIAS ISSUES

While students from minority groups are overrepresented in special education programs, they are often underrepresented in programs for the gifted and talented. This seems to be tied to the fact that the minority groups of African Americans, Native Americans, and Hispanic Americans tend to have low socioeconomic status. Lack of resources means inferior health care, poor nutrition, and poor living conditions, all of which will contribute to poor academic performance.

Biased assessments also may account for this overrepresentation. The assessments to identify students' special-education needs may contain items that are culturally sensitive, and so it will be biased against those from minority cultures. There also may be inconsistencies between home culture and school culture that lead to conflict with classroom expectations. This means students are identified as having behavioral problems when in fact they are behaving in a manner that they believe to be appropriate.

Research also shows that students from different cultures learn differently. Students who are African American, for example, tend to learn intuitively, through social environments. They benefit from cooperative learning where they learn through hands-on activities. Caucasian students, on the other hand, have been found to work well within independent and competitive classroom settings. Because educators tend to be from the majority culture, they may mistakenly identify students with learning styles similar to theirs as being academically advanced and those with very different learning styles as needing extra help.

How can this change? The first way is through creating unbiased assessments. The lawsuit *Larry P. v. Riles* ruled that IQ tests that are culturally biased cannot be used to determine educational placements. Unbiased assessments are, in fact, required by IDEA, and special educators must ensure that they choose assessments which fairly evaluate students from all cultural backgrounds.

Teachers also should take into account student cultures when developing instructional objectives and activities. Addressing all student needs in the classroom takes effort, but with the proper thought and planning it can be done.

REFERENCES

29th Annual Report to Congress on the Implementation of the Individuals with Disabilities Education Act, 2007. Vol. 2. Washington, D.C.: U.S. Department of Education, 2010. www2.ed.gov/about/reports/annual/osep/2007/parts-b-c/29th-vol-2.pdf

"A Guide to Disability Rights Laws." *U.S. Department of Justice.* Last modified February 16, 2006. www.ada.gov/cguide.htm

Bowe, Frank. Making Inclusion Work. New Jersey: Pearson Education, 2005.

"Building the Legacy: IDEA 2004." *U.S. Department of Education.* Retrieved November 1, 2011. http://idea.ed.gov/explore/view/p/,root,regs,300,A,300%252E8,c,.

"Categories of Disability under IDEA." *National Dissemination Center for Children with Disabilities.* Last modified April 2009. http://nichcy.org/disability/categories.

"CEC Standards for Professional Practice." *Council for Exceptional Children.* Retrieved November 9, 2011. www.cec.sped.org/Content/NavigationMenu/ProfessionalDevelopment/ProfessionalStandards/PracticeStandards/default.htm.

Gargiulo, Richard M. *Special Education in Contemporary Society,* 3rd ed. California: SAGE Publications, 2009.

"No Child Left Behind." *Education Week.* Last modified September 19, 2011. www.edweek.org/ew/issues/no-child-left-behind/.

"Oberti." *Kids Together, Inc.* Last modified June 29, 2010. www.kidstogether.org/right-ed_files/oberti.htm.

Wright, Pam, and Pete Wright. *Wrightslaw: From Emotions to Advocacy,* 2nd ed. Virginia: Harbor House Law Press, 2007.

Wright, Pamela Darr, and Peter W. D. Wright. *Wrightslaw: Special Education Law,* 2nd ed. Virginia: Harbor House Law Press, 2007.

Practice Test 1

Education of Exceptional Students: Core Content Knowledge (0353)

This test is also on CD in our special interactive TestWare® for the Praxis II Education of Exceptional Students: Core Content Knowledge (0353). It is highly recommended that you first take this exam on computer. You will then have the additional study features and benefits of enforced timed conditions and instantaneous, accurate scoring. See page 6 for instructions on how to get the most out of our book and software.

Visit www.rea.com for updates and additional resources

1. Ⓐ Ⓑ Ⓒ Ⓓ
2. Ⓐ Ⓑ Ⓒ Ⓓ
3. Ⓐ Ⓑ Ⓒ Ⓓ
4. Ⓐ Ⓑ Ⓒ Ⓓ
5. Ⓐ Ⓑ Ⓒ Ⓓ
6. Ⓐ Ⓑ Ⓒ Ⓓ
7. Ⓐ Ⓑ Ⓒ Ⓓ
8. Ⓐ Ⓑ Ⓒ Ⓓ
9. Ⓐ Ⓑ Ⓒ Ⓓ
10. Ⓐ Ⓑ Ⓒ Ⓓ
11. Ⓐ Ⓑ Ⓒ Ⓓ
12. Ⓐ Ⓑ Ⓒ Ⓓ
13. Ⓐ Ⓑ Ⓒ Ⓓ
14. Ⓐ Ⓑ Ⓒ Ⓓ
15. Ⓐ Ⓑ Ⓒ Ⓓ

16. Ⓐ Ⓑ Ⓒ Ⓓ
17. Ⓐ Ⓑ Ⓒ Ⓓ
18. Ⓐ Ⓑ Ⓒ Ⓓ
19. Ⓐ Ⓑ Ⓒ Ⓓ
20. Ⓐ Ⓑ Ⓒ Ⓓ
21. Ⓐ Ⓑ Ⓒ Ⓓ
22. Ⓐ Ⓑ Ⓒ Ⓓ
23. Ⓐ Ⓑ Ⓒ Ⓓ
24. Ⓐ Ⓑ Ⓒ Ⓓ
25. Ⓐ Ⓑ Ⓒ Ⓓ
26. Ⓐ Ⓑ Ⓒ Ⓓ
27. Ⓐ Ⓑ Ⓒ Ⓓ
28. Ⓐ Ⓑ Ⓒ Ⓓ
29. Ⓐ Ⓑ Ⓒ Ⓓ
30. Ⓐ Ⓑ Ⓒ Ⓓ

31. Ⓐ Ⓑ Ⓒ Ⓓ
32. Ⓐ Ⓑ Ⓒ Ⓓ
33. Ⓐ Ⓑ Ⓒ Ⓓ
34. Ⓐ Ⓑ Ⓒ Ⓓ
35. Ⓐ Ⓑ Ⓒ Ⓓ
36. Ⓐ Ⓑ Ⓒ Ⓓ
37. Ⓐ Ⓑ Ⓒ Ⓓ
38. Ⓐ Ⓑ Ⓒ Ⓓ
39. Ⓐ Ⓑ Ⓒ Ⓓ
40. Ⓐ Ⓑ Ⓒ Ⓓ
41. Ⓐ Ⓑ Ⓒ Ⓓ
42. Ⓐ Ⓑ Ⓒ Ⓓ
43. Ⓐ Ⓑ Ⓒ Ⓓ
44. Ⓐ Ⓑ Ⓒ Ⓓ
45. Ⓐ Ⓑ Ⓒ Ⓓ

46. Ⓐ Ⓑ Ⓒ Ⓓ
47. Ⓐ Ⓑ Ⓒ Ⓓ
48. Ⓐ Ⓑ Ⓒ Ⓓ
49. Ⓐ Ⓑ Ⓒ Ⓓ
50. Ⓐ Ⓑ Ⓒ Ⓓ
51. Ⓐ Ⓑ Ⓒ Ⓓ
52. Ⓐ Ⓑ Ⓒ Ⓓ
53. Ⓐ Ⓑ Ⓒ Ⓓ
54. Ⓐ Ⓑ Ⓒ Ⓓ
55. Ⓐ Ⓑ Ⓒ Ⓓ
56. Ⓐ Ⓑ Ⓒ Ⓓ
57. Ⓐ Ⓑ Ⓒ Ⓓ
58. Ⓐ Ⓑ Ⓒ Ⓓ
59. Ⓐ Ⓑ Ⓒ Ⓓ
60. Ⓐ Ⓑ Ⓒ Ⓓ

PRACTICE TEST 1

EDUCATION OF EXCEPTIONAL STUDENTS: CORE CONTENT KNOWLEDGE (0353)

TIME: 1 Hour
            60 Multiple-choice questions

In this section, you will find examples of test questions similar to those you are likely to encounter on the Praxis II Education of Exceptional Students: Core Content Knowledge (0353) Exam.

1. Under which disability are students with ADHD often classified?

    (A) Attention deficit/hyperactivity disorder
    (B) Specific learning disability
    (C) Other health impairment
    (D) Conduct disorder

2. Which categorical area represents the largest proportion of children served under IDEA?

    (A) Intellectual disabilities
    (B) Hearing impairments
    (C) Learning disabilities
    (D) Emotional disturbance

3. Most people who are legally blind

    (A) have no vision.
    (B) were born that way.
    (C) have some sight.
    (D) use large-print documents.

4. Which of the following symptoms are almost always present when a child's nervous system is damaged?

    (A) Poor adaptive skills
    (B) Muscular weakness or paralysis
    (C) Long- and short-term memory loss
    (D) Cognitive impairments

5. Which special education category is the identification used for children between the ages of 3 and 9 who are otherwise not categorized?

    (A) Developmental delay
    (B) Specific learning disability
    (C) Multiple disabilities
    (D) Other health impairment

6. Which of the following is the LEAST prevalent among American school children?

    (A) Deaf-blindness
    (B) Emotional behavior disturbance
    (C) Speech or language impairments
    (D) Specific learning disability

7. Which of the following is NOT a high-incidence disability?

    (A) Emotional and behavioral disorders
    (B) Intellectual disabilities
    (C) Other health impairments
    (D) Specific learning disability

8. To be classified as having speech or language impairment, a student who speaks two languages must demonstrate the impairment

    (A) only in school.
    (B) in both languages.
    (C) only in the English language.
    (D) in the home and in school.

9. Which of the following disabilities describes a student who has unintelligible speech that interferes with communication?

    (A) Speech delay
    (B) Speech impairment
    (C) Language impairment
    (D) Semantics deficits

10. Which of the following disabilities also occurs concurrently with language impairment in the

majority of students with this disability, making them vulnerable to academic learning problems?

(A) Learning disabilities
(B) Behavior disorders
(C) Visual impairments
(D) Hearing impairments

11. Although this characteristic does not require documentation, the federal definition indicates that a learning disability may be due to

(A) minimal brain dysfunction.
(B) poor instruction.
(C) heredity.
(D) hyperactivity.

12. A child with a learning disability will probably be identified

(A) when he starts preschool.
(B) by first grade.
(C) in third grade.
(D) soon after birth.

13. Students with ADHD are eligible for services under IDEA if

(A) their disability adversely affects their educational performance.
(B) they are referred by their pediatrician.
(C) they are prescribed medicine for ADHD.
(D) they display disruptive behavior.

14. Which child is more likely to be determined eligible for ADHD?

(A) A boy
(B) A girl
(C) A girl who stares out the window in class
(D) A boy who disrupts the class

15. What does it mean if a student is determined to have a learning disability with comorbidity?

(A) The student cannot be served in the general education classroom.
(B) The student's learning disability is a result of heredity.
(C) The student's learning disability is present with another disability.

(D) The student must be diagnosed by a physician.

16. In order to qualify for special education services, the IEP team must determine that a student with emotional and behavioral disorders

(A) is socially maladjusted.
(B) does not have schizophrenia.
(C) has his or her educational performance adversely affected.
(D) was identified before the age of 10.

17. An example of an externalizing behavioral problem is

(A) bullying.
(B) depression.
(C) learning disability.
(D) bulimia.

18. According to IDEA 2004, a student who is diagnosed as HIV+ and whose academics are affected because of the illness should be classified as having which of the following?

(A) Terminal illness.
(B) Other health impairment.
(C) Multiple disability.
(D) Learning disability.

19. Who is considered the father of special education?

(A) Thomas Hopkins Gallaudet
(B) Edouard Seguin
(C) Jean-Marc-Gaspard Itard
(D) Leo Kanner

20. The first federal court case guaranteeing special education services for children with intellectual disabilities (mental retardation) was

(A) *Mills v. Board of Education* (1972).
(B) *Larry P. v. Riles* (1972).
(C) *Honig v. Doe* (1988).
(D) *Pennsylvania Association for Retarded Children v. Commonwealth of Pennsylvania* (1972).

21. In the passage of the Education of All Handicapped Children Act (1975), which later became IDEA, which provision was NOT included?

(A) Increase in the range of ages of children considered eligible for special education services

(B) Guarantee of legal fees to parents who sue and win disputes regarding special education services

(C) Least restrictive environment through consideration of placement in general education classrooms

(D) Responsibility of the school system to locate students with disabilities

22. The role of the parent in the development of the individualized education plan (IEP) is best described by which of the following statements?

(A) The parent is invited to attend the IEP meeting, but is not an important part of the IEP development process.

(B) While the parent may make suggestions, the recommendations of the professionals are paramount.

(C) The parent may offer recommendations only through legal counsel.

(D) Parents play an active role in the development of the IEP and may make recommendations for inclusion in the plan.

23. Parents have the right to each of the following EXCEPT

(A) a due process hearing.
(B) the refusal of services or assessment of their child.
(C) the examination of all school records.
(D) preventing their child from attending school.

24. The most important component of an effective and productive parent-teacher partnership is

(A) sharing the same ethnicity.
(B) having a friendship.
(C) good communication.
(D) having similar value systems.

25. Transitions in the life of a child with a disability are difficult because

(A) parents of children with disabilities are especially controlling.

(B) additional service providers become involved in their lives and this adds to and creates more stress.

(C) most parents of children with disabilities do not trust the professionals.

(D) parents of children with disabilities are ill equipped to do what is best for their child.

26. Which of the following court cases determined that school districts must provide beneficial instructional services to student with disabilities:

(A) *Rowley v. Hendrick Hudson School District*
(B) *Irving Independent School District v. Tatro*
(C) *Honig v. Doe*
(D) *Cedar Rapids Community School District v. Garret F*

27. Which of the following actions is supported under ADA?

(A) Existing buildings being renovated for accessibility
(B) Parent participation in IEP meetings
(C) Child Find
(D) Accessibility to new buses, trains, and subways

28. Section 504 and the ADA are considered to be all of the following EXCEPT

(A) civil rights laws.
(B) anti-discrimination laws.
(C) educational laws.
(D) laws that ensure accessibility for people with disabilities.

29. If a student has ADHD, but does not qualify for special education services, which of the following options is available?

(A) The parents should request reassessment.
(B) The student's physician should contact the school.
(C) The teacher may choose to provide special education services anyway.
(D) The student may receive accommodations, such as preferential seating and extended time, under a Section 504 plan.

30. The category of ADHD was first identified in which legislative act?

    (A) No Child Left Behind Act
    (B) Vocational Rehabilitation Act
    (C) 2004 reauthorization of IDEA
    (D) 1997 reauthorization of IDEA

31. Continuum of services requires

    (A) that students be placed in the setting most like that of their nondisabled peers.
    (B) that students begin placement in the most restrictive environment.
    (C) that a full range of service options for students with disabilities will be provided.
    (D) early intervention services.

32. Most students with learning disabilities receive the majority of their instruction in

    (A) resource programs.
    (B) self-contained classes.
    (C) a regular classroom inclusive environment.
    (D) in separate schools.

33. A written request to evaluate a student to determine whether a disability is present is known as

    (A) a referral.
    (B) a transition plan.
    (C) full inclusion.
    (D) special education.

34. IFSPs are generated for

    (A) infants/toddlers.
    (B) young adults.
    (C) school-age children.
    (D) high school students.

35. Students with learning disabilities have scores on standardized tests

    (A) within the normal range.
    (B) two standard deviations below the norm.
    (C) that can be from two standard deviations below to two standard deviations above the norm.
    (D) usually above the normal range.

36. Barry has a learning disability and has difficulty memorizing math facts. Twice each week, he takes a one-minute timed math fact test. His teacher collects the data from these tests and makes instructional decisions based upon his progress. This procedure is called

    (A) due process.
    (B) sequential learning.
    (C) assistive technology.
    (D) progress monitoring.

37. In which component of Response to Intervention are all students assessed?

    (A) Universal screening
    (B) Tier 1
    (C) Tier 2
    (D) Tier 3

38. Mr. Sheppard teaches all the students in his sixth-grade social studies class the same content, but he uses different instructional methods that match various learning needs, preferences, and styles. What is Mr. Sheppard using?

    (A) Accommodations
    (B) Procedural safeguards
    (C) Modifications
    (D) Differentiated instruction

39. Cindy is in a general education class for most of the day, but goes to a special education class for help with reading and language arts. What type of service delivery is Cindy receiving?

    (A) Resource room
    (B) Full inclusion
    (C) Self-contained special education
    (D) Consultation

40. Ms. Woodward designs lessons that use grouping practices that include either heterogeneous or homogeneous groups. The pace of instruction varies as the groups solve problems or complete assignments together. Ms. Woodward has differentiated the instructional

    (A) delivery.
    (B) content.

(C)   scope and sequence.
(D)   curriculum.

41. Toderick is a seventh grader with a visual impairment. An appropriate accommodation for Toderick is to

(A)   have Toderick listen to the lectures in class but do not assign the class readings.
(B)   let him watch movies and videos about the content in place of the assigned readings.
(C)   provide him with the textbook on audio-tape and let him listen to his assignments.
(D)   have another student give copies of his or her lecture notes to Toderick and let him use those for testing.

42. The prereferral stage is designed to

(A)   notify the parents that their child is in danger of being retained.
(B)   notify the teachers that the student has skill deficits.
(C)   conduct assessments to determine the child's present level of performance.
(D)   avoid unnecessary assessments and placements in special education.

43. What two issues must be identified during the eligibility step of the IEP process?

  I.   Whether the child has a disability
  II. Whether the child qualifies for special education services
  II. Whether the school has the resources to provide the services
  III Whether related services are necessary
  IV. Which disability the child qualifies for

(A)   I only
(B)   I and II
(C)   I and IV
(D)   III and IV

44. Student participation in development of their IEPs promotes behaviors needed for independent living such as making decisions, choosing preferences, and practicing self-advocacy. This is considered

(A)   self-determination.
(B)   accommodations.
(C)   partial participation.
(D)   community-based instruction.

45. One important principle when developing an IEP is that

(A)   services that are too expensive for the school system may be left off the IEP.
(B)   all services listed do not have to be related to the student's goals.
(C)   no mention of unavailable services should occur.
(D)   all of the student's needs must be met.

46. Students' IEPs are available to

(A)   the special education teacher and parent only.
(B)   district assessment personnel.
(C)   researchers with the superintendent's permission.
(D)   any educator who interacts with the child.

47. Which of the following is NOT an example of a testing accommodation for a student?

(A)   Reading the test aloud
(B)   Reducing the number of answer choices
(C)   Having an assistant provide the answers
(D)   Testing in a small group

48. Tonisha's special education teacher evaluates her learning outcomes using class assignments, writing samples, and observational data. Which of the following assessments is Tonisha's teacher using?

(A)   Authentic assessment
(B)   Portfolio assessments
(C)   Norm-referenced testing
(D)   Performance standards

49. Which curriculum is one that includes lessons that demonstrate aspects of many different cultures to help teach concepts and enhance the learning of a diverse population?

(A)   Culturally responsive
(B)   Evidence-based
(C)   Culturally focused
(D)   Bicultural

50. Who of the following provides the usual source of referral to special education for school-age children?

    (A) Parents
    (B) General education teachers
    (C) Special education teachers
    (D) School nurse

51. Which of the following is a guideline for determining which testing accommodations to provide for a student who is learning English as a second language?

    (A) Always include a bilingual translator in testing situations.
    (B) Provide the test in his native language.
    (C) Begin with the translator, and add other accommodations as the need arises.
    (D) Provide the same accommodations used for instruction.

52. Cooperative learning is an effective strategy to use with culturally and linguistically diverse students for all of the following reasons EXCEPT

    (A) peers are more likely to know how to reach the other students.
    (B) peers can assist each other with assignments.
    (C) not all teachers can offer bilingual education or support in a child's native language.
    (D) children who come from cultures that do not value individual competition feel more comfortable.

53. DeMarco is taught a reading comprehension strategy in his reading resource room and remembers how and when to use it when reading his science and social studies texts. He is demonstrating

    (A) motivation.
    (B) learned helplessness.
    (C) attention-seeking behaviors.
    (D) generalization.

54. What should occur in order for collaboration among school professionals to be effective?

    (A) Individual students' progress must be carefully monitored.
    (B) The special education teacher must be in the room with the students on his or her caseload.
    (C) Building administrators should assign teachers to collaborative pairs.
    (D) The general education teacher must allow the special education teacher to teach in the classroom.

55. Which professional would work with a student who had difficulty holding a pencil, cutting with scissors, and other fine-motor tasks required in elementary school?

    (A) Occupational therapist
    (B) School nurse
    (C) School counselor
    (D) Adaptive physical education teacher

56. A student takes her test in a distraction-free area outside of her regular classroom. Which type of accommodation is she receiving?

    (A) Curriculum accommodation
    (B) Accommodations regarding content
    (C) Accommodations during testing
    (D) Setting accommodation

57. Which of the following is the most common accommodation to testing situations for students with ADHD?

    (A) Extended time
    (B) Testing done over more days, but for shorter periods of time
    (C) Preferential seating
    (D) Test questions read aloud

58. Mr. Roberts believes that one of his students is displaying disruptive behaviors more often in the morning than the afternoon. What validated practice can Mr. Roberts use to determine the occurrence of the behaviors?

    (A) Content mapping
    (B) Goal setting
    (C) Curriculum-based measurement
    (D) Functional behavior assessment

59. One important premise of positive behavior support is

    (A) medication.
    (B) addressing disproportionality.
    (C) rewarding appropriate behavior.
    (D) prevention.

60. Students with intellectual disabilities (mental retardation) are often unable to learn incidentally, which refers to

    (A) learning from ordinary or "everyday" experiences.
    (B) the ability to generalize tasks.
    (C) learning from models presented in the classroom.
    (D) learning by following their job coach.

Answer Explanations
for Practice Test 1

Education of Exceptional Students: Core Content Knowledge (0353)

1. (C)	13. (A)	25. (B)	37. (A)	49. (A)
2. (C)	14. (D)	26. (A)	38. (D)	50. (B)
3. (C)	15. (C)	27. (D)	39. (A)	51. (D)
4. (B)	16. (C)	28. (C)	40. (A)	52. (A)
5. (A)	17. (A)	29. (D)	41. (C)	53. (D)
6. (A)	18. (B)	30. (D)	42. (D)	54. (A)
7. (C)	19. (C)	31. (C)	43. (B)	55. (A)
8. (B)	20. (D)	32. (C)	44. (A)	56. (D)
9. (B)	21. (B)	33. (A)	45. (D)	57. (A)
10. (A)	22. (D)	34. (A)	46. (D)	58. (D)
11. (A)	23. (D)	35. (A)	47. (C)	59. (D)
12. (C)	24. (C)	36. (D)	48. (A)	60. (A)

ANSWER KEY ALIGNED TO CONTENT CATEGORIES

Question	Answer	Content Category
1	C	I. Understanding Exceptionalities
2	C	I. Understanding Exceptionalities
3	C	I. Understanding Exceptionalities
4	B	I. Understanding Exceptionalities
5	A	I. Understanding Exceptionalities
6	A	I. Understanding Exceptionalities
7	C	I. Understanding Exceptionalities
8	B	I. Understanding Exceptionalities
9	B	I. Understanding Exceptionalities
10	A	I. Understanding Exceptionalities
11	A	I. Understanding Exceptionalities
12	C	I. Understanding Exceptionalities
13	A	I. Understanding Exceptionalities
14	D	I. Understanding Exceptionalities
15	C	I. Understanding Exceptionalities
16	C	I. Understanding Exceptionalities
17	A	I. Understanding Exceptionalities
18	B	I. Understanding Exceptionalities
19	C	II. Legal and Societal Issues
20	D	II. Legal and Societal Issues

(continued)

Question	Answer	Content Category
21	B	II. Legal and Societal Issues
22	D	II. Legal and Societal Issues
23	D	II. Legal and Societal Issues
24	C	II. Legal and Societal Issues
25	B	II. Legal and Societal Issues
26	A	II. Legal and Societal Issues
27	D	II. Legal and Societal Issues
28	C	II. Legal and Societal Issues
29	D	II. Legal and Societal Issues
30	D	II. Legal and Societal Issues
31	C	III. Delivery of Services to Students with Disabilities
32	C	III. Delivery of Services to Students with Disabilities
33	A	III. Delivery of Services to Students with Disabilities
34	A	III. Delivery of Services to Students with Disabilities
35	A	III. Delivery of Services to Students with Disabilities
36	D	III. Delivery of Services to Students with Disabilities
37	A	III. Delivery of Services to Students with Disabilities
38	D	III. Delivery of Services to Students with Disabilities
39	A	III. Delivery of Services to Students with Disabilities
40	A	III. Delivery of Services to Students with Disabilities
41	C	III. Delivery of Services to Students with Disabilities
42	D	III. Delivery of Services to Students with Disabilities
43	B	III. Delivery of Services to Students with Disabilities

(*continued*)

Question	Answer	Content Category
44	A	III. Delivery of Services to Students with Disabilities
45	D	III. Delivery of Services to Students with Disabilities
46	D	III. Delivery of Services to Students with Disabilities
47	C	III. Delivery of Services to Students with Disabilities
48	A	III. Delivery of Services to Students with Disabilities
49	A	III. Delivery of Services to Students with Disabilities
50	B	III. Delivery of Services to Students with Disabilities
51	D	III. Delivery of Services to Students with Disabilities
52	A	III. Delivery of Services to Students with Disabilities
53	D	III. Delivery of Services to Students with Disabilities
54	A	III. Delivery of Services to Students with Disabilities
55	A	III. Delivery of Services to Students with Disabilities
56	D	III. Delivery of Services to Students with Disabilities
57	A	III. Delivery of Services to Students with Disabilities
58	D	III. Delivery of Services to Students with Disabilities
59	D	III. Delivery of Services to Students with Disabilities
60	A	III. Delivery of Services to Students with Disabilities

1.   (C)

The question tests the knowledge of the classification of students with disabilities. Option C is correct because ADHD does not have its own category in IDEA 2004, and is classified under the umbrella OHI.

2.   (C)

The question tests the knowledge of the incidence of disabilities. Option C is correct because over half of all students with disabilities are classified as learning disabled (LD).

3.   (C)

The question tests the knowledge of the characteristics of students with disabilities. Option C is correct because those students who are legally blind typically have some vision, were blinded adventitiously (not at birth) and use assistive technology, not large-print documents.

4.   (B)

The question tests the knowledge of the characteristics of students with disabilities. Option B is correct because damage to the nervous system (as in the case of cerebral palsy) almost always presents muscular weakness or paralysis, and does not affect cognition or adaptive skills.

5.   (A)

The question tests the knowledge of the classification system of IDEA. Option A is correct because developmental delay is the specific non-categorical classification given to children between the ages of 3 and 9 who cannot be reliably assessed for other disabilities, such as intellectual disabilities and learning disabilities.

6.   (A)

The question tests the knowledge of the prevalence of disabilities. Option A is correct because this disability affects less than 0.001% of all children found eligible for special education services.

7.   (C)

The question tests the knowledge of the incidence of disabilities. Students found eligible under EBD represent around 6%, SLD 43%, and ID 9%, combined with speech and language disorders, make up nearly 90% of all students receiving special education and are considered high incidence. Students with OHI make up about 5%.

8.   (B)

The question tests the knowledge of the definition of students with language impairments. Option B is correct because a student who is bilingual must have a language impairment that occurs in both languages, not just showing slowness in learning English.

9.   (B)

The question tests the knowledge of the definition of students with speech and language impairments. Option B is correct because unintelligible speech is a characteristic of those students identified under the subset of speech impairments.

10.   (A)

The question tests the knowledge of concomitant disabilities. Option A is correct because the majority of students with learning disabilities are also found to have language impairment.

11. (A)

The question tests the knowledge of the federal definition of learning disabilities. Option A is correct because the federal definition clearly states that a learning disability may be a result of minimal brain dysfunction.

12. (C)

The question tests the knowledge of the classification of students. Option C is correct because as many as 40% of students with learning disabilities are identified in the third grade, when academic tasks become more demanding.

13. (A)

The question tests the knowledge of the definition of students with ADHD. Option A is correct because, as is true for most disabilities, educational performance must be adversely affected to qualify for services under IDEA 2004.

14. (D)

The question tests the knowledge of prevalence. Option D is correct because male students who have received office referrals or who have been identified by their teachers as "disruptive" are more likely to be referred for determined eligible for services because they are diagnosed as ADHD.

15. (C)

The question tests the knowledge of presence of multiple exceptionalities. Option C is correct because comorbidity means two or more disabilities present in an individual.

16. (C)

The question tests the knowledge of the definition of emotional and behavioral disorders. Option C is correct because educational performance must be adversely affected to qualify for services under IDEA 2004.

17. (A)

The question tests the knowledge of the nature of behaviors associated with students with disabilities. Option A is correct because bullying is an externalizing behavior, while depression and bulimia are more likely to be internalizing behaviors, and a learning disability is a disability related to deficits in academics.

18. (B)

The question tests the knowledge of the definition of other health impairments. Option B is correct because while students who are HIV+ may be comorbid with other disabilities, a singular diagnosis would qualify them under OHI.

19. (C)

The question tests the knowledge of the history of special education. Option C is correct because Itard and his work with the "wild boy" of Aveyron is considered the first professional to design special educational services.

20. (D)

The question tests the knowledge of the important court cases that affect students with disabilities. Option D is correct because the PARC case set the precedent that students with mental retardation should be provided a free appropriate public education.

21. (B)

The question tests the knowledge of the federal law and legislation related to special education. The correct answer is option B because parents are not guaranteed legal fees in lawsuits, while the other choices are included.

22. (D)

The question tests the knowledge of the school's connections with parental partnerships and roles. The correct answer is option D because the parents are guaranteed and encouraged to participate in all facets of their child's education, and are not required to have legal counsel.

23. (D)

The question tests the knowledge of the right of parents. The correct answer is option D because parents cannot prevent their child from attending school, while they do have the right to all of the other choices.

24. (C)

The question tests the knowledge of the roles of parents and the collaborative relationship with parents. The correct answer is option C because parents and teachers will have the most successful partnership when there is open communication. Ethnicity, friendship, and value systems will not guarantee a successful partnership.

25. (B)

The question tests the knowledge of the cooperative nature of the transition planning process. The correct answer is option B because the addition of more service providers adds stress to both the student with the disabilities and the parents of the child.

26. (A)

The question tests the knowledge of the important court cases that affect students with disabilities. Option A is correct because the Rowley case outlined free and appropriate public education as a responsibility of the school district and determined that the school must provide services with "some educational benefit," not simply warehouse the student in the public school.

27. (D)

The question tests the knowledge of the important legislation that affects students with disabilities. Option D is correct because under ADA: old buildings are not required to be renovated for accessibility, but any new public transportation must be accessible to individuals with disabilities, including those who are in wheelchairs, and those who have visual or hearing impairments.

28. (C)

The question tests the knowledge of the important legislation that affects students with disabilities. Option C is correct because ADA and Section 504 of the Vocational Rehabilitation Act are considered civil rights laws, anti-discrimination laws, and laws that address accessibility, but are not considered educational laws.

29. (D)

The question tests the knowledge of advocacy for students with disabilities and the application of the federal law. Option D is correct because a student may receive accommodations under a Section 504 plan even if the student does not qualify for special education services under IDEA 2004.

30. (D)

The question tests the knowledge of federal legislation that affects students with disabilities. Option D is correct because the reauthorization of IDEA in 1997 was the first time that the category was mentioned in the federal legislation as it was categorized under OHI.

31. (C)

The question tests the knowledge of placement and program issues that affect students with disabilities. Continuum of services is not related to where or how the placement will occur, nor is it related to when the services are provided, as in early intervention. Therefore option C is correct because the continuum of services is the range of services that must be available to the students of a school district so that they may be served in the least restrictive environment.

32. (C)

The question tests the knowledge of placement and program issues that affect students with disabilities. Option C is correct because the majority of students with LD receive most of their instruction in the general education classroom.

33. (A)

The question tests the knowledge of curriculum and instruction including the IEP process. Option A is correct because a referral is the written request for evaluation. A transition plan is the part of the IEP that addresses a student's movement through points in his or her education and life process, while full inclusion is the philosophy of including all students, regardless of their disability in the general education classroom, and special education is the individualized instruction designed for students with disabilities.

34. (A)

The question tests the knowledge of curriculum and instruction including the IFSP process. Option A is correct because the IFSP is created specifically for infants and toddlers who display behaviors and disabilities that make them eligible for special education services.

35. (A)

The question tests the knowledge of procedures and test materials typically used for prereferral for a learning disabled student. Option A is correct because students with learning disabilities must have scores that fall within the normal range (70-130) in order to be classified as having a learning disability. A score falling below 70 would be considered a severe disability.

36. (D)

The question tests the application of procedures and test materials used for ongoing program monitor-ing. Option D is correct because the process described is the manner in which a teacher monitors a student's progress and makes decisions about what to teach next based on the student outcomes.

37. (A)

The question tests the knowledge of the use of assessment for making instructional decisions. The correct answer is Option A because in universal screening, all students are assessed for appropriate research-based interventions. The tiers are used for more selective assessments to determine the level of intervention appropriate for students.

38. (D)

The question tests the knowledge of instructional format and components. Option D is correct because the use of different instructional methods that match learning styles is a major component of differentiated instruction, which is not dependent on whether the student has a disability or not.

39. (A)

The question tests the knowledge of placement and program issues. Option A is correct because the "pull-out" model of providing specialized support services is most commonly known as a resource room model.

40. (A)

The question tests the knowledge of teaching strategies and methods related to facilitated group strategies. Option A is correct because Ms. Woodward has modified how she presents or delivers the instruction, and has not changed the content, scope, and sequence or curriculum.

41. (C)

The question tests the knowledge of technology for teaching and learning, integrating best practices.

Option C is correct because Toderick requires modifications that promote his integration into the general education classroom, which is accomplished with books on tape. He does not require curriculum modification or a change in the expectations for mastery of the objectives.

42. (D)

The question tests the knowledge of curriculum and instruction including the IEP. The correct answer is option D because the prereferral stage is designed to support a student with academic and/or behavioral deficits who might not have a disability so that the student will not be assessed for or placed in special education. The prereferral stage promotes the use of research-based interventions to address needs of students who might be struggling academically, but do not have a disability.

43. (B)

The question tests the knowledge of curriculum and instruction including the IEP. The correct answer is option B because the two-pronged test for eligibility, as outlined in *Daniel R.R.* is that the child must have a disability, and that the child requires specialized instruction to have access to the curriculum.

44. (A)

The question tests the knowledge of transition of students and IEPs. The correct answer is option A because self-determination is an attribute of students with disabilities, which promotes self-care and self-advocacy.

45. (D)

The question tests the knowledge of development of the IEP. Option D is correct because the IEP must first address the needs of the student, regardless of cost, and that the student's goals must be related to the services provided.

46. (D)

The question tests the knowledge of curriculum and instruction including the IEP. Option D is correct because IEPs are available to those educators who have interaction with the child, and are not restricted to the special education teacher, the parent, or the diagnostician. Finally, researchers must have parent permission, not district permission, in order to access a child's IEP.

47. (C)

The question tests the knowledge of assessment, including how to modify tests. The correct answer is option C, because giving a student the answers does not allow for assessment of the student's mastery of the content.

48. (A)

The question tests the knowledge of assessment, including alternatives to norm-referenced testing. Option A is correct because authentic assessment allows the teacher to evaluate curriculum-based assessments that occur in the student's usual instructional day.

49. (A)

The question tests the knowledge of best practices from multidisciplinary research and professional literature. Option A is correct because a culturally responsive curriculum is one that is based on the idea that culture is central to student learning.

50. (B)

The question tests the knowledge of referrals to special education. Option B is correct because most students are placed in a general education classroom, and the teacher in this classroom has contact with students who may demonstrate problems with behaviors or academics.

51. (D)

The question tests the knowledge of assessment, including appropriate modifications for students who are ELL. Option D is correct because the accommodations used in testing should be those accommodations used in instruction.

52. (A)

This question tests instructional format and components, including ESL and limited English proficiency. Option A is correct because there is no evidence that ELL peers are more equipped to teach culturally and linguistically diverse students, though they can help with assignments.

53. (D)

This question tests instructional format and components, including concept generalization. Option D is correct because generalization is the ability to take skills learned in one setting or environment and apply those skills, such as a reading comprehension strategy, into another setting.

54. (A)

This question tests instructional format and components, including teaching strategies and methods. Option A is correct because collaboration is successful only when the students' progress is monitored. The setting, logistics of pairing teachers, and teaching assignments are secondary to the student outcomes.

55. (A)

This question tests background knowledge, including roles of other professionals. Option A is correct because the OT is responsible for fine-motor skill instruction while the other choices, which are all school professionals who may provide related services, are not trained for this type of intervention.

56. (D)

This question tests application of modification of assessments. Option D is correct because moving a student to a preferential seating area free of distraction is a setting accommodation, while the other choices identify changes to the content and curriculum or the test itself.

57. (A)

This question tests application of modification of assessments. Option A is correct because extended time is used as an accommodation for over half of all students with ADHD.

58. (D)

The question tests knowledge of assessments, including how to select appropriate assessments. Option D is correct because it is the initial assessment used to determine the frequency, duration, intensity, and severity of behaviors and can provide data to teachers to develop a behavior intervention plan.

59. (D)

This question tests background knowledge, including conceptual approaches to behavior. Option D is correct because PBS is based on the concept that if the function of disruptive behaviors can be identified, those behaviors can be prevented.

60. (A)

This question tests instructional format and components, including learning strategy instruction. Option A is correct because incidental learning is the ability to learn from completing everyday tasks outside of direct instruction. Students with intellectual disabilities typically do not have generalizing skills and this prevents them from using life skills in other settings.

Practice Test 2

Special Education:
Core Content Knowledge (0354)

This test is also on CD in our special interactive TestWare® for the Praxis II Special Education: Core Content Knowledge (0354). It is highly recommended that you first take this exam on computer. You will then have the additional study features and benefits of enforced timed conditions and instantaneous, accurate scoring. See page 6 for instructions on how to get the most out of our book and software.

Visit www.rea.com for updates and additional resources

ANSWER SHEET

1. Ⓐ Ⓑ Ⓒ Ⓓ	34. Ⓐ Ⓑ Ⓒ Ⓓ	67. Ⓐ Ⓑ Ⓒ Ⓓ	100. Ⓐ Ⓑ Ⓒ Ⓓ
2. Ⓐ Ⓑ Ⓒ Ⓓ	35. Ⓐ Ⓑ Ⓒ Ⓓ	68. Ⓐ Ⓑ Ⓒ Ⓓ	101. Ⓐ Ⓑ Ⓒ Ⓓ
3. Ⓐ Ⓑ Ⓒ Ⓓ	36. Ⓐ Ⓑ Ⓒ Ⓓ	69. Ⓐ Ⓑ Ⓒ Ⓓ	102. Ⓐ Ⓑ Ⓒ Ⓓ
4. Ⓐ Ⓑ Ⓒ Ⓓ	37. Ⓐ Ⓑ Ⓒ Ⓓ	70. Ⓐ Ⓑ Ⓒ Ⓓ	103. Ⓐ Ⓑ Ⓒ Ⓓ
5. Ⓐ Ⓑ Ⓒ Ⓓ	38. Ⓐ Ⓑ Ⓒ Ⓓ	71. Ⓐ Ⓑ Ⓒ Ⓓ	104. Ⓐ Ⓑ Ⓒ Ⓓ
6. Ⓐ Ⓑ Ⓒ Ⓓ	39. Ⓐ Ⓑ Ⓒ Ⓓ	72. Ⓐ Ⓑ Ⓒ Ⓓ	105. Ⓐ Ⓑ Ⓒ Ⓓ
7. Ⓐ Ⓑ Ⓒ Ⓓ	40. Ⓐ Ⓑ Ⓒ Ⓓ	73. Ⓐ Ⓑ Ⓒ Ⓓ	106. Ⓐ Ⓑ Ⓒ Ⓓ
8. Ⓐ Ⓑ Ⓒ Ⓓ	41. Ⓐ Ⓑ Ⓒ Ⓓ	74. Ⓐ Ⓑ Ⓒ Ⓓ	107. Ⓐ Ⓑ Ⓒ Ⓓ
9. Ⓐ Ⓑ Ⓒ Ⓓ	42. Ⓐ Ⓑ Ⓒ Ⓓ	75. Ⓐ Ⓑ Ⓒ Ⓓ	108. Ⓐ Ⓑ Ⓒ Ⓓ
10. Ⓐ Ⓑ Ⓒ Ⓓ	43. Ⓐ Ⓑ Ⓒ Ⓓ	76. Ⓐ Ⓑ Ⓒ Ⓓ	109. Ⓐ Ⓑ Ⓒ Ⓓ
11. Ⓐ Ⓑ Ⓒ Ⓓ	44. Ⓐ Ⓑ Ⓒ Ⓓ	77. Ⓐ Ⓑ Ⓒ Ⓓ	110. Ⓐ Ⓑ Ⓒ Ⓓ
12. Ⓐ Ⓑ Ⓒ Ⓓ	45. Ⓐ Ⓑ Ⓒ Ⓓ	78. Ⓐ Ⓑ Ⓒ Ⓓ	111. Ⓐ Ⓑ Ⓒ Ⓓ
13. Ⓐ Ⓑ Ⓒ Ⓓ	46. Ⓐ Ⓑ Ⓒ Ⓓ	79. Ⓐ Ⓑ Ⓒ Ⓓ	112. Ⓐ Ⓑ Ⓒ Ⓓ
14. Ⓐ Ⓑ Ⓒ Ⓓ	47. Ⓐ Ⓑ Ⓒ Ⓓ	80. Ⓐ Ⓑ Ⓒ Ⓓ	113. Ⓐ Ⓑ Ⓒ Ⓓ
15. Ⓐ Ⓑ Ⓒ Ⓓ	48. Ⓐ Ⓑ Ⓒ Ⓓ	81. Ⓐ Ⓑ Ⓒ Ⓓ	114. Ⓐ Ⓑ Ⓒ Ⓓ
16. Ⓐ Ⓑ Ⓒ Ⓓ	49. Ⓐ Ⓑ Ⓒ Ⓓ	82. Ⓐ Ⓑ Ⓒ Ⓓ	115. Ⓐ Ⓑ Ⓒ Ⓓ
17. Ⓐ Ⓑ Ⓒ Ⓓ	50. Ⓐ Ⓑ Ⓒ Ⓓ	83. Ⓐ Ⓑ Ⓒ Ⓓ	116. Ⓐ Ⓑ Ⓒ Ⓓ
18. Ⓐ Ⓑ Ⓒ Ⓓ	51. Ⓐ Ⓑ Ⓒ Ⓓ	84. Ⓐ Ⓑ Ⓒ Ⓓ	117. Ⓐ Ⓑ Ⓒ Ⓓ
19. Ⓐ Ⓑ Ⓒ Ⓓ	52. Ⓐ Ⓑ Ⓒ Ⓓ	85. Ⓐ Ⓑ Ⓒ Ⓓ	118. Ⓐ Ⓑ Ⓒ Ⓓ
20. Ⓐ Ⓑ Ⓒ Ⓓ	53. Ⓐ Ⓑ Ⓒ Ⓓ	86. Ⓐ Ⓑ Ⓒ Ⓓ	119. Ⓐ Ⓑ Ⓒ Ⓓ
21. Ⓐ Ⓑ Ⓒ Ⓓ	54. Ⓐ Ⓑ Ⓒ Ⓓ	87. Ⓐ Ⓑ Ⓒ Ⓓ	120. Ⓐ Ⓑ Ⓒ Ⓓ
22. Ⓐ Ⓑ Ⓒ Ⓓ	55. Ⓐ Ⓑ Ⓒ Ⓓ	88. Ⓐ Ⓑ Ⓒ Ⓓ	
23. Ⓐ Ⓑ Ⓒ Ⓓ	56. Ⓐ Ⓑ Ⓒ Ⓓ	89. Ⓐ Ⓑ Ⓒ Ⓓ	
24. Ⓐ Ⓑ Ⓒ Ⓓ	57. Ⓐ Ⓑ Ⓒ Ⓓ	90. Ⓐ Ⓑ Ⓒ Ⓓ	
25. Ⓐ Ⓑ Ⓒ Ⓓ	58. Ⓐ Ⓑ Ⓒ Ⓓ	91. Ⓐ Ⓑ Ⓒ Ⓓ	
26. Ⓐ Ⓑ Ⓒ Ⓓ	59. Ⓐ Ⓑ Ⓒ Ⓓ	92. Ⓐ Ⓑ Ⓒ Ⓓ	
27. Ⓐ Ⓑ Ⓒ Ⓓ	60. Ⓐ Ⓑ Ⓒ Ⓓ	93. Ⓐ Ⓑ Ⓒ Ⓓ	
28. Ⓐ Ⓑ Ⓒ Ⓓ	61. Ⓐ Ⓑ Ⓒ Ⓓ	94. Ⓐ Ⓑ Ⓒ Ⓓ	
29. Ⓐ Ⓑ Ⓒ Ⓓ	62. Ⓐ Ⓑ Ⓒ Ⓓ	95. Ⓐ Ⓑ Ⓒ Ⓓ	
30. Ⓐ Ⓑ Ⓒ Ⓓ	63. Ⓐ Ⓑ Ⓒ Ⓓ	96. Ⓐ Ⓑ Ⓒ Ⓓ	
31. Ⓐ Ⓑ Ⓒ Ⓓ	64. Ⓐ Ⓑ Ⓒ Ⓓ	97. Ⓐ Ⓑ Ⓒ Ⓓ	
32. Ⓐ Ⓑ Ⓒ Ⓓ	65. Ⓐ Ⓑ Ⓒ Ⓓ	98. Ⓐ Ⓑ Ⓒ Ⓓ	
33. Ⓐ Ⓑ Ⓒ Ⓓ	66. Ⓐ Ⓑ Ⓒ Ⓓ	99. Ⓐ Ⓑ Ⓒ Ⓓ	

PRACTICE TEST 2

SPECIAL EDUCATION: CORE CONTENT KNOWLEDGE (0354)

TIME: 2 Hours
120 Multiple-choice questions

In this section, you will find examples of test questions similar to those you are likely to encounter on the Praxis II Special Education: Core Content Knowledge (0354) Exam.

1. A teacher is delivering a lesson to a group of students. One of the students has a hearing impairment. To meet the needs of the student with a hearing impairment, the teacher should be cognizant of all of the following EXCEPT

   (A) the location where the hearing impaired student is seated.
   (B) the necessity for the teacher to speak in a clear voice.
   (C) minimizing audible and visual distractions.
   (D) providing the students with large-print materials.

2. Students with visual impairments would likely benefit from class materials that feature

   I. colored overlays
   II. tests with fewer questions
   III. enlarged print

   (A) I only
   (B) I and II only
   (C) I and III only
   (D) II and III only

3. Which of the following is not a designated category under IDEA?

   (A) Hearing impairment
   (B) Visual impairment
   (C) Diabetes
   (D) Autism

4. The Kubler-Ross model of death and dying is often extended to parents of students identified as having a cognitive impairment because the model

   (A) outlines an approach to fixing the impairment permanently.
   (B) helps parents understand the process of accepting a loved one's disability.
   (C) assists parents in funeral planning for children who will most likely die as a result of their impairment.
   (D) instructs parents how to talk to children about the dying process so they are able to cope when a loved one passes.

5. When determining the appropriate educational placement for a student with a cognitive impairment, it is important to consider

   I. free and appropriate public education
   II. least restrictive environment
   III the student's ability to "fit in" with peers

   (A) I only
   (B) I and II only
   (C) I, II and III
   (D) II and III only

6. The United States Department of Education tracks the data provided by individual school districts regarding the racial and ethnic backgrounds of special education students in an effort to

   (A) prove the theory that minorities are at a greater risk of being impaired.

(B) ensure that school districts are considering the cultural backgrounds of students before placing them in special education.

(C) identify the minority population of students so funding and programming can be increased to meet their needs.

(D) provide data to immigration officials and limit immigration.

7. A multidisciplinary evaluation team would likely determine that a student has an emotional disturbance in accordance with IDEA if the student has demonstrated all of the following EXCEPT

(A) an inability to learn that cannot be explained by intellectual, sensory, or health factors.

(B) an inability to build and maintain satisfactory relationships with students and teachers.

(C) a general pervasive mood of unhappiness.

(D) a conduct disorder.

8. Which of the following would be the best technique to use when trying to maximize success for a student who is identified as having ADHD?

(A) Developing a plan in which the student is the helper, distributing materials, delivering messages, and running errands.

(B) Allowing the student to take as many breaks as he or she needs throughout the day

(C) Allowing students to run or play in the recess yard whenever they feel the need to release energy

(D) Creating an area within the classroom full of stimulating activities so students can access the materials whenever they need to release energy

9. Students who are identified as being autistic are most likely to receive which of the following school related services?

(A) Speech services and social work

(B) Social work and hearing services

(C) Physical therapy and speech therapy

(D) One-on-one time with a paraprofessional

10. While state guidelines differ, federal law mandates that all states provide special education services to students identified as having impairment, outlined within the Individuals with Disabilities Education Act, from age

(A) 0–26.

(B) 3–26.

(C) 3–21.

(D) 0–18.

11. Which of the following is an example of a developmental disability?

(A) Autism

(B) Vision Impairment

(C) Depression diagnosed in the toddler years

(D) Traumatic brain injury

12. When students are identified as having a specific learning disability, they are likely to have a deficit in all of the areas described below EXCEPT

(A) listening.

(B) speaking.

(C) writing.

(D) IQ.

13. At what point is a manifestation determination review to be conducted for a student receiving special education services?

(A) After every five suspensions

(B) Before ten suspensions have occurred

(C) After ten suspensions in an academic year

(D) Each time the student is suspended

14. A multidisciplinary evaluation team would likely determine that a student has a cognitive impairment according to IDEA provided the student has demonstrated all of the following EXCEPT

(A) an intellectual quotient of 70 or below.

(B) a deficit in adaptive behavior.

(C) a deficit in social awareness.

(D) scores much lower than the mean in academic areas.

15. Federal law mandates that students receiving special education services are to have a standard IEP developed how often?

(A) Once a semester.

(B) Each year.
(C) Every month.
(D) Once a decade.

16. Federal law mandates that students receiving special education services are required to have a more thorough IEP, which involves academic testing, every

(A) 3 years.
(B) 2 years.
(C) 5 years.
(D) 4 years.

17. Teachers of students with special education certification must familiarize themselves with, create lessons for, and formally evaluate the students'

(A) hopes and dreams.
(B) needs and wants.
(C) goals and objectives.
(D) modifications and accommodations.

18. Which of the following are examples of special education categories as outlined within the federal law?

I. emotional disturbance
II. specific learning disability
III. socially maladjusted disorder

(A) I only
(B) I and II only
(C) I and III only
(D) I, II and III

19. The teaching technique that involves breaking a problem down, or simplifying a task in a step-by-step fashion is called

(A) chunking.
(B) task analysis.
(C) description.
(D) task assessment.

20. Which of the following statements can you conclude about a student who is identified as being severely cognitively impaired?

(A) The student will require one-on-one instruction with multiple paraprofessionals.
(B) The student likely has secondary disabilities.
(C) The student needs intense instruction by trained professionals to improve scores.
(D) The student likely has serious behavioral problems.

21. Which of the following is NOT a component of a well-planned behavior intervention plan?

(A) Functional behavior assessment
(B) Use of positive behavior interventions
(C) Program modifications and supplementary aids
(D) A manifestation determination review

22. Highly effective lesson plans are comprised of

I. objectives for student learning
II. teaching and learning activities
III. strategies to check for understanding
IV. scripts which instructors read verbatim

(A) I and II only
(B) II and III only
(C) I, II and III only
(D) II and IV only

23. Which of the following should an educator NOT consider when planning the learning environment with special learners in mind?

(A) The need for an orderly environment that is pleasing to the eye
(B) Seating arrangements that allow certain students to have preferred seating
(C) Designating an area of the room where students can go for punishment
(D) Bulletin boards decorated with educationally stimulating material

24. Which of the following is the BEST technique for encouraging a student with special needs to share answers orally in the classroom?

(A) Assuring students they will only be called upon when the teacher knows they have the correct answer

(B) Telling students in concrete terms that they must participate orally in order to receive all of their participation points

(C) Calling on the student and using the appropriate wait time until demanding an answer

(D) Having all students participate in the order in which they are seated so students with special needs have plenty of notice

25. When completing an ABC log for a student with a suspected emotional impairment, the teacher should consider all of the following EXCEPT

(A) the anger the student experiences when provoked.

(B) the antecedent.

(C) the behavior.

(D) the consequence of the behavior.

26. The key to gaining students' attention when introducing a new concept is to have a well-developed

(A) anticipatory set.

(B) lesson.

(C) group activity.

(D) individual assignment.

27. When anticipating a fire drill, it is prudent for the special education teacher to

I. explain the upcoming fire drill to the students

II. discuss the fact that drills are for practice, and there is no need for the students to worry

III. say nothing to the students and study how they react so you can address issues

(A) I only

(B) I and II only

(C) I and III only

(D) II and III only

28. A student has access to a resource room in his or her IEP. It is important to allow the student to use the resource room when

(A) instruction is being given in the classroom.

(B) the student is avoiding work and needs a break from assignments.

(C) the student has participated in the lesson and is completing an assignment.

(D) the student has a question about the lesson given and requires further instruction.

29. Which of the following terms describes placing students with special needs in an appropriate program and setting based on their physical, emotional, and cognitive needs?

(A) Accommodation

(B) Least restrictive environment

(C) Modification

(D) Self-contained environment

30. Which of the following is the least effective teaching method for a student with a learning disability in mathematics?

(A) Large group instruction

(B) Skill drill

(C) Modeling

(D) Direct instruction

31. Planning the classroom environment for your students should include

I. rules

II. consequences

III. expectations

(A) I and II only

(B) I and III only

(C) II and III only

(D) I, II and III

32. Which of the following is NOT an accommodation for a student with ADHD within the classroom environment?

(A) Movement breaks during class

(B) Extended test-taking time

(C) Preferential seating near the teacher during instruction

(D) Removing difficult content from a social-studies unit

33. Which of the following would a teacher use to determine if a student is progressing and if the program being used is effective?

(A) Summative evaluation

(B) Psychological evaluation
(C) Formative evaluation
(D) Special education evaluation

34. When determining the most appropriate class-room placement of a student with special needs, the teacher must take into account

    I. the student's background history
    II. previous evaluations and assessments
    III. the student's extracurricular activities and hobbies

    (A) I and II only
    (B) I and III only
    (C) II and III only
    (D) I, II and III

35. If a student is blurting out and disrupting instruction, which of the following steps should a teacher take first to eliminate the behavior?

    (A) Reprimand the student in front of his/her classmates
    (B) Collect data about the behavior, such as frequency and antecedents
    (C) Gather counselors and administrators to discuss the behavior and solutions
    (D) Have a meeting with the student's parents and/or guardian

36. Having learning centers set up in your classroom will help students

    I. become more independent
    II. gain more responsibility for their learning
    III. have more time to do homework

    (A) I only
    (B) II only
    (C) I and II only
    (D) I and III only

37. Which of the following is NOT a part of a self-contained classroom for students with moderate to severe autism?

    (A) One-on-one instruction from paraprofessionals
    (B) Structure and routine
    (C) Full inclusion of the student
    (D) Lessons on communication and social skills

38. What would be an appropriate seating choice for a student with a visual impairment?

    I. Seating near the instructor
    II. Seating near an air vent or heater
    III. Seating near bright or natural light

    (A) I and II only
    (B) I and III only
    (C) II and III only
    (D) I, II and III

39. Which of the following is a teacher LEAST likely to do to immediately reinforce positive behavior in the classroom?

    (A) Reward the student a with a tangible item
    (B) Offer verbal praise in front of the student's peers
    (C) Write a positive comment in the student's next report card
    (D) Send the student's guardian a positive note about the behavior

40. When giving directions for an assignment, which of the following steps would be most beneficial for a student with a central auditory processing disorder?

    (A) Announcing the directions to the entire class
    (B) Telling the student one-on-one directions the day before
    (C) Recording the directions so the student can listen to them
    (D) Giving the student directions in written form the day before

41. Which of the following characteristics are associated with ADHD?

    I. Inattention
    II. Hyperactivity
    III. Impulsive behavior

    (A) I and II only
    (B) II and III only
    (C) III only
    (D) I, II and III

42. Which of the following is NOT a learning strategy?

    (A) Competence
    (B) Elaboration
    (C) Megacognition
    (D) Rehearsal

43. To meet NCLB regulations, teachers must

    I. provide school safety
    II. provide scientifically based methods of teaching
    III. provide self-advocacy skills for students

    (A) I only
    (B) II only
    (C) I and II only
    (D) I, II and III

44. Which of the following can provide accommodations to students within the school setting, but with no federal funding attached?

    (A) 504 services
    (B) Speech and language services
    (C) Social work services
    (D) Occupational therapy services

45. When finding job placement for a student in a post-secondary education program, which of the following is LEAST likely to be considered?

    (A) The student's career goals and aspirations
    (B) The student's past statewide assessment scores
    (C) The student's current abilities in reading and math
    (D) The student's criminal background and history

46. The use of achievement assessments provides teachers with

    I. medical history
    II. instructional decisions
    III. diagnosis of a student

    (A) II only
    (B) III only
    (C) II and III only

(D) I and III only

47. For which of the following would a teacher want to create a behavior intervention plan?

    (A) A ninth-grade student is performing at a second-grade level on vocabulary assessments.
    (B) A fourth-grade student has a poor attendance record over the duration of the school year.
    (C) An eleventh-grade student experiences anxiety during finals week.
    (D) A second-grade student pushes her peers during class transition time.

48. Co-teaching instruction can include which of the following strategies?

    I. Parallel teaching
    II. Supportive teaching
    III. Team teaching

    (A) I only
    (B) II only
    (C) II and III only
    (D) I, II and III

49. Which of the following would be the most effective instruction for teaching vocabulary to a child who is an English language learner?

    (A) Giving out vocabulary flash cards for students to study
    (B) Having students write about their lives in vocabulary journals
    (C) Sending students to learning centers geared toward vocabulary
    (D) Repeating vocabulary by listening, speaking, and writing

50. Which of the following is NOT one of Vygotsky's strategies of instruction?

    (A) Modeling
    (B) Scaffolding
    (C) Apprenticeship
    (D) Guided participation

51. A teacher of a math class that includes students with diverse levels of ability should try all of the following strategies EXCEPT

    (A) dividing learners into small groups by abilities.
    (B) accommodating math work for high and low abilities.
    (C) gaining a co-teacher to help with instruction of students.
    (D) giving all students the same amount of work at the same level.

52. Tracking and instruction of IEP goals can be done through

    I. state assessments
    II. progress monitoring
    III. the scaffolding method

    (A) II only
    (B) III only
    (C) II and III only
    (D) I, II and III

53. Which of the following strategies would be best for teaching sight words?

    (A) K-W-L
    (B) Books on tape
    (C) Incremental rehearsal
    (D) Teacher modeling and demonstration

54. When instructing students who are autistic, a teacher must keep in mind all of the following EXCEPT

    (A) poor communication skills.
    (B) limited language skills.
    (C) hyperactive and violent behaviors.
    (D) repetitive and ritualistic behaviors.

55. When giving instruction within a special education classroom, teachers are encouraged to use

    I. timers
    II. microphones
    III. smartboards

    (A) I and II only

(B) II and III only
(C) III only
(D) I, II and III

56. Which of the following is NOT considered assistive technology in the classroom?

    (A) Braille
    (B) iPad
    (C) Trackball
    (D) Joystick

57. When working with students on their IEP goals, teachers must

    I. instruct at the students' IEP goal level
    II. work one on one with students
    III. monitor progress

    (A) I only
    (B) II only
    (C) I and III only
    (D) I, II and III

58. A teacher is giving directions on an upcoming science project. Several students in the class have a low processing speed. Which of the following would be inappropriate for the teacher to use?

    (A) Concept cards
    (B) Peer notes
    (C) Written instruction
    (D) Verbal directions

59. Which of the following would be inappropriate in a post-secondary program for students with cognitive impairments?

    (A) Teaching students how to do laundry
    (B) Teaching students how to grocery shop
    (C) Having students tutor their general education peers
    (D) Having students open and maintain bank accounts

60. Instruction for students with special needs should take place in

    I. the community
    II. general education classrooms

III. social environments

(A) I and II only
(B) III only
(C) II and III only
(D) I, II and III

61. Which of the following must a teacher employ to meet NCLB guidelines?

(A) Use of assistive technology in the classroom
(B) Use of scientifically based methods
(C) Use of visual, auditory, and kinesthetic approaches
(D) Use of previously successful practices

62. Which of the following best describes differentiated instruction?

(A) Accommodating all student work and challenges that arise within the classroom
(B) Modifying all curriculum and content being taught in a classroom
(C) Adapting instruction, materials, and content to meet the needs of all learners
(D) Changing the learning environment, setting, and curriculum to increase learning

63. The use of social stories would be inappropriate for which type of students?

(A) Students with learning disabilities
(B) Students with autism spectrum disorder
(C) Students with cognitive impairments
(D) Students with emotional impairments

64. Which of the following would NOT be considered differentiated instruction?

(A) Having classroom books at a variety of reading levels
(B) Giving choices for a project, such as letter, debate, or PowerPoint
(C) Use of assistive technology within the classroom
(D) Giving all students the same amount of time to complete a test

65. Which of the following describes a method used to provide early academic support and assistance to students who are having learning difficulties?

(A) Response to interactions
(B) Response to instruction
(C) Response to intervention
(D) Response to inattentiveness

66. Which of the following graphic organizers would be best suited to sequencing events from a storybook?

I. K-W-L chart
II. timeline
III. flow chart

(A) I and II only
(B) II and III only
(C) II only
(D) III only

67. When working with students, parents, guardians, and colleagues, teachers must use which of the following types of language to communicate properly and respectfully?

(A) English as a second language
(B) People-first language
(C) Semantic proper language
(D) Language-based learning

68. Which of the following types of instruction will NOT help to build reading comprehension?

(A) Teaching decoding skills
(B) Teaching vocabulary
(C) Teaching text structure
(D) Teaching systematic listing

69. Which of these problem-solving strategies are recommended when teaching mathematics?

I. Working backwards
II. Logical reasoning
III. Drawing a model

(A) I only
(B) I and II only
(C) I and III only
(D) I, II and III

70. Which of the following instructional approaches would be best for teaching students how to communicate effectively with peers and adults?

    (A) Peer tutoring
    (B) Social groups
    (C) Group projects
    (D) Peer mediation

71. Cooperative and collaborative instruction with colleagues includes

    I.   providing insight and problem-solving techniques together
    II. developing and sharing common instructional goals
    III. creating curriculum based on one's personal viewpoint

    (A) I only
    (B) II only
    (C) I and II only
    (D) I, II and III

72. Which of the following may occur when teaching new mathematics skills to a student with a learning disability in the area of mathematics?

    (A) Student will become violent.
    (B) Student will become impulsive.
    (C) Student will become frustrated.
    (D) Student will become self-directed.

73. Which of the following is NOT a benefit of monitoring and assessing reading instruction in your classroom?

    (A) Helping to create behavior intervention plans for students
    (B) Helping to find ways to change or adapt instruction
    (C) Helping to see growth and progress of students
    (D) Helping to provide current levels and skills of students

74. When planning instruction for a student with special needs, what reports would be useful to read?

    I.   Previous teacher reports
    II. Psychological reports
    III. Social worker reports

    (A) I and II only
    (B) I and III only
    (C) II and III only
    (D) I, II and III

75. All of the following are examples of authentic assessment EXCEPT a

    (A) presentation.
    (B) performance.
    (C) written response.
    (D) multiple-choice test.

76. An instructionally supportive test is characterized as

    I.   providing informative results to guide instruction
    II. having only a few highly significant curricular aims
    III. supplying clear descriptions of what is to be assessed

    (A) I only
    (B) I and II only
    (C) I, II and III
    (D) I and III only

77. Which of the following is NOT an example of an accommodation made for assessment purposes?

    (A) Changing the setting in which the assessment occurs
    (B) Changing the method of response to the assessment
    (C) Altering the constructs being tested by the assessment
    (D) Allowing more time for the assessment to be completed

78. In regard to assessment, which of the following represents an accommodation in presentation?

    (A) A student is provided large print to read.
    (B) A student is tested alone in a separate room.
    (C) A student uses a brailler to respond to questions.

(D) A student is allowed frequent breaks while testing.

79. Of what value is progress monitoring to teachers?

(A) Teachers can be informed of adjustments to instruction to help students succeed.
(B) Teachers need only measure student achievement periodically rather than frequently.
(C) Teachers can eliminate the use of accommodations for students who are having difficulty.
(D) Teachers can use a single instructional approach with a student until it has the desired effect.

80. What is Curriculum-Based Measurement (CBM)?

(A) A universal screening of academics and behavior for all students within a school
(B) A method teachers use to determine how students are progressing in basic academic areas
(C) An observational checklist of teaching behaviors focused on the individual providing instruction
(D) A comparison of students' learning rates and achievement in different classrooms of similar grade level

81. Following a brief assessment, a student with a disability shows a low rate of progress. The student's teacher can modify by

I.   increasing instructional time
II. changing a teaching technique
III. lowering expectations for performance

(A) I only
(B) I and II only
(C) I, II and III
(D) I and III only

82. Which of the following tells when Tier Two intervention begins?

(A) After a student undergoes a lengthy referral process
(B) Before progress monitoring of a student is analyzed

(C) When a student fails to progress in the general classroom
(D) Before a student receives core instruction in general education

83. A teacher will assess a student with a disability on a regular basis to

(A) measure the student's mastery of a series of single short-term objectives.
(B) predict when the student will meet the year-end benchmark for math or reading.
(C) determine whether the student is profiting from the typical instructional program.
(D) continue with the typical instructional program to improve the student's outcomes.

84. An at-risk student who is making progress in Tier One instruction will MOST likely require

(A) intensive intervention through Tier Two instruction.
(B) careful monitoring by the general classroom teacher.
(C) evaluation to determine a specific learning disability.
(D) immediate individualized instruction from a specialist.

85. Response to Intervention (RTI) helps schools

I.   monitor student progress
II. provide evidence-based interventions
III. identify students at risk for poor learning outcomes

(A) I only
(B) I and II only
(C) I, II and III
(D) I and III only

86. A student with a disability must take an examination. Which of the following is NOT a reasonable adjustment?

(A) Split testing sessions
(B) Unsupervised rest breaks
(C) Use of personal computer
(D) Separate examination area

87. Which of the following assessment strategies allows students to choose their own topic for exploration?

   (A) Lab experiment
   (B) Multiple-choice test
   (C) Project-based exercise
   (D) Short-answer responses

88. Students who continually fail on assessments are likely to

   (A) stop trying.
   (B) practice with focus.
   (C) seek new approaches.
   (D) persist despite obstacles.

89. Portfolio assessment programs are used to

   I. invite students to reflect upon their growth as learners
   II. provide quantitative evaluations of student achievement
   III. aid in the diversification of approaches to learning styles

   (A) I only
   (B) I and II only
   (C) I, II and III
   (D) I and III only

90. Which is NOT a typical classroom accommodation when giving a test to a student with a disability?

   (A) Use of notes
   (B) Use of technology
   (C) Use of a calculator
   (D) Use of peer editing

91. Which of the following should be avoided when administering an accommodation during testing?

   (A) Making the accommodation available to every student out of convenience
   (B) Knowing the parameters within which the accommodation can be provided
   (C) Being familiar with the particular accommodation given to a student
   (D) Considering an accommodation essential if only one student needs it

92. When choosing accommodations for a student with a disability, the IEP team should

   I. make decisions based on the student's individualized needs
   II. be specific about how and when accommodations will be provided
   III. assume the same accommodations should remain in place each year

   (A) I only
   (B) I and II only
   (C) I, II and III
   (D) I and III only

93. A teacher who uses progress monitoring will do all of the following EXCEPT

   (A) exclude accommodations.
   (B) chart a student's progress.
   (C) assess a student frequently.
   (D) adjust instructional approaches.

94. Which of the following is a common assessment-related difficulty for a student with a hearing impairment?

   (A) Extreme stress
   (B) Reduced concentration
   (C) Inability to write with a pen
   (D) Difficulty communicating orally

95. When adjustments to assessments are made, students with a disability will

   (A) pass or fail based on performance.
   (B) be exempt from failure.
   (C) pass an assignment.
   (D) master a course.

96. Which is NOT a form of assessment variation?

   (A) Giving assignments instead of exams
   (B) Coaching while administering an exam
   (C) Providing short-answer instead of multiple-choice exams
   (D) Allowing audio-taped instead of written answers to exams

97. Which of the following was typical of special education in the United States during the 1800s?

   (A) Agencies such as asylums and hospitals practiced isolation of children with special needs.
   (B) Students with disabilities were in schools with all other children but in separate classrooms.
   (C) Institutions grouped children with disabilities together but separated them from regular schools.
   (D) Children with disabilities were integrated into regular classrooms at schools as much as possible.

98. Parents who sought passage of the Education for All Handicapped Children Act of 1975 wanted

   I.   mainstreaming for children with disabilities
   II. fair assessment for children with disabilities
   III. participation in the special education process

   (A) I only
   (B) I and II only
   (C) I, II and III
   (D) I and III only

99. Since 1975, the ONLY children eligible for special education support in the United States have been those

   (A) with a qualifying disability such as autism or mental retardation.
   (B) whose parents can afford to pay for specially designed services.
   (C) who live in select states that have a state education department.
   (D) who attend private schools providing special education services.

100. Which of the following defines due process as it relates to special education?

   (A) A system of checks and balances for fair treatment of students with disabilities
   (B) A written education plan created by a team especially for a child with a disability
   (C) A mandate to provide an environment most like a normal classroom to a disabled child

   (D) A nondiscriminatory set of standards used to locate, assess, and place disabled children

101. Measurable goals on an IEP may include all of the following EXCEPT

   (A) academic goals.
   (B) social skills.
   (C) behaviors.
   (D) attitudes.

102. Which of the following is an example of a specific goal that can be measured objectively on an IEP?

   (A) John will learn typing skills with progress determined by teacher observation.
   (B) Megan will increase in-seat, on-task behavior as reported through teacher judgment.
   (C) Leroy will stop overreacting to normal classroom stimuli to the degree achievable by other students in the classroom.
   (D) Taylor will increase her passage reading of text orally from the 10th to the 25th percentile as measured by XYZ test.

103. The Individuals with Disabilities Education Act (IDEA) requires an IEP to have

   I.   a listing of measurable goals, such as benchmarks, for the student
   II. a statement of the student's present levels of educational performance
   III. a detailing of modifications for the student within the educational environment

   (A) I only
   (B) I and II only
   (C) I, II and III
   (D) I and III only

104. According to federal regulation, the goals contained in an IEP are best described as

   (A) broad weekly goals.
   (B) purposeful daily goals.
   (C) measurable annual goals.
   (D) direction-setting monthly goals.

105. Which is NOT included in the options for becoming a highly qualified special education teacher in a core academic subject?

    (A) The teacher holds a bachelor's or a more advanced college degree.
    (B) The teacher holds appropriate professional credentials related to impairments.
    (C) The teacher has obtained full state certification as a special education teacher.
    (D) The teacher has participated in an alternative route to special education certification.

106. Which of the following is excluded as a service related to special education?

    (A) interpreting services
    (B) occupational therapy
    (C) parent counseling and training
    (D) checking an implanted medical device

107. Psychological services of students with a disability include all of the following EXCEPT

    (A) interpreting psychological assessment results.
    (B) developing positive behavioral intervention strategies.
    (C) psychological counseling for children and their parents.
    (D) preventing further impairment or loss of physical function.

108. By law, native language for a student with deafness or blindness is

    I.   Braille
    II. sign language
    III. oral communication

    (A) I only
    (B) I and II only
    (C) I, II and III
    (D) I and III only

109. Federal regulation mandates use of assistive technology if

    (A) it is kept at a child's home.
    (B) a child desires to use a device.
    (C) it is required by a child's IEP.

    (D) a child's parents purchase a device.

110. Present levels of performance (PLAAFP) for a child with a disability can be measurable on an IEP by

    I.   specifying a grade-level performance
    II. indicating a rate
    III. limiting goals to areas of academic needs

    (A) I only
    (B) I and II only
    (C) I, II and III
    (D) I and III only

111. Which of the following is required for an IEP meeting to take place?

    (A) The parent must participate by conference call.
    (B) The parent must agree to purchase a copy of the IEP.
    (C) The IEP team must include an interpreter if needed by a parent.
    (D) The IEP team must convince the parents that they must attend.

112. Which is NOT a primary responsibility of a regular education teacher of a child with a disability?

    (A) Provide appropriate behavioral interventions and supports
    (B) Personally review and implement the student's IEP plan
    (C) Instruct the student in curricula within areas of content specialization
    (D) Assist in the determination of supplementary aids and services for a child

113. When is a teacher at risk of being out of compliance with federal law?

    I.   When the teacher willfully fails to implement a child's IEP
    II. When the teacher fails to provide proof that he or she is implementing a child's IEP
    III. When the teacher fails to memorize what is enumerated in the child's IEP documents

(A) I only
(B) I and II only
(C) I, II and III
(D) I and III only

114. A special education teacher has the role of

(A) suggesting modifications to testing for a child with a disability.
(B) allotting transition service resources for a child with a disability.
(C) providing related services to a child with a disability such as physical therapy.
(D) teaching general curriculum in the regular classroom to a child with a disability.

115. Parents who disagree with their child's IEP have the right to do all of the following EXCEPT

(A) ask for mediation to try to reach an agreement.
(B) ask for due process before an impartial officer.
(C) file a complaint with the state education agency.
(D) change their child's current educational placement.

116. Which of the following is a role of the classroom teacher?

(A) Notifying personnel to request an evaluation for a struggling student
(B) Evaluating the safety of a classroom for a visually impaired student
(C) Co-teaching with a content area teacher in an inclusive classroom
(D) Holding small reading recovery groups for several grades

117. What decision was made by the U.S. courts in the case of *Oberti v. Board of Education*?

(A) Segregated placements of children with disabilities are inappropriate.
(B) Inclusion of a child with a disability is mandated as a requirement of IDEA.
(C) The aim of IDEA is to place a student with a disability in the least restrictive environment.

(D) Mainstreaming a child with a disability with non-disabled peers is the preference of IDEA.

118. In the case of *Irving Independent School District v. Tatro*, the court decided

I. Clean Intermittent Catheterization (CIC) is a related service under the Education of the Handicapped Act
II. the provision of CIC is not subject to exclusion as a medical service under the Education of the Handicapped Act
III. related services such as CIC must be documented within an IEP as required by the Education of the Handicapped Act

(A) I only
(B) I and II only
(C) I, II and III
(D) I and III only

119. The decision in the Rowley Case asserted that Amy Rowley, a deaf student, was

(A) a well-adjusted child and therefore needed no interpreter.
(B) performing better than average and therefore needed no interpreter.
(C) experiencing a poor rapport with her teachers and therefore needed an interpreter.
(D) understanding less than she would without her disability and therefore needed an interpreter.

120. Which of the following pieces of legislation guarantees equal opportunity for all individuals with disabilities?

(A) Section 504 of the Rehabilitation Act of 1973
(B) Americans with Disabilities Act of 1990
(C) No Child Left Behind Act of 2001
(D) Education America Act of 1994

Answer Explanations
for Practice Test 2

Special Education: Core Content Knowledge (0354)

1.	(D)	31.	(D)	61.	(B)	91.	(A)
2.	(C)	32.	(D)	62.	(C)	92.	(B)
3.	(C)	33.	(C)	63.	(A)	93.	(A)
4.	(B)	34.	(A)	64.	(D)	94.	(D)
5.	(B)	35.	(B)	65.	(C)	95.	(A)
6.	(B)	36.	(C)	66.	(B)	96.	(B)
7.	(D)	37.	(C)	67.	(B)	97.	(A)
8.	(A)	38.	(B)	68.	(D)	98.	(C)
9.	(A)	39.	(C)	69.	(D)	99.	(A)
10.	(C)	40.	(D)	70.	(B)	100.	(A)
11.	(A)	41.	(D)	71.	(C)	101.	(D)
12.	(D)	42.	(A)	72.	(C)	102.	(D)
13.	(C)	43.	(C)	73.	(A)	103.	(C)
14.	(C)	44.	(A)	74.	(D)	104.	(C)
15.	(B)	45.	(B)	75.	(D)	105.	(B)
16.	(A)	46.	(C)	76.	(C)	106.	(D)
17.	(C)	47.	(D)	77.	(C)	107.	(D)
18.	(B)	48.	(D)	78.	(A)	108.	(C)
19.	(B)	49.	(D)	79.	(A)	109.	(C)
20.	(B)	50.	(A)	80.	(B)	110.	(B)
21.	(D)	51.	(D)	81.	(B)	111.	(C)
22.	(C)	52.	(A)	82.	(C)	112.	(D)
23.	(C)	53.	(C)	83.	(C)	113.	(B)
24.	(A)	54.	(C)	84.	(B)	114.	(A)
25.	(A)	55.	(D)	85.	(C)	115.	(D)
26.	(A)	56.	(A)	86.	(B)	116.	(A)
27.	(B)	57.	(C)	87.	(C)	117.	(C)
28.	(C)	58.	(D)	88.	(A)	118.	(C)
29.	(B)	59.	(C)	89.	(D)	119.	(D)
30.	(A)	60.	(D)	90.	(D)	120.	(B)

ANSWER KEY ALIGNED TO CONTENT CATEGORIES

Question	Answer	Content Category
1	D	I. Development and Characteristics of Learners
2	C	I. Development and Characteristics of Learners
3	C	I. Development and Characteristics of Learners
4	B	I. Development and Characteristics of Learners
5	B	I. Development and Characteristics of Learners
6	B	I. Development and Characteristics of Learners
7	D	I. Development and Characteristics of Learners
8	A	I. Development and Characteristics of Learners
9	A	I. Development and Characteristics of Learners
10	C	I. Development and Characteristics of Learners
11	A	I. Development and Characteristics of Learners
12	D	I. Development and Characteristics of Learners
13	C	I. Development and Characteristics of Learners
14	C	I. Development and Characteristics of Learners
15	B	I. Development and Characteristics of Learners
16	A	I. Development and Characteristics of Learners
17	C	I. Development and Characteristics of Learners
18	B	I. Development and Characteristics of Learners
19	B	I. Development and Characteristics of Learners
20	B	I. Development and Characteristics of Learners
21	D	II. Planning and the Learning Environment
22	C	II. Planning and the Learning Environment
23	C	II. Planning and the Learning Environment
24	A	II. Planning and the Learning Environment
25	A	II. Planning and the Learning Environment
26	A	II. Planning and the Learning Environment
27	B	II. Planning and the Learning Environment
28	C	II. Planning and the Learning Environment
29	B	II. Planning and the Learning Environment
30	A	II. Planning and the Learning Environment
31	D	II. Planning and the Learning Environment
32	D	II. Planning and the Learning Environment
33	C	II. Planning and the Learning Environment
34	A	II. Planning and the Learning Environment
35	B	II. Planning and the Learning Environment

(continued)

Question	Answer	Content Category
36	C	II. Planning and the Learning Environment
37	C	II. Planning and the Learning Environment
38	B	II. Planning and the Learning Environment
39	C	II. Planning and the Learning Environment
40	D	II. Planning and the Learning Environment
41	D	II. Planning and the Learning Environment
42	A	II. Planning and the Learning Environment
43	C	II. Planning and the Learning Environment
44	A	II. Planning and the Learning Environment
45	B	II. Planning and the Learning Environment
46	C	II. Planning and the Learning Environment
47	D	II. Planning and the Learning Environment
48	D	III. Instruction
49	D	III. Instruction
50	A	III. Instruction
51	D	III. Instruction
52	A	III. Instruction
53	C	III. Instruction
54	C	III. Instruction
55	D	III. Instruction
56	A	III. Instruction
57	C	III. Instruction
58	D	III. Instruction
59	C	III. Instruction
60	D	III. Instruction
61	B	III. Instruction
62	C	III. Instruction
63	A	III. Instruction
64	D	III. Instruction
65	C	III. Instruction
66	B	III. Instruction
67	B	III. Instruction
68	D	III. Instruction
69	D	III. Instruction
70	B	III. Instruction
71	C	III. Instruction
72	C	III. Instruction
73	A	III. Instruction

(*continued*)

Question	Answer	Content Category
74	D	III. Instruction
75	D	IV. Assessment
76	C	IV. Assessment
77	C	IV. Assessment
78	A	IV. Assessment
79	A	IV. Assessment
80	B	IV. Assessment
81	B	IV. Assessment
82	C	IV. Assessment
83	C	IV. Assessment
84	B	IV. Assessment
85	C	IV. Assessment
86	B	IV. Assessment
87	C	IV. Assessment
88	A	IV. Assessment
89	D	IV. Assessment
90	D	IV. Assessment
91	A	IV. Assessment
92	B	IV. Assessment
93	A	IV. Assessment
94	D	IV. Assessment
95	A	IV. Assessment
96	B	IV. Assessment
97	A	V. Foundations and Professional Responsibilities
98	C	V. Foundations and Professional Responsibilities
99	A	V. Foundations and Professional Responsibilities
100	A	V. Foundations and Professional Responsibilities
101	D	V. Foundations and Professional Responsibilities
102	D	V. Foundations and Professional Responsibilities
103	C	V. Foundations and Professional Responsibilities
104	C	V. Foundations and Professional Responsibilities
105	B	V. Foundations and Professional Responsibilities
106	D	V. Foundations and Professional Responsibilities
107	D	V. Foundations and Professional Responsibilities
108	C	V. Foundations and Professional Responsibilities
109	C	V. Foundations and Professional Responsibilities
110	B	V. Foundations and Professional Responsibilities
111	C	V. Foundations and Professional Responsibilities

(continued)

Question	Answer	Content Category
112	D	V. Foundations and Professional Responsibilities
113	B	V. Foundations and Professional Responsibilities
114	A	V. Foundations and Professional Responsibilities
115	D	V. Foundations and Professional Responsibilities
116	A	V. Foundations and Professional Responsibilities
117	C	V. Foundations and Professional Responsibilities
118	C	V. Foundations and Professional Responsibilities
119	D	V. Foundations and Professional Responsibilities
120	B	V. Foundations and Professional Responsibilities

1. (D)

The correct answer is option D, because it is unlikely the student would require large-print materials as a result of a hearing impairment. The other examples provided would be good techniques to utilize.

2. (C)

The correct answer is option C, because colored overlays and materials with enlarged print would be excellent ways to assist the student with a visual impairment. Option II suggests that the student has a learning problem in addition to the visual impairment. Teachers should never assume a learning problem when working with students with visual impairments.

3. (C)

The correct answer is option C because although diabetic students can receive special education services under the Other Health Impairment category, by itself, diabetes is not a category of special education.

4. (B)

The correct answer is option B because this model shows the range of emotions one goes through when experiencing a "death" of the dreams the parents once had for their child.

5. (B)

The correct answer is option B because the federal law clearly states that persons receiving special education services are entitled to a "free and appropriate public education" within the "least restrictive environment." The student's social awareness shouldn't be a factor in determining placement.

6. (B)

The correct answer is option B because the federal government works hard to ensure there are not a disproportionate number of minorities receiving special education services. If a district is found to have a disproportion, it is believed that cultural differences were not taken into consideration when evaluating students. The data is tracked to ensure that students who are behind as a result of a language difference, or who have not been exposed to certain culturally foreign concepts, are not placed into special education classes.

7. (D)

The correct answer is option D because conduct disorders are different from emotional impairment, and as such, students with conduct disorders are not guaranteed special education services under the Individuals with Disabilities Education Act.

8. (A)

The correct answer is option A because best practices suggest allowing students with ADHD to assist in activities that allow for kinesthetic movement to release energy so they are more likely to focus when needed.

9. (A)

The correct answer is option A because best practices suggest that persons with autism perform better with speech and language services as well as with social work support.

10. (C)

The correct answer is option C because IDEA asserts that states must provide services to students identified as requiring special education support. The students must receive services between the ages of

3–21. States can choose to exceed the federal guidelines if they desire.

11. (A)

The correct answer is option A. Autism is a developmental disability, a chronic condition that is due to a mental or physical impairment. Traumatic brain injuries, depression, and vision impairment are not developmental disabilities.

12. (D)

The correct answer is option D because the other options are included in the seven categories of specific learning disabilities as outlined by the federal law.

13. (C)

The correct answer is option C because IDEA states that students receiving special education services who are suspended ten days during an academic year are entitled to a manifestation determination review to evaluate whether the students' suspensions are a direct result of their disability.

14. (C)

The correct answer is option C because choices (A), (B), and (D) are components of the process for determining special education eligibility under federal law. Social awareness is not an aspect of the eligibility guidelines.

15. (B)

The correct answer is option B because IDEA states that students receiving special education services must have an IEP developed once per academic year. It must be addressed within one calendar year of the previous IEP. If the IEP were to be conducted even one day more than a year after the previous annual IEP, the district would be in violation of federal law.

16. (A)

The correct answer is option A because IDEA states that every three years a student receiving special education services is required to have a more thorough IEP. This IEP typically involves academic testing to measure whether the student still requires special education services. Parents can choose to waive testing if the team feels the student is appropriately placed.

17. (C)

The correct answer is option C because IDEA states that students receiving special education are to have individual goals and objectives within their IEP document and they are to be addressed and evaluated by the teacher on a basis stated within the IEP.

18. (B)

The correct answer is option B because options I and II are stated in IDEA. Socially maladjusted behavior is not a designated category of special education.

19. (B)

The correct answer is option B because task analysis is defined as the breaking down a task into its component parts. Once accomplished, the analysis should include including a detailed description of both manual and mental activities.

20. (B)

The correct answer is option B because in general, when intellectual quotients are below 40, it is likely that the student will have additional disabilities and will probably require more services such as speech and language, occupational, and/or physical therapy.

21. (D)

The correct answer is option D. A manifestation determination review is typically used when determining whether the student's behavior or misconduct was the result of his or her disability, rather than a willful act to behave in a manner inconsistent with the rules. The other options are all aspects of a well-planned behavior intervention plan.

22. (C)

The correct answer is option C. An effective lesson plan would not include scripts from which the teacher reads. Options I, II, and III are key components of an effective lesson plan.

23. (C)

The correct answer is option C. Best practices in education suggest that students do not benefit from being singled out and punished. Rather, methods should allow for dignity to be maintained by the misbehaving student. Time Out areas are an antiquated management technique. The current trend is to manage in a way that does not encourage embarrassment to be associated with discipline so students feel safe in the classroom.

24. (A)

The correct answer is option A. Students with special needs suffer anxiety when sharing their answers with the class. They often fear being incorrect. In fact, many general education students share this fear. By assuring students they will be called upon only when the teacher is certain their answer is correct, students' anxiety is alleviated. This method allows students to enjoy the pride of having the correct answer.

25. (A)

The correct answer is option A. When completing an ABC log, the evaluator must track the antecedent (if known), the behavior that follows, and the consequence of the behavior.

26. (A)

The correct answer is option A because although lessons, group activities, and individual assignments are all important parts of the learning process, the anticipatory set is intended to get the students' attention prior to delivering the lesson.

27. (B)

The correct answer is option B because many special education students have fear and anxiety with respect to drills. They benefit from advance notice whenever possible.

28. (C)

The correct answer is option C because resource rooms are designed to assist students once they have participated in a classroom lesson. They are not meant to be an avenue whereby a special education teacher gives instruction; rather, the special educator offers support within the resource room and frequently offers assistance during assignments.

29. (B)

The correct answer is option B because a least-restrictive environment means finding the appropriate program and setting based on a student's physical, emotional, and cognitive needs. Making accommodations involves placing strategies and tools into students' programs to help them gain success. Modifications means taking material and content out of curriculum based on the student's abilities. Mainstreaming is when a student with special needs is placed within the general education setting with all general education students.

30. (A)

The correct answer is option A because students with learning disabilities in mathematics have difficulty following along, keeping up, asking questions, and understanding the material. With direct instruction by the teacher, the student would find it easier to ask questions, keep up, and follow the material. Modeling is a good strategy to show how a math problem or process is carried out. Skill drill is a good method to reinforce mathematic processes, routine, and practice.

31. (D)

The correct answer is option D because in order to have a productive and successful classroom the teacher must create all three elements—rules, consequences, and expectations—for students. The other answer choices do not combine all three elements.

32. (D)

The correct answer is option D because removing content from a social studies unit is a modification to a student's work materials. The other choices are clear and appropriate accommodations for a student with ADHD because they relate to the behaviors ADHD can cause.

33. (C)

The correct answer is option C because a formative evaluation will show the student's progress and the effectiveness of the program. Summative evaluations measure students' mastery skills and suggest whether students should continue to the next grade. Psychological evaluation is not performed by teachers, but will give results about cognitive abilities. Special education evaluation is the process of testing a student who may qualify for services.

34. (A)

The correct answer is option A, I and II only, because in order to determine the least restrictive environment of a student, you need to know the student's previous placement, academic history, school, and family history. You will also want to know how the student is performing. Evaluation and assessments will help determine which classroom or setting fits best with the student's abilities. Number III would be incorrect

because the hobbies a student has outside of school are not be a factor for at-school classroom placement.

35. (B)

The correct answer is option B because collecting data on the behavior helps to determine where the behavior is manifesting and helps provide clear reasoning and effective solutions. Once teachers have information, they should call a meeting or contact the parents to discuss the behavior. Answer choice A would be incorrect because reprimanding a student in front of peers may have a negative effect. The student may enjoy the attention and increase this behavior further. Answer choice C is incorrect because counselors and administrators do not get involved until data is collected to help the team come to a clear solution. Answer choice D is incorrect because talking to a parent without data is an ineffective approach.

36. (C)

The correct answer is option C because learning centers are used to give students independence to work on their own, and increase the responsibility of working on their own to gain better understanding. Number III is incorrect because working on homework is not part of the learning centers' purpose.

37. (C)

The correct answer is option C because full inclusion of the student would entail students attending general education classes full time with their general ed peers. The rest of the choices are incorrect because they are appropriate strategies and elements for a self-contained classroom for students with moderate to severe autism.

38. (B)

The correct answer is option B because students with visual impairments need correct and clear lighting depending on the severity of their disability. These students also would benefit from being close to the instructor to hear more easily. Statement II is incorrect because of the noise and distraction inherent in sitting close to a vent or heater.

39. (C)

The correct answer is option C because the student's gratification will not be immediate. The student has to wait for positive reinforcement, thus decreasing the chances of the behavior continuing. All other choices are do not answer the question because they are immediate; therefore, they result in the student experiencing a direct effect of positive behavior.

40. (D)

The correct answer is option D because students with central auditory processing disorders have an inability to understand and process verbal language. These students benefit from written directions, especially if they receive the materials ahead of time and can discuss them with the teacher one on one. Answer choices A through C are incorrect because they rely on verbal language for directions.

41. (D)

The correct answer is option D because all of the listed characteristics are associated with attention deficit hyperactivity disorder (ADHD).

42. (A)

The correct answer is option A because competence is not a learning strategy; it is a part of developing self-skills. The rest of the choices are learning strategies.

43. (C)

The correct answer is option C because providing school safety and scientifically based methods of teaching are factors of the No Child Left Behind (NCLB) Act. Statement III is incorrect because providing self-advocacy skills for students does not fall under NCLB.

44. (A)

The correct answer is option A because a 504 plan allows accommodations for students who struggle, but no federal money is attached to the services. The rest of the choices are correct because they can be included as part of special education services and the student IEP, which is a funded service.

45. (B)

The correct answer is option (B) because past statewide assessment scores are the least helpful qualifier in determining job placement and effective postsecondary success in the workforce. The rest of the choices are do not answer the question because they connect directly to a job the student will be working on currently.

46. (C)

The correct answer is option C because achievement assessments can provide information about what area the student may qualify for and what instructional method(s) will work best for the student's abilities. Statement I is incorrect because medical history needs to be provided by parents or guardians or a medication professional.

47. (D)

The correct answer is option D because the behavior is consistent and disruptive to peers. Answer choice A is incorrect because the student is having an academic struggle that would be addressed with remediation. Answer choice B is incorrect because the main office can care for attendance problems. Answer choice C is incorrect because the student is facing an emotional issue that a social worker or counselor may handle privately.

48. (D)

The correct answer is option D because parallel, supportive, and team teaching are all different ways to effectively co-teach and provide instruction in the classroom. In supportive teaching, one teacher takes the lead role, while another teacher circulates among the students to provide additional support. Parallel teaching involves dividing the classroom students so different teachers can instruct different groups of students. In team teaching, the members of the team co-teach together and share responsibility for the planning, teaching, and assessing of the class.

49. (D)

The correct answer is option D because repetition using listening, speaking, and writing is ideal when working with a student who is an English language learner. The other choices are inferior because they do not guarantee or provide repetition using listening, speaking, and writing.

50. (A)

The correct answer is option A because Vygotsky discusses three instruction strategies: scaffolding, apprenticeship, and guided participation. Modeling is not one of Vygotsky's strategies, although it can be used as an instructional strategy within the classroom.

51. (D)

The correct answer is option D because all of the other choices would benefit a classroom made up of diverse learners. Dividing the class into small groups by abilities would help students learn with peers at their own level to help eliminate frustration and the frustration of anyone falling behind. Accommodating high and low learners would help students feel challenged and work at their own ability level. Having a co-teacher would help provide more assistance to students, and co-teaching strategies would help reach all learners.

52. (A)

The correct answer is option A because progress monitoring is a way to track and help instruct students in regards to IEP goals. State assessments cannot be used to monitor goals because they cover a vast area of academics and may not be at the student's ability level. The scaffolding method is an instruction strategy by Vygotsky. Scaffolding involves putting in supports for effective instruction so that new and old skills can develop.

53. (C)

The correct answer is option C because incremental rehearsal builds fluency and retention with new skills. K-W-L is incorrect because this strategy is used for teaching large chucks of information in a student-directed activity. Books on tape are incorrect because they do not build fluency or retention. Teacher modeling and demonstration are incorrect because these strategies fail to promote fluency and retention strength in students.

54. (C)

The correct answer is option C because hyperactivity is a characteristic associated with ADHD, and violent behaviors can be associated with a variety of disabilities based on the individual student. The other choices are all characteristics of students that are on the autistic spectrum.

55. (D)

The correct answer is option D because all of the listed items are used to meet the needs of special education students. The items can be used as visual and auditory aids to help increase learning.

56. (A)

The correct answer is option A because Braille is not a technological device; it is used as a reading and writing method for those who are visually impaired.

Trackballs, iPads, and joysticks are all technological devices that assist and enhance learning for students with disabilities.

57. (C)

The correct answer is option C because teachers are not required to work independently with students on their IEP goals. Teachers can instruct in groups if the students have similar abilities and goals. Teachers must instruct at students' goal levels to measure progress and growth. The teacher must also monitor the progress and growth the student shows weekly, bi-weekly, etc.

58. (D)

The correct answer is option D because giving verbal directions to students with a low processing speed would not benefit their understanding of the project. Low processing speed slows down the process for understanding information. Students with low processing speed need time, concept cards, notes, and written directions to accommodate their disability by having tangible documentation.

59. (C)

The correct answer is option C because students with cognitive impairments are not comparable to their same-age general education peers. Students with cognitive impairments are inappropriate candidates for tutoring because their skills are below age and grade level. The other choices are all appropriate. A post-secondary program would focus on daily and vocational skills to help their students function in the community.

60. (D)

The correct answer is option D because community, general education classrooms, and social environments are all settings to instruct on academic, social, emotional, daily, and vocational skills. These settings are great places to instruct on new skills or build on old skills for students.

61. (B)

The correct answer is option B because scientifically based methods are part of No Child Left Behind guidelines. The use of assistive technology, all learning modalities, and previous practices do not answer the question because they are not covered in NCLB. All of the listed methods *can* be used for instruction, but they are not required under NCLB guidelines.

62. (C)

The correct answer is option C because differentiated instruction means adapting all of the instruction, materials, and content to benefit a variety of different learners. The other answers would be incorrect because they do not discuss meeting the special needs of all learners.

63. (A)

The correct answer is option A because students with learning disabilities do not respond well to social stories. Students with learning disabilities have weaknesses in academic areas. The other choices are correct because students with disabilities such as autism spectrum disorder, cognitive impairments, and emotional impairments usually have weak social skills.

64. (D)

The correct answer is option D because giving all students the same amount of time to take a test may not meet their personal needs. Students may need different time limits and expectations. The other choices would be incorrect because they provide different levels and choices to satisfy the needs of a variety of learners.

65. (C)

The correct answer is option C because response to intervention is described as a method to provide early academic support and assistance to students who are having learning difficulties.

66. (B)

The correct answer is option B because a timeline and flow chart will help organize information in a visual and sequential format. The format helps to recreate a story from beginning to end. A K-W-L chart asks students, what they **Know**, what they **Want** to learn, and what they've **Learned**. This organizer would not help to sequence a story.

67. (B)

The correct answer is option B because people-first language requires putting the person before the disability, aiming to eliminate prejudices and hurtful descriptors. This language is the most respectful and proper way to communicate. The other answers would be incorrect because they are language instruction terms that do not relate to the question.

68. (D)

The correct answer is option D because systematic listing is a common strategy for math problem solving. Systematic listing is a way to organize steps and use them as a checklist when performing mathematic processes. All the other choices are appropriate and successful ways to develop reading comprehension. Decoding skills helps to break down unknown words within reading. Vocabulary helps to understand words when reading. Text structures help students identify what they're reading and organize the information correctly.

69. (D)

The correct answer is option D because all of the choices listed are correct strategies to use when teaching mathematics problem solving. Working backwards involves solving problems from end to beginning. Logical reasoning means properly applying the correct operation to math problems. Drawing a model means creating a visual picture of how to tackle a math problem.

70. (B)

The correct answer is option B because social groups combine a variety of students who need to focus on social and communication issues in social environments. These groups work on social cues, peer relationships, and appropriate communication skills. A social worker, counselor, or teacher usually facilitates these groups. Peer tutoring, group projects, and peer mediation would be incorrect because teaching specific social and appropriate communication skills needs to come first, and from a trained professional before students can work effectively with peers and groups.

71. (C)

The correct answer is option C because providing insight, problem-solving techniques, developing, and sharing instructional goals are a part of cooperative and collaborative instruction with colleagues. Creating curriculum based on one's personal viewpoint would be incorrect because it does not combine a variety of colleagues' insight, ideas, and techniques.

72. (C)

The correct answer is option C because students with a learning disability can become frustrated with the material due to their inability to understand it correctly and immediately. Violent behavior is incorrect because violence does not normally occur with students with a learning disability. Impulsive behavior is incorrect because it is associated with students with ADHD. Self-direction is incorrect because students with a learning disability need support and additional assistance with academics.

73. (A)

The correct answer is option A because a behavior intervention plan does not relate to the monitoring and assessing of reading instruction within the classroom. Helping to change instruction, seeing growth and progress of students, and providing a student's current level and skills are associated with monitoring and assessing of reading instruction.

74. (D)

The correct answer is option D because all reports have information related to the student. Previous teacher reports will help provide background information about the student's abilities, behaviors, strengths, and weaknesses. Psychological reports will help provide information regarding I.Q., processing speed, memory, etc. Social worker reports will help provide social and emotional concerns a teacher should be aware of for instruction.

75. (D)

The correct answer is option D because the question requires an exception to authentic assessment. Answer D is NOT an example of authentic assessment requiring a student to demonstrate skills in a real world context, but rather is typical of a test. Therefore, D is the exception. Each example A, B, and C describes a task included in authentic assessment and therefore, does not answer the question.

76. (C)

The correct answer is option C because it includes all three correct statements. Instructionally supportive tests are those which (I) have only a few highly significant curricular aims, (II) supply clear descriptions of what is to be assessed, and (III) provide informative results to guide instruction. Since I, II, and III are all characteristics of instructionally supportive tests, all three must be included when choosing the correct answer.

77. (C)

The correct answer is option C because the question requires an exception to a testing accommodation. Answer C is NOT an example of a testing accommodation because accommodations do not alter the constructs being tested. The other examples (A, B, and D) describe accommodations made to remove obstacles to test-taking presented by a disability and so cannot be a correct answer.

78. (A)

The correct answer is option A because accommodations in presentation affect the way content is delivered to students. In option A, the student is provided with large print to read to better engage in the content of the assessment. Answer choices B-D represent other types of accommodations such as those in response, setting, and timing/scheduling.

79. (A)

The correct answer is option A because progress monitoring is a strategy that measures student achievement through the use of targeted instruction and frequent assessment of academic performance. The other answer choices represent ideas contrary to the goals of progress monitoring.

80. (B)

The correct answer is option B because CBM is a method for the progress monitoring of students. The other answer choices represent core features of strong RTI other than progress monitoring such as universal screening and fidelity measures.

81. (B)

The correct answer is option B because it includes the two possible correct statements. The teacher of a student exhibiting a low rate of progress can (I) increase instructional time or (II) change a teaching technique. Since I and II are both possible changes called for in responses to a low rate of learning progress, both must be included when choosing the correct answer. Option III is not an appropriate response as the teacher's goal is to help the student make sufficient progress toward meeting academic goals.

82. (C)

The correct answer is option C because Tier Two Intervention is for students for whom Tier One instruction is insufficient and who are falling behind on benchmark skills. The other answer choices mostly describe steps that occur during Tier One intervention.

83. (C)

The correct answer is option C because a teacher will assess the progress of a student on a regular basis for the purpose of determining whether the student is profiting appropriately from the typical instructional program. The other answer choices represent purposes of classroom assessment such as mastery measurement or are contrary to the purpose of progress monitoring.

84. (B)

The correct answer is option B because the scenario states that the student is making progress in Tier One, indicating that he or she is responding to the instruction. The qualifier asks what the student MOST needs, and since the student is progressing, the answer is continued monitoring by the teacher. The other options would only be needed if the student was unresponsive to Tier One instruction and required further interventions.

85. (C)

The correct answer is option C because it includes all three correct statements. RTI helps schools (I) identify students at risk for poor learning outcomes, (II) monitor student progress, and (III) provide evidence-based interventions. Since I, II, and III are all ways that RTI helps schools, all three must be included when choosing the correct answer.

86. (B)

The correct answer is option B because it gives the exception by NOT being a reasonable adjustment to an examination situation. A reasonable adjustment would be supervised rest breaks with a clear understanding between the supervisor and student as to their purpose. The other answer choices represent reasonable adjustments to an exam situation.

87. (C)

The correct answer is option C because a project-based exercise allows students to choose their own topics and thus allows flexibility in assessment. The other answer choices represent more traditional means of classroom assessment.

88. (A)

The correct answer is option (A) because a student who fails often generally succumbs to hopelessness and stops trying. The other options relate to the emotional experience of students who succeed on assessments.

89. (D)

The correct answer is option D because it includes the two correct statements. Portfolio assessments are used to (I) invite students to reflect upon their growth as learners and (III) aid in the diversification of approaches to learning styles. Since I and III are both reasons why portfolio assessments are used, both must be included when choosing the correct answer. Answer (II) is true of standardized evaluations such as test scores.

90. (D)

The correct answer is option D because accommodations should help students but not give them an unfair advantage. A student whose assessment is edited by a peer has an unfair advantage and the assessment will not reflect what the student being tested knows. The other options all are acceptable classroom accommodations.

91. (A)

The correct answer is option A because making an accommodation available to all students during an exam does not adhere to strict accommodation guidelines. The other answer options are examples appropriate to administering assessment accommodations.

92. (B)

The correct answer is option B because it includes the two correct statements. Accommodations should be chosen (I) based on the student's individualized needs and (II) be specified as to their use. Since I and II are both suggested for choosing accommodations, both must be included when choosing the correct answer. Answer (III) is not suggested when making accommodation decisions.

93. (A)

The correct answer is option A because it gives the exception by NOT being supportive of progress monitoring. Progress monitoring is a way of continually checking on student growth and adjusting instruction to match student need. One option available to teachers is the use of accommodations. The other answer options are examples appropriate to progress monitoring.

94. (D)

The correct answer is option D because students who are deaf, hard of hearing, or who have an auditory processing disorder may have trouble participating in discussions or have speech that is difficult for others to understand. The other answer options are examples of assessment-related difficulties associated with other disability types such as mental illness.

95. (A)

The correct answer is option A because despite adjustments being made, a student with a disability may not pass an exam or assignment, just like any other student. He or she must still meet the necessary standard to pass an assignment or course.

96. (B)

The correct answer is option B because it gives the exception by NOT being a form of assessment variation. The other answer choices represent fair and effective forms of varying assessments for all students.

97. (A)

The correct answer is option A because special education history in the 1800s was shaped by agencies that all tended toward isolation of children with disabilities. The other options describe later movements in special education history, from segregation to integration.

98. (C)

The correct answer is option C because it includes all three correct statements. The Education for All Handicapped Children Act of 1975 led to crucial new elements in special education including (I) mainstreaming for children with disabilities, (II) fair assessment for children with disabilities, and (III) parental participation in the special education process. Since I, II, and III are all improvements sought by parents who supported EAHCA, all three must be included when choosing the correct answer.

99. (A)

The correct answer is option A because special education support is a right of all children in the United States and its territories who have a qualifying disability such as autism, speech impairment, learning disability, etc. The other answer options are erroneous because once a child is qualified, he or she can receive specially designed instruction at no cost to parents regardless of state or school district.

100. (A)

The correct answer is option A because due process is the system of checks and balances that assures fair treatment and accountability to students with disabilities. The other options describe other key elements of the Education for All Children Act, including Least Restrictive Environment and Individualized Education Program.

101. (D)

The correct answer is option D because it gives the exception by NOT being a measurable goal. Attitudes cannot be measured, as they represent a state of mind. The other answer choices are goals that can be devised as specific and measurable.

102. (D)

The correct answer is option D because it is the only goal stated specifically and objectively taking into consideration the child's deficits. The other examples are measured in subjective terms such as teacher observation/judgment, or are probably unattainable if the child's current skills are below average.

103. (C)

The correct answer is option C because it includes all three correct statements. IDEA requires about eight specific elements of an IEP including (I) a listing of measurable goals for the student such as benchmarks, (II) a statement of the student's present levels of educational performance, and (III) a detailing of modifications for the student within the educational environment. Since I, II, and III are components of the IEP within IDEA, all three must be included when choosing the correct answer.

104. (C)

The correct answer is option C because there is no limit to the number of goals contained in an IEP. Rather, law requires goals to be measurable annual goals related to the child's progress in the general curriculum. They are direction-setting goals that support plans, rather than being daily, weekly, or monthly lesson plans.

105. (B)

The correct answer is option B because it gives the exception by NOT being among the requirements for special education teachers in general. The other answer choices represent requirements for becoming a special education teacher.

106. (D)

The correct answer is option D because the law limits the checking of a surgically implanted device needed to maintain the health and safety of a child. The other options describe services required to assist a child with a disability to benefit from special education.

107. (D)

The correct answer is option D because it gives the exception by NOT being among the services included as psychological but is rather an occupational therapy service. The other answer choices are included as federally regulated examples of psychological services provided to children with disabilities.

108. (C)

The correct answer is option C because it includes all three correct statements. By law, the native language for individuals with deafness or blindness can include (I) braille, (II) sign language, and (III) oral communication. Since I, II, and III are means by which individuals with no written language might communicate, all three must be included when choosing the correct answer.

109. (C)

The correct answer is option C because by law a child with a disability is entitled to assistive technology if its use is determined useful by his or her IEP team. The device would be purchased by the school and available in a child's home or other setting.

110. (B)

The correct answer is option B because it includes two correct statements. The members of an IEP Team can make annual goals measurable by (I) specifying a grade level performance or (II) indicating a rate. Since I and II are ways to measure present level of performance, both must be included when choosing the correct answer. Since PLAAFP also includes functional performance, III would need to include academic and non-academic areas (behavior, motor, communication, etc.).

111. (C)

The correct answer is option C because federal regulations require that the IEP team takes appropriate action to make sure the parent understands the proceedings, such as arranging for an interpreter for parents with deafness or whose native language is other than English.

112. (D)

The correct answer is option D because it gives the exception by *not* being among the primary responsibilities of a general education teacher but is rather a primary responsibility of a special education teacher. The other answer choices are important responsibilities of general education teachers of students with disabilities.

113. (B)

The correct answer is option B because it includes the two correct statements. A teacher becomes at risk of personal liability if he or she (I) fails to implement or (II) fails to provide proof of implementation of a child's IEP. Lastly, teachers are not required to memorize the documents, but they must remember what they say.

114. (A)

The correct answer is option A because the special education teacher is uniquely qualified in the education of students with disabilities. He or she can therefore suggest how to modify testing so students can show what they have learned. The other answer choices are roles of the general education teacher, representative

of transition service agencies or related service professionals.

115. (D)

The correct answer is option D because parents have all of the rights listed in (A) through (C). The exception is (D), as parents cannot change their child's educational placement while a complaint about his or her IEP is pending.

116. (A)

The correct answer is option A because the classroom teacher is the person who will recommend a child for special education. The classroom teacher is typically the first person to notice a possible learning problem because he or she spends the most time with a student in a learning environment. The other answers are roles of specialists, such as special education teachers and teachers of the visually impaired.

117. (C)

The correct answer is option C because the court ruled in the Oberti case that a disabled child named Rafael should be considered for the full continuum of placement options under IDEA. The court determined that the school district had failed to implement services that might avoid Rafael's "unnecessary segregation," thus upholding the LRE (Least Restrictive Environment) component of IDEA.

118. (C)

The correct answer is option C because it includes all three correct statements. In the case of an 8-year-old child with a catheter, the court ruled that clean intermittent catheterization (CIC) was (I) a related medical service, (II) not excluded, and (III) in accordance with the child's IEP. Since I, II, and III are all decisions made by the court, all three must be included when choosing the correct answer.

119. (D)

The correct answer is option D because although Amy Rowley was performing well academically, the court decided there was a disparity between Amy's achievement and her potential. Providing an interpreter in all her academic classes would allow Amy to comprehend what was said in the classroom, rather than her comprehending less than half of what other children would comprehend, thus making her opportunity to learn equal.

120. (B)

The correct answer is option (B) because the ADA was landmark legislation regarding equal opportunity and civil rights for all individuals with disabilities. This law mandates reasonable accommodations in areas of employment, access to public facilities, and more. The other answer choices represent other federal legislation to support people with disabilities.

Practice Test 3

Special Education: Core Knowledge and Mild to Moderate Applications (0543)

1. Ⓐ Ⓑ Ⓒ Ⓓ
2. Ⓐ Ⓑ Ⓒ Ⓓ
3. Ⓐ Ⓑ Ⓒ Ⓓ
4. Ⓐ Ⓑ Ⓒ Ⓓ
5. Ⓐ Ⓑ Ⓒ Ⓓ
6. Ⓐ Ⓑ Ⓒ Ⓓ
7. Ⓐ Ⓑ Ⓒ Ⓓ
8. Ⓐ Ⓑ Ⓒ Ⓓ
9. Ⓐ Ⓑ Ⓒ Ⓓ
10. Ⓐ Ⓑ Ⓒ Ⓓ
11. Ⓐ Ⓑ Ⓒ Ⓓ
12. Ⓐ Ⓑ Ⓒ Ⓓ
13. Ⓐ Ⓑ Ⓒ Ⓓ
14. Ⓐ Ⓑ Ⓒ Ⓓ
15. Ⓐ Ⓑ Ⓒ Ⓓ
16. Ⓐ Ⓑ Ⓒ Ⓓ
17. Ⓐ Ⓑ Ⓒ Ⓓ
18. Ⓐ Ⓑ Ⓒ Ⓓ
19. Ⓐ Ⓑ Ⓒ Ⓓ
20. Ⓐ Ⓑ Ⓒ Ⓓ
21. Ⓐ Ⓑ Ⓒ Ⓓ
22. Ⓐ Ⓑ Ⓒ Ⓓ
23. Ⓐ Ⓑ Ⓒ Ⓓ

24. Ⓐ Ⓑ Ⓒ Ⓓ
25. Ⓐ Ⓑ Ⓒ Ⓓ
26. Ⓐ Ⓑ Ⓒ Ⓓ
27. Ⓐ Ⓑ Ⓒ Ⓓ
28. Ⓐ Ⓑ Ⓒ Ⓓ
29. Ⓐ Ⓑ Ⓒ Ⓓ
30. Ⓐ Ⓑ Ⓒ Ⓓ
31. Ⓐ Ⓑ Ⓒ Ⓓ
32. Ⓐ Ⓑ Ⓒ Ⓓ
33. Ⓐ Ⓑ Ⓒ Ⓓ
34. Ⓐ Ⓑ Ⓒ Ⓓ
35. Ⓐ Ⓑ Ⓒ Ⓓ
36. Ⓐ Ⓑ Ⓒ Ⓓ
37. Ⓐ Ⓑ Ⓒ Ⓓ
38. Ⓐ Ⓑ Ⓒ Ⓓ
39. Ⓐ Ⓑ Ⓒ Ⓓ
40. Ⓐ Ⓑ Ⓒ Ⓓ
41. Ⓐ Ⓑ Ⓒ Ⓓ
42. Ⓐ Ⓑ Ⓒ Ⓓ
43. Ⓐ Ⓑ Ⓒ Ⓓ
44. Ⓐ Ⓑ Ⓒ Ⓓ
45. Ⓐ Ⓑ Ⓒ Ⓓ
46. Ⓐ Ⓑ Ⓒ Ⓓ

47. Ⓐ Ⓑ Ⓒ Ⓓ
48. Ⓐ Ⓑ Ⓒ Ⓓ
49. Ⓐ Ⓑ Ⓒ Ⓓ
50. Ⓐ Ⓑ Ⓒ Ⓓ
51. Ⓐ Ⓑ Ⓒ Ⓓ
52. Ⓐ Ⓑ Ⓒ Ⓓ
53. Ⓐ Ⓑ Ⓒ Ⓓ
54. Ⓐ Ⓑ Ⓒ Ⓓ
55. Ⓐ Ⓑ Ⓒ Ⓓ
56. Ⓐ Ⓑ Ⓒ Ⓓ
57. Ⓐ Ⓑ Ⓒ Ⓓ
58. Ⓐ Ⓑ Ⓒ Ⓓ
59. Ⓐ Ⓑ Ⓒ Ⓓ
60. Ⓐ Ⓑ Ⓒ Ⓓ
61. Ⓐ Ⓑ Ⓒ Ⓓ
62. Ⓐ Ⓑ Ⓒ Ⓓ
63. Ⓐ Ⓑ Ⓒ Ⓓ
64. Ⓐ Ⓑ Ⓒ Ⓓ
65. Ⓐ Ⓑ Ⓒ Ⓓ
66. Ⓐ Ⓑ Ⓒ Ⓓ
67. Ⓐ Ⓑ Ⓒ Ⓓ
68. Ⓐ Ⓑ Ⓒ Ⓓ
69. Ⓐ Ⓑ Ⓒ Ⓓ

70. Ⓐ Ⓑ Ⓒ Ⓓ
71. Ⓐ Ⓑ Ⓒ Ⓓ
72. Ⓐ Ⓑ Ⓒ Ⓓ
73. Ⓐ Ⓑ Ⓒ Ⓓ
74. Ⓐ Ⓑ Ⓒ Ⓓ
75. Ⓐ Ⓑ Ⓒ Ⓓ
76. Ⓐ Ⓑ Ⓒ Ⓓ
77. Ⓐ Ⓑ Ⓒ Ⓓ
78. Ⓐ Ⓑ Ⓒ Ⓓ
79. Ⓐ Ⓑ Ⓒ Ⓓ
80. Ⓐ Ⓑ Ⓒ Ⓓ
81. Ⓐ Ⓑ Ⓒ Ⓓ
82. Ⓐ Ⓑ Ⓒ Ⓓ
83. Ⓐ Ⓑ Ⓒ Ⓓ
84. Ⓐ Ⓑ Ⓒ Ⓓ
85. Ⓐ Ⓑ Ⓒ Ⓓ
86. Ⓐ Ⓑ Ⓒ Ⓓ
87. Ⓐ Ⓑ Ⓒ Ⓓ
88. Ⓐ Ⓑ Ⓒ Ⓓ
89. Ⓐ Ⓑ Ⓒ Ⓓ
90. Ⓐ Ⓑ Ⓒ Ⓓ

TIME: 2 hours
90 Multiple-choice questions
3 Integrated Constructed-Response Questions

In this section, you will find examples of test questions similar to those you are likely to encounter on the Special Education: Core Knowledge and Mild to Moderate Applications (0543) test.

1. High incidence disabilities include all of the following EXCEPT

 (A) intellectual disabilities.
 (B) autism.
 (C) speech impairments.
 (D) learning disabilities.

2. Students with autism differ from those with Asperger's syndrome because those with classic autism have

 (A) difficulties in social interactions.
 (B) cognitive and language deficits.
 (C) difficulties in school.
 (D) restricted, repetitive, all-involving interests or behaviors.

3. The largest percentage of cases of intellectual disabilities are identified

 (A) during infancy.
 (B) evenly across the age periods during the developmental period (0–18).
 (C) in the preschool years.
 (D) in the elementary school years.

4. The term "developmental delay" may be used as a classification when

 (A) the parents refuse to accept the classification of intellectual disabilities.

 (B) a child aged 0–9 requires intervention for significant delays in one or more functional areas.
 (C) the intellectual disability is from a biological cause.
 (D) the intellectual disability is in the mild range.

5. According to IDEA 2004, which of the following is NOT required to determine if a child has a learning disability?

 (A) Assessing the child's ability to learn
 (B) Evaluating academic functioning in a variety of academic areas
 (C) Determining if the child has had the opportunity to learn
 (D) Evaluating the discrepancy between the ability and achievement measures

6. Critics of the current IDEA definition of emotional disturbance have criticized it because of its

 (A) overly precise terminology.
 (B) exclusion of students identified as socially maladjusted.
 (C) exacting assessment requirements.
 (D) attention to cultural differences.

7. Mike's mother is concerned that his attention problems are hindering his outcomes in class. His teacher noted that he seems to listen when instructions are given but then he seems to lose focus before the activity is completed. The teacher hypothesizes that Mike's problems relate primarily to deficits in

 (A) coming to attention.
 (B) alertness.

(C) selective attention.

(D) sustained attention.

8. Which theory suggests that for learning to be most effective and efficient, teachers must determine the appropriate level to begin teaching a student and also determine the amount the student can learn with support?

(A) Social constructivism

(B) Biological constructivism

(C) Mastery learning theory

(D) Behavioral theory

9. To be successful at learning and thinking, what must students use to direct their use of thinking strategies for most effective learning?

(A) Mnemonic strategies

(B) Constructivist strategies

(C) Accommodation and assimilation strategies

(D) Executive functions

10. With regard to social cognition, students with mild disabilities tend to

(A) have much less trouble functioning than they do in academic learning.

(B) be able to manage their social responses, despite their disability.

(C) demonstrate considerable variability in their social functioning.

(D) display deficits in developing age-appropriate social cognitive skills.

11. Which of the following is NOT generally true of students with significant maladaptive behaviors?

(A) Learners with maladaptive behaviors are more likely than other learners to fail classes in school.

(B) Learners with maladaptive behaviors are more likely than other learners to drop out of school.

(C) Learners with maladaptive behaviors are more likely than learners with other disabilities to be placed in general education classrooms.

(D) Learners with problem behaviors frequently exhibit symptoms of depression.

12. Parental engagement is vital to the educational process. Which of the following is NOT an action that would help with such involvement?

(A) Offer parenting skills workshops

(B) Discourage involvement in learning activities at home

(C) Coordinate with community agencies to provide family services

(D) Include parents in important school decisions

13. According to Piaget, all children follow the same developmental stages in the same order, but at a different pace. Therefore, the teaching strategy that would work best for a student at the concrete stage of development is

(A) experimentation with materials.

(B) drill and repetition activities.

(C) memorization activities.

(D) the lecture type of instruction.

14. To what type of disorders are specific learning disabilities primarily attributed?

(A) Environmental

(B) Cultural

(C) Economic

(D) Neurological

15. Schools discourage parents' involvement by

(A) providing child care services during parent meetings.

(B) disregarding parent work schedules.

(C) overcoming communication barriers.

(D) scheduling open houses during the day.

16. Which does NOT appear to be a major contributing factor toward achieving an effective family-school partnership?

(A) Encourage parental decision making whenever possible.

(B) Encourage parents to be at the schools as much of the time as possible.

(C) Involve parents in meaningful activities.

(D) Collaborate with community organizations.

17. The best source of information about developmental, social, and academic problems is

    (A) the family.
    (B) other teachers.
    (C) a school psychologist.
    (D) a child.

18. Modified curricula may include all of the following EXCEPT

    (A) accommodations to procedures required for a learner to benefit from instruction.
    (B) alternative curricular goals for particular students with special learning needs.
    (C) substitution of alternative classroom objectives for a given student with a disability.
    (D) substitution of an alternative skill or topic of instruction for a student with a disability.

19. According to IDEA, each student with a disability must be provided with a program of individualized instruction. In this context, individualized instruction refers to

    (A) private tutoring.
    (B) instruction by a special education teacher.
    (C) instructional experiences selected to meet the student's needs.
    (D) instruction that differs in significant ways from that which is generally provided and that involves the use of specialized materials.

20. Which of the following is an example of a universal design for learning action?

    (A) Selecting a textbook that all students in the class can read
    (B) Using only audiovisual media to present content so that nonreaders are not disadvantaged
    (C) Requiring all students to do a multiplication facts test each day until everyone in the class has attained mastery
    (D) Assessing the learning in the social studies class by allowing students to design a way to demonstrate what they learned

21. James has attained mastery on his multiplication facts, demonstrating the ability to correctly answer 70% in less than two seconds. His teacher should now plan practice activities with the goal of helping him to

    (A) retain the skill over time.
    (B) use the skill in other settings.
    (C) learn a new skill.
    (D) retain and generalize the skill in other applications.

22. Maximizing academic learning time is essential for students with mild disabilities whose learning rate is generally slower than other students. Factors of concern to teachers should include all of the following EXCEPT

    (A) starting school as early as possible in the morning to capitalize on the students' energy.
    (B) reducing transition time between learning activities through efficient management techniques.
    (C) minimizing the time lost in moving from general education classes to special classes.
    (D) planning activities to actively involve the learners and minimize losses due to inattention.

23. Instruction in cognitive learning strategies is particularly useful to learners with disabilities because learning strategies

    (A) make the content to be learned explicit and clear.
    (B) assist students in becoming independent learners.
    (C) convey content area learning more effectively.
    (D) help the teacher structure the content learning for easier learning.

24. Positive behavior intervention support (PBIS) is a system that does what?

    (A) Uses problem solving to prevent inappropriate behavior through teaching and supporting appropriate behavior

(B) Uses problem solving to prevent appropriate behavior through teaching and supporting appropriate behavior

(C) Intervenes to model inappropriate behavior to teach inappropriate behavior

(D) Intervenes to exclude students with inappropriate behavior

25. When considering classroom organization barriers, all of the following are examples of physical space issues EXCEPT the

(A) size of the room and seating availability.
(B) temperature in the space.
(C) placement of whiteboard and materials.
(D) windows, doorways, and hallway traffic.

26. Which of the following is NOT part of teaching students the process of project work?

(A) Project management skills
(B) Teaching students to work collaboratively
(C) Showing which jobs have the least amount of responsibility
(D) Group decision-making strategies

27. Which of the following is the best way to guarantee individual accountability in the group environment?

(A) Each member must demonstrate specific knowledge or skills before the group can move to the next step of the PBL.
(B) Each member evaluates the other members of the group.
(C) Each member must reach mastery level of the PBL learning goals before the project is considered finished.
(D) There is no way to guarantee individual accountability in the group environment.

28. Strategies for modifying general education classroom instruction include all of the following EXCEPT

(A) presenting information in a manner that is relevant to the student.
(B) providing students with concrete illustrations of their progress.
(C) varying the format of tests to prepare students for standardized testing experiences.

(D) giving frequent feedback on student performance.

29. Recommendations for teaching students with emotional/behavioral disturbances include all of the following EXCEPT

(A) presenting lessons in a format that connects to the personal experiences of your students.
(B) developing a rigid, unchanging classroom routine to which students must adapt.
(C) considering diet, allergies, and other physical causes for disturbing behaviors.
(D) looking for lessons and discipline procedures that may contribute to behavior problems.

30. To improve the attentiveness of students with attention deficit disorders, which of the "principles of remediation" has NOT been recommended?

(A) Decrease the length of required assignments and tasks
(B) Increase the novelty especially of longer tasks
(C) Identify the entry-level skills for each academic area
(D) Make assignments and school tasks interesting

31. Inclusion programs work best when

(A) teachers are coerced to comply with mandates about mainstreaming.
(B) general and special education teachers are told how they can best work together.
(C) students are taught through transitional preparatory classes to follow directions, wait for teacher assistance, and concentrate on learning tasks with minimum adult supervision.
(D) students with mild disabilities are seated next to students without disabilities.

32. In preparing for a change from a special education to a general education classroom, a student will have to adjust to all of the following changes EXCEPT

(A) larger classes.
(B) different educational materials.
(C) more individualized attention from the teacher.
(D) less adult supervision.

33. All of the following would be observed in a student-centered classroom EXCEPT

(A) four students creating a play at the writing center.
(B) three students sitting on pillows reading library book in the "quiet corner."
(C) a student working on a brain teaser at the math center.
(D) all students sitting at their desks completing worksheets on the use of commas.

34. Which of the following are NOT specified by curriculum-based objectives for learning?

(A) The conditions under which performance is obtained
(B) The desired learning behaviors
(C) The persons responsible for student learning
(D) The criteria for success

35. Which of the following activities helps students become accepted members of the classroom?

(A) Successfully completing a worksheet
(B) Taking part in a spelling bee
(C) Writing a play in a cooperative small group
(D) Playing kickball on the playground

36. One modification that could be made in materials used by students with mild disabilities is

(A) increasing the number of problems required for seatwork to provide more practice.
(B) keeping the procedure of giving spelling tests consistent.
(C) altering instructional formats.
(D) having students read the instructions of a worksheet aloud before they begin.

37. Objectives are

(A) annual projections of student performance.
(B) behavioral and measurable.

(C) long-range plans.
(D) made up of at least two goals.

38. Assistive technology devices can help students with mild to moderate disabilities increase their ability to learn in the classroom. An example of an assistive technology that can help students meet their learning need is

(A) a book on tape
(B) a wheelchair
(C) a modified toothbrush
(D) a seat cushion

39. Transition services are designed to promote students with mild to moderate disabilities successful movement from school to adult life. Accordingly, a transition plan for students with mild to moderate disabilities must be addressed in their IEP beginning at what age?

(A) 12, or younger if determined by IEP team
(B) 14, or younger if determined by IEP team
(C) 16, or younger if determined by IEP team
(D) 18, or younger if determined by IEP team

40. Deverett is a 10th-grade student who has been found eligible for special education under the classification of intellectual disability. While attending the meeting for planning his transition services, Deverett stated that one of his goals is to obtain a job as a cashier at a local hardware store. In what transition planning domain should Deverett's special education teacher focus her instruction to help support his transition goal?

(A) Post-secondary education
(B) Daily living
(C) Employment
(D) Community participation

41. In Mr. Woods's classroom, Jeongae is a third-grade student whose primary language is not English. After monitoring Jeongae's performance in her core academic subject, Mr. Woods realizes that Jeongae is experiencing academic difficulties. In order to improve her performance, he has decided to provide Jeongae with some prereferral

interventions to determine whether they will improve her academic performance. Which type of prereferral intervention strategies should he employ?

- (A) Strategies to promote language acquisition
- (B) Strategies to promote mastery of curricular objectives
- (C) Strategies to promote academic development
- (D) Strategies to promote social development

42. Which of the following is the best example of direct instruction?

- (A) All students use varying materials and are involved in different activities.
- (B) Students work in small groups to complete the same activity.
- (C) Students derive their own knowledge and meaning from the experiences the teacher creates.
- (D) All students use the same materials and are involved in the same activity.

43. Which of these is NOT a preteaching strategy that could be used to orient students with disabilities to a new topic?

- (A) Recalling prior experience and knowledge
- (B) Allowing students to write an essay on the new topic
- (C) Using advanced organizers
- (D) Teaching new vocabulary

44. Kathleen, a seventh-grade teacher, starts a lesson on Native Americans by showing a documentary. She then provides artifacts such as beads, bracelets, and poster once used by Native Americans. After discussing the documentary and artifacts, Kathleen provides skeleton guided notes with important facts and dates. At the end of the lesson, Kathleen asks how the Native American influences are seen in contemporary life, and the students are asked to create their own artifact to represent their lifestyle. Which of the following describes the strategy Kathleen is using to teach this content?

- (A) Modeling different processes

- (B) Using several memory strategies to assess students in information retention
- (C) Presenting information in multiple ways to address students' learning styles
- (D) Using self-regulation activities

45. Kitty has observed that Craig, a student with communication disorders in her second-grade class, has a very limited vocabulary. What strategies can Kitty use to help Craig develop a more robust vocabulary?

- (A) Graphic organizers
- (B) Elaboration and modeling
- (C) Self-recording
- (D) Choral responding

46. Shelley is providing guided notes in her art history class and recognizes that her students with mild disabilities often have a difficult time keeping up with the information to complete their guided notes. Which strategy would be helpful in filling in the gaps for those students whose notes may not be complete?

- (A) Homogeneous grouping
- (B) Provide the students with the teacher's notes
- (C) Provide students with copies of student's notes
- (D) Conduct collaborative open-note quizzes

47. What is the best way to describe co-teaching?

- (A) When general and special educators work cooperatively to teach heterogeneous groups of students in the general education classrooms
- (B) When teachers consult with each other about case loads
- (C) When general educators work with teachers from different grade levels to address scope and sequence
- (D) When special educators are present in general education classrooms in case modifications are needed

48. Which of the following is the best way to determine vocabulary that is essential to objectives?

- (A) Semantic webbing

(B) Expository writing
(C) Instructional devices
(D) Text highlighting

(A) Self-concept
(B) Aggression
(C) Anger management
(D) Social perception

49. Pam is an intelligent and well-behaved ninth grader who is reading four grade levels below the rest of the science class. In planning her instruction, the IEP team proposed several accommodations. Which of the following would NOT be appropriate for Pam?

(A) Allow Pam to have her science tests read orally, or allow her to use technology that would "read" print for her.
(B) Pair Pam with a lab partner who can help with the reading, but hold Pam accountable for completing the labs and writing up her results.
(C) Allow Pam to complete easier science labs from the fifth-grade science book because this book is at her reading level.
(D) Provide Pam with audiotapes of the labs and textbook chapters, so she may listen to them at her convenience.

50. Partial participation refers to

(A) general educators partially participating in the education of students with disabilities.
(B) special educators partially participating in activities in the general education classroom.
(C) students with disabilities being included in the general education classroom part of the day.
(D) students with disabilities participating on a somewhat diminished basis in essentially all activities in the general education classroom.

51. Angie found out that Eric, a second grader with moderate intellectual disabilities who often seeks attention by acting out in the classroom, has just earned a Boy Scout badge in fly-fishing. Angie asks Eric about fly-fishing, and asks him to bring his fishing flies and demonstrate his technique to the class. What is Angie helping Eric with?

52. In which of the following classrooms would a student with problems learning how to read find success?

(A) One where the teacher teaches to the reading test
(B) One where there is an emphasis on pre-packed curricular materials
(C) In a print-rich classroom that is student- and materials-centered
(D) In one where there are opportunities for reading aloud

53. When teaching math facts to students with mild to moderate disabilities, it is important for the teacher to monitor their progress because they are less likely to learn math skills incidentally. Students with disabilities have difficulty learning math facts and computations

(A) through lectures.
(B) with a buddy.
(C) by reading the text.
(D) through the process of problem solving.

54. Ms. Harris, a seventh-grade mathematics teacher, always asks her students to "turn and talk" to their neighbor about what she just taught. Why does she do this?

(A) To teach comprehension
(B) To increase the student's vocabulary
(C) As an alternative instructional delivery system
(D) To move her students through the abstract stage of math comprehension

55. Mr. Morrick has his students turn to the glossary whenever they encounter a word they do not know in their reading of the textbook. The glossary is an example of

(A) a modification.
(B) a metacognitive strategy.

(C) guided notes.

(D) an instructional device.

56. Mrs. Liu has several students with ADHD in her class, and has recently learned that providing optimal stimulation can facilitate their learning in her classroom. What should she do to provide optimal stimulation?

(A) Use heterogeneous grouping

(B) Apply task analysis

(C) Play music while the students are completing a worksheet

(D) Provide enough guided practice during class so that the students do not need homework

57. When interpreting a student's assessment results, *inter-individual* interpretation involves comparing the student

(A) with other students in the norm group.

(B) with his/her own performance.

(C) to other students in the school.

(D) with other students in the criterion-referenced group.

58. When interpreting assessment results, *intra-individual* interpretation involves comparing the student

(A) with other students in the norm group.

(B) with his/her own performance.

(C) to other students in the school.

(D) with other students in the criterion-referenced group.

59. The regulations of the 1997 amendments to IDEA require that assessment data be interpreted and used to develop educational and behavioral interventions that will be which of the following?

(A) Utilized as part of the school code of conduct

(B) Of benefit to the student

(C) Kept in the student's file

(D) Evidence of student's progress

60. Achievement tests are designed to measure what a student has learned. Which of these is an example of an achievement test?

(A) Woodcock-Johnson III NU Form C/Brief Battery

(B) Key Math 3—Diagnostic Assessment

(C) Gray Oral Reading Tests—Fourth Edition

(D) Test of Written Spelling—4

61. The Woodcock-Johnson III Tests of Achievement NU is appropriate for what age range?

(A) Ages 0–12

(B) Ages 4–19

(C) Ages 2–90

(D) Ages 5–21

62. What tests are used to obtain further information about a specific skill or area of academic achievement?

(A) Diagnostic test

(B) Achievement test

(C) Aptitude test

(D) Screening test

63. Which of the following tests assesses areas of math functioning typically NOT addressed by other instruments?

(A) Test of Mathematical Abilities—Second Edition

(B) Key Math—Diagnostic Assessment

(C) Peabody Individual Achievement Test—Revised

(D) Kaufmann Test of Educational Achievement—Second Edition

64. Which of the following assessments is used to evaluate receptive vocabulary using no reading or writing?

(A) Test of Language Development

(B) Peabody Picture Vocabulary Test—4

(C) Peabody Individual Achievement Test—Revised

(D) Kaufmann Test of Educational Achievement, Second Edition

65. Which of the following assessments is used to determine the function or purpose of a student's behavior?

(A) Positive behavior support system

(B) Behavior intervention plan

(C) Functional behavior assessment

(D) Functional behavior analysis

66. Which of the following assessments analyzes the student's total learning environment?

(A) Ecological assessment

(B) Rating scale assessment

(C) Checklist assessment

(D) Projective assessment

67. Sammie is an 8-year-old girl in a local school. Her teacher reports that Sammie has difficulty completing tasks in school due to a lack of focus and impulsive behaviors. What assessment might help Sammie's teacher better understand her behaviors?

(A) Behavior rating profile—2

(B) Behavior assessment system for children, second edition

(C) Functional behavior assessment

(D) Connors rating scales—revised

68. Which of the following is the best example of a formative assessment?

(A) A math teacher administers a test following the introduction of each new concept in algebra.

(B) The special education teacher requires her students to take a test at the end of the school year to determine how much they have learned.

(C) In World History, the teacher administers a unit test and uses the score as part of the end-of-term grade.

(D) A fifth-grade language arts teacher administers a unit test and uses the score as part of the end-of-term grade.

69. Which of the following is the best example of a summative assessment?

(A) A math teacher administers a test following the introduction of a new concept in algebra.

(B) The special education teacher requires her students to read oral passages twice a week to determine their rate of fluency and accuracy of reading.

(C) In World History, the teacher administers a unit test and uses the score as part of the end-of-term grade.

(D) A fifth-grade language arts teacher uses curriculum-based measurement twice each week to determine if students are correctly sequencing the letters in the spelling words.

70. The assessment of infants and young children requires different methods than those used when assessing school-aged children. A technique that places the child and the facilitator in the center of the multidisciplinary team during the assessment is known as

(A) play evaluations.

(B) early childhood assessment.

(C) arena assessment.

(D) early intervention assessment.

71. The best practice in assessing infants and toddlers as well as preschool-age children involves which of the following?

(A) Multiple measures, multiple examiners, and multiple situations

(B) Interviewing parents

(C) Direct observations and surveys

(D) Cognitive assessment, speech evaluation, and behavioral assessment

72. Which of these assessments is NOT appropriate for children who are suspected of having characteristics of an autism spectrum disorder?

(A) Behavior rating profile (BRP-2)

(B) Gilliam autism rating scale (GARS-2)

(C) PDD behavior inventory (PDDBI)

(D) Childhood autism rating scale (CARS2)

73. When interpreting assessment results, it is best to organize data to see how the data cluster. What is this process called?

(A) Measures of dispersion

(B) Measures of central tendency

(C) Frequency

(D) Normal distribution

74. As defined in IDEA, what does *special education* refer to?

    (A) A written statement describing the special education and related services that a school will provide
    (B) Specifically designed instruction, provided by the school, to meet the unique needs of the student
    (C) Special schools providing instruction on the general education curriculum
    (D) A well-written statement on the strengths and weaknesses of the student

75. Assistance required to enable students to benefit from special education (e.g., speech/language pathology, occupational therapy, transportation) is called what?

    (A) Related services
    (B) Supplementary aids
    (C) Supplementary services
    (D) Service plan

76. According to IDEA, the document that outlines and describes all of the special education services a student who is in first grade is to receive is called what?

    (A) Individualized family service plan
    (B) Individualized evaluation protocol
    (C) Individualized education program
    (D) Service plan

77. Which provision of the Individuals with Disabilities Education Improvement Act 2004 states that schools must ensure, to the maximum extent appropriate, that students with disabilities be educated in a setting most like that of their peers without disabilities in which the student can be successful with appropriate supports?

    (A) Individualized education environment
    (B) Local education agency
    (C) Most restrictive environment
    (D) Least restrictive environment

78. Which of these statements best describes an assistive technology device?

    (A) Any item used to maintain or improve functional capabilities
    (B) Any service used to maintain or improve functional capabilities
    (C) Services that directly assist students in the selection of assistive technology devices
    (D) Services that directly assist students in the selection of assistive technology devices

79. Which of the following was the first federal special education legislation that set federal guidelines for special education in 1975?

    (A) Individuals with Disabilities Education Act
    (B) Vocational Rehabilitation Act
    (C) Americans with Disabilities Act
    (D) Public Law 94–142, Education for All Handicapped Children Act

80. Public Law 108–446 was signed into law in 2004 and implemented further refinements in special education such as the need for teachers to be highly qualified in core academic subjects and the need for students to have transition services addressed in their IEP beginning at age 16. What is the name of this legislation?

    (A) Individuals with Disabilities Education Act
    (B) Individuals with Disabilities Education Improvement Act
    (C) Americans with Disabilities Act
    (D) No Child Left Behind Act

81. Which of the following groups of students are NOT included in IDEA?

    (A) Students with specific learning disabilities
    (B) Students with attention deficit-hyperactivity disorder
    (C) Students with developmental delays
    (D) Students with visual impairments

82. These students have average or above-average intelligence, but often encounter difficulty learning how to read, write, and compute. These students may have what type of disability?

    (A) Specific learning disability
    (B) Hearing impairment

(C) Orthopedic impairment

(D) Speech or language impairment

83. Special education teachers have many roles. Which of these is NOT one of a special education teacher's roles?

(A) Provide day-to-day instruction

(B) Provide support for students with disabilities

(C) Prepare adapted materials to meet students' needs

(D) Design interventions to address speech needs

84. Which of these is NOT a professional who may deliver related special education services?

(A) Speech/language pathologist

(B) Occupational therapist

(C) School principal

(D) School psychologist

85. What group is responsible for determining whether a student is eligible for special education services?

(A) Teacher, school principal, and occupational therapist

(B) Parents

(C) Intervention assistance team

(D) Multidisciplinary team

86. Which of the following is NOT a component of an individualized education program?

(A) Short-term objectives

(B) Annual goals

(C) Intervention assistance

(D) Present level of performance

87. According to IDEA, this must be offered to parents, at no cost to them, as a means to resolve disputes.

(A) Due process hearing

(B) Early intervening services

(C) Informal dispute resolution meeting

(D) Mediation

88. Which of the following factors may NOT contribute to the disproportionate representation of culturally and linguistically diverse students (CLD) in special education?

(A) High-quality instruction

(B) Poverty

(C) Teacher attitude

(D) Systematic bias

89. In order to avoid unintended bias in the referral of students for special education services, alternative assessment strategies have been recommended. Which of these is NOT an example of an alternative assessment strategy?

(A) Portfolio assessment

(B) Standardized test

(C) Performance assessment

(D) Curriculum-based assessment

90. Sophia is a student in Ms. Huddleston's fourth-grade classroom. Sophia's teacher provides her with instruction on the general education curriculum with strategies such as general teaching methods, remedial instruction, and tutoring, when necessary. However, Sophia's performance is markedly discrepant from that of her peers. Her teacher feels she may be at-risk of academic problems. According to the three-tier model of intervention, Sophia should

(A) receive tier 1 interventions.

(B) receive tier 2 interventions.

(C) receive tier 3 interventions.

(D) be referred for evaluation for special education eligibility.

Answer Explanations for Practice Test 3

Special Education: Core Knowledge and Mild to Moderate Applications (0543)

1. (B)	19. (D)	37. (B)	55. (D)	73. (B)
2. (B)	20. (D)	38. (A)	56. (C)	74. (B)
3. (D)	21. (D)	39. (C)	57. (A)	75. (A)
4. (B)	22. (A)	40. (C)	58. (B)	76. (C)
5. (D)	23. (B)	41. (A)	59. (B)	77. (D)
6. (B)	24. (A)	42. (D)	60. (A)	78. (A)
7. (D)	25. (B)	43. (B)	61. (C)	79. (D)
8. (A)	26. (C)	44. (C)	62. (A)	80. (B)
9. (D)	27. (A)	45. (B)	63. (A)	81. (B)
10. (C)	28. (C)	46. (D)	64. (B)	82. (A)
11. (C)	29. (B)	47. (A)	65. (C)	83. (D)
12. (B)	30. (C)	48. (A)	66. (A)	84. (C)
13. (A)	31. (C)	49. (C)	67. (D)	85. (D)
14. (D)	32. (C)	50. (D)	68. (A)	86. (C)
15. (B)	33. (D)	51. (A)	69. (C)	87. (D)
16. (B)	34. (C)	52. (C)	70. (C)	88. (A)
17. (A)	35. (C)	53. (D)	71. (A)	89. (B)
18. (A)	36. (C)	54. (A)	72. (A)	90. (B)

ANSWER KEY ALIGNED TO CONTENT CATEGORIES

Question	Answer	Content Category
1	B	I. Development and Characteristics of Learners
2	B	I. Development and Characteristics of Learners
3	D	I. Development and Characteristics of Learners
4	B	I. Development and Characteristics of Learners
5	D	I. Development and Characteristics of Learners
6	B	I. Development and Characteristics of Learners
7	D	I. Development and Characteristics of Learners
8	A	I. Development and Characteristics of Learners
9	D	I. Development and Characteristics of Learners
10	C	I. Development and Characteristics of Learners
11	C	I. Development and Characteristics of Learners
12	B	I. Development and Characteristics of Learners
13	A	I. Development and Characteristics of Learners
14	D	I. Development and Characteristics of Learners
15	B	I. Development and Characteristics of Learners
16	B	I. Development and Characteristics of Learners
17	A	I. Development and Characteristics of Learners
18	A	II. Planning and Learning Environment
19	D	II. Planning and Learning Environment
20	D	II. Planning and Learning Environment
21	D	II. Planning and Learning Environment
22	A	II. Planning and Learning Environment
23	B	II. Planning and Learning Environment
24	A	II. Planning and Learning Environment
25	B	II. Planning and Learning Environment
26	C	II. Planning and Learning Environment
27	A	II. Planning and Learning Environment
28	C	II. Planning and Learning Environment
29	B	II. Planning and Learning Environment
30	C	II. Planning and Learning Environment

(*continued*)

Question	Answer	Content Category
31	C	II. Planning and Learning Environment
32	C	II. Planning and Learning Environment
33	D	II. Planning and Learning Environment
34	C	II. Planning and Learning Environment
35	C	II. Planning and Learning Environment
36	C	II. Planning and Learning Environment
37	B	III. Instruction
38	A	III. Instruction
39	C	III. Instruction
40	C	III. Instruction
41	A	III. Instruction
42	D	III. Instruction
43	B	III. Instruction
44	C	III. Instruction
45	B	III. Instruction
46	D	III. Instruction
47	A	III. Instruction
48	A	III. Instruction
49	C	III. Instruction
50	D	III. Instruction
51	A	III. Instruction
52	C	III. Instruction
53	D	III. Instruction
54	A	III. Instruction
55	D	III. Instruction
56	C	IV. Assessment
57	A	IV. Assessment
58	B	IV. Assessment
59	B	IV. Assessment
60	A	IV. Assessment
61	C	IV. Assessment
62	A	IV. Assessment
63	A	IV. Assessment

(*continued*)

Question	Answer	Content Category
64	B	IV. Assessment
65	C	IV. Assessment
66	A	IV. Assessment
67	D	IV. Assessment
68	A	IV. Assessment
69	C	IV. Assessment
70	C	IV. Assessment
71	A	IV. Assessment
72	A	IV. Assessment
73	B	V. Foundations and Professional Responsibilities
74	B	V. Foundations and Professional Responsibilities
75	A	V. Foundations and Professional Responsibilities
76	C	V. Foundations and Professional Responsibilities
77	D	V. Foundations and Professional Responsibilities
78	A	V. Foundations and Professional Responsibilities
79	D	V. Foundations and Professional Responsibilities
80	B	V. Foundations and Professional Responsibilities
81	B	V. Foundations and Professional Responsibilities
82	A	V. Foundations and Professional Responsibilities
83	D	V. Foundations and Professional Responsibilities
84	C	V. Foundations and Professional Responsibilities
85	D	V. Foundations and Professional Responsibilities
86	C	V. Foundations and Professional Responsibilities
87	D	V. Foundations and Professional Responsibilities
88	A	V. Foundations and Professional Responsibilities
89	B	V. Foundations and Professional Responsibilities
90	B	III. Instruction

1. **(B)**

This question tests understanding of the occurrence of disabilities in the populations. Answer option B is the correct answer because, while cases of autism are on the rise, they are still not categorized as high incidence.

2. **(B)**

The question tests the knowledge of characteristics of students with high-functioning and low-functioning autism, and the comparison of those two. Answer option B is correct because student with classic autism also experience lower cognitive functioning coupled with language deficits.

3. **(D)**

The question tests the knowledge of the prevalence of identification of students with intellectual disabilities (ID). Answer option D is correct because prior to elementary school, many students are identified as developmentally delayed, and it is not until elementary school that the intelligence tests, coupled with adaptive behavior tests, identify students as ID.

4. **(B)**

This question tests the knowledge of characteristics of young children with intellectual and behavioral deficits. Answer option B is correct because this label is used only on those children prior to age 10.

5. **(D)**

This question tests knowledge of the current law and how it applies to the characteristics of children with LD. Answer option D is correct because this descriptor reflects the prior assessment of the discrepancy model no longer used.

6. **(B)**

This question tests the knowledge of current law and how it applies to the exclusion of some students under the emotional/behavioral disorders (EBD) label. Answer option B is correct because the current law does not allow for students to be classified and receive services under the classification socially maladjusted, though clearly these students have benefited from special education.

7. **(D)**

This question tests the knowledge of learning styles of children with attention problems. Answer option D is correct because the description of Mike's problem indicates that he cannot stay on topic after some time has passed.

8. **(A)**

This question tests the knowledge of learning theories. Answer option A is correct because this theory is based on the teacher's ability to supply challenging tasks and support the student's learning.

9. **(D)**

This question tests the knowledge of learning strategies as related to students' characteristics. Answer option D is correct because a student's ability to use his or her executive function promotes metacognition.

10. **(C)**

This question tests the characteristics of students with mild disabilities. Answer option C is correct because there is no one "typical" characteristic of students with mild disabilities, as this group of students is very heterogeneous.

11. (C)

This question tests the knowledge of placement of students with behavior problems. Answer option C answers the question because students with behavioral issues are less likely to be placed with their non-disabled peers.

12. (B)

This question tests the knowledge of the development of learners with mild disabilities, and the importance of the parents in the development process. Answer option B is correct because involvement of the parents at home is a vital component of the educational process.

13. (A)

This question tests knowledge of developmental stages. Answer option A is correct because children at the concrete stage of development require hands-on learning.

14. (D)

This question tests knowledge of the causes of LD. Answer option D is correct because most special learning disabilities are neurological in cause.

15. (B)

This question tests knowledge of successful school-parent partnerships. Answer option B is correct because it is important to know and be mindful of parent schedules when encouraging parent involvement

16. (B)

This question tests knowledge of successful school-parent partnerships. Answer option B is correct because it is not necessary for parents to be at school in order for a good relationship to develop.

17. (A)

This question tests knowledge of successful school-parent partnerships. Answer option A is correct because no matter how much school personnel may know about a child, the family still provides the best source of information.

18. (A)

This question tests knowledge about modifying curriculum for learners. Answer option A is correct because modifications are done so that the student can benefit from the instruction, not be given differing tests or objectives.

19. (D)

This question tests basic knowledge of what defines special education. Answer option D is correct because instruction must be significantly different with specialized material in order for it to be considered special education.

20. (D)

This question tests application of designing the learning environment. Answer option D is correct because when planning using UDL, it is important to allow the student to demonstrate mastery in a way that reflects his or her learning.

21. (D)

This question tests knowledge of sequence of mastery of objectives. Answer option D is correct because it is necessary to first practice retention and generalize the skill.

22. (A)

This question tests knowledge of how to plan instruction. Answer option A is incorrect, as there is no research that indicates that starting school early increases academic learning time.

23. (B)

This question tests knowledge of how to integrate learning strategies in the learning environment. Answer option B is correct because the teacher's intention is to make it possible for the learner to become more independent.

24. (A)

This question tests knowledge of successful classroom management. Answer option A is correct because PBIS teaches problem solving as a way to identify other ways to react to situations that promote misbehavior.

25. (B)

This question tests knowledge of possible classroom barriers, specifically physical space barriers. Answer option B is correct because the temperature of the classroom, while part of the comfort level of the learning environment, is not a physical barrier.

26. (C)

This question tests the demonstration of organizing small-group work. Answer option C is correct because all jobs should have equitable responsibilities, and all students should have equal accountability.

27. (A)

This question tests the demonstration of organizing small-group work with problem-based learning. Answer option A is correct because all members must meet mastery before the whole group can move on. This supports intra-dependent group contingencies to support group membership.

28. (C)

This question tests the knowledge of application of appropriate modifications in the general education classroom. Answer option C is correct because modify-ing tests for the sake of standardized test practice is not appropriate.

29. (B)

This question tests the knowledge of learning environments for students with EBD. Answer option B is the right answer because rigid classrooms routines do not promote the learning styles of these students who do best when offered choice rather than rigid structure.

30. (C)

This question tests the knowledge of learning environments for students with ADD. Answer option C is correct because identifying entry levels for each academic area will not promote learning, though it may be some type of early assessment.

31. (C)

The question tests the knowledge of learning environments, specifically inclusion. Answer option C is correct because students should be taught expectations of general education classes and how to generalize the skills necessary to be successful.

32. (C)

The question tests the knowledge of learning environments, specifically inclusion. Answer option C is correct because typically students will receive less individualized attention, not more.

33. (D)

The question tests the knowledge of learning environments, specifically those that are learning centered. Answer option D answers the question, as students typically are not asked to complete worksheets in a learning-centered environment.

34. (C)

The question tests the knowledge of learning environments, specifically lesson plans. Answer option C is correct because objectives list the performance criteria, the mastery criteria, and the conditions for learning, but not the person who is responsible for instruction.

35. (C)

The question tests the knowledge of learning environments, specifically inclusion of students with disabilities. Answer option C is correct because the use of cooperative groups in developing a class climate where members are accepted is essential.

36. (C)

The question tests the knowledge of teaching in differing learning environments, specifically inclusion. Answer option C is correct, because by using a variety of instructional materials, students with disabilities can be instructed with their nondisabled peers.

37. (B)

The question tests the knowledge of learning environments, specifically lesson plans and IEPs. Answer option B is correct because mastery must be determined by operational terms that are measureable and behavioral.

38. (A)

This question tests understanding of options for assistive technology. Answer option A is the correct answer because a "book on tape" is an example of an assistive technology that would address students' learning needs.

39. (C)

This question tests understanding of transition practices. Answer option C is correct because "16, or younger if determined by IEP team" is the federally mandated age, according to the Individuals with Disabilities Education Improvement Act 2004, in which

IEP teams must begin transition planning for students with disabilities.

40. (C)

This question tests understanding of instructional strategies that support transition goals. Answer option C is correct because the "employment" domain focuses on skills that enable student's access to employment.

41. (A)

This question tests understanding of preventative strategies and intervention strategies for at-risk learners. Answer option A is correct because students with cultural and linguistic differences (CLD) may lack the level of proficiency with the English language necessary to perform academic work.

42. (D)

This question tests understanding of instructional techniques that are appropriate, considering students' ages and abilities. Answer option D is correct because direct instruction involves teaching students a specific skill or material using highly structured, teacher-directed lessons and "all students use the same materials and are involved in the same activity."

43. (B)

This question tests understanding of instructional techniques that are appropriate, considering students' ages and abilities. Answer option B is correct because "allowing students to write an essay on the new topic" is not an effective strategy to orient students with disabilities to a new topic.

44. (C)

This question tests understanding of differentiation within a singular lesson to address differing learning styles including visual, kinesthetic, and artistic. Answer option C is correct because "Presenting information in multiple ways to address students' learning styles" describes the multiple methods used in this lesson of instruction.

45. (B)

The question tests knowledge of how to increase a student's vocabulary. Answer option B is correct because by elaborating on provided responses and modeling how to use a variety of synonyms and antonyms, Kitty can provide Craig with more vocabulary that is age-appropriate.

46. (D)

The question tests knowledge of how to modify instructional devices to meet the needs of diverse learners. Answer option D is correct because it allows students to demonstrate the knowledge that they have encoded, while providing peer assistance on those parts of the notes that they may not have completed.

47. (A)

The question tests ability to recognize the correct co-teaching model, not the models that may be in practice. Answer option A is correct because co-teaching means the sharing and collaboration of the general and special education teachers in addressing the needs of all students.

48. (A)

The question tests knowledge of preteaching vocabulary to diverse learners. Answer option A is correct because semantic webbing allows the teacher to probe how much vocabulary students currently know so that he or she can better adjust instruction.

49. (C)

The question tests knowledge of appropriate accommodations that address grade-level standards, while accommodating a student for her disability.

Answer option C is correct because providing a lower-level science book changes the lesson objective instead of accommodating for a student's disability.

50. (D)

The question tests understanding of inclusion for students who may not be able to meet all the criteria for mastery in a general education classroom, but who would benefit from interaction with their nondisabled peers. Answer option D is correct because partial participation refers to taking part in the classroom activities, though some activities may need to be modified to accommodate a student's disabilities.

51. (A)

The question tests the understanding of managing student behavior and social acceptance. Answer option A is correct because it describes Angie's discovery of Eric's talents and abilities and her recognition of these, which is how teachers enhance a student's self-concept.

52. (C)

The question tests the knowledge of print-rich classrooms and their role in promoting reading skills. Answer option C is correct because a print-rich classroom affords students multiple opportunities to read without having an "assigned" reading task.

53. (D)

The question tests the knowledge of students with disabilities in mathematics which may range from dyscalculia to more mild manifestations. Answer option D is correct because while other students are able to deduce facts and mathematic computations through repeated practice, students with learning problems have difficulty are not. Unfortunately, research attempting to classify the specific problems has yet to be validated or widely accepted, so caution is required when considering descriptions of differing degrees of math disability. Still, it seems evident that students do experience not only differing intensities of math dilemmas, but also different types, which require diverse classroom emphases, adaptations and sometimes even divergent methods.

54. (A)

This question tests the understanding of teaching higher order thinking skills. Answer option A is correct because as the students explain what the teacher just taught, the teacher can monitor the students' abilities to put the information in their own words, thus increasing their comprehension.

55. (D)

This question tests knowledge of instructional materials that are helpful in teaching all students, but especially students with disabilities, who are taught how to use existing instructional devices provided within text. Answer option D is correct because a glossary is a learning tool, or instructional device, provided by the authors of textbooks.

56. (C)

The question tests the knowledge of appropriate teaching strategies for students with ADHD. Answer option C is correct because it is an example of optimal stimulation.

57. (A)

This question tests understanding of the interpretation of assessment results. Answer option A is correct because inter-individual interpretation involves comparing the student to a peer norm group to determine how different the student is from that group.

58. (B)

This question tests understanding of the interpretation of assessment results. Answer option B is correct because intra-individual interpretation involves comparing the student with his or her own performance to determine strengths and weaknesses; hence the term *intra*, which means "within."

59. (B)

This question tests understanding and use of the results of assessments. Answer option B is correct because IDEA regulations require that assessment data be interpreted and used to develop educational and behavioral interventions that will be of benefit to the student.

60. (A)

This question tests the ability to define and use various assessments. Answer option A is correct because the "Woodcock-Johnson III NU Form C/Brief Battery" is an achievement test that assesses basic academic skills and is the shorter version of the Woodcock-Johnson III Tests of Achievement NU.

61. (C)

This question tests the ability to define and use various assessments. Answer option C is correct because the norm group for this test ranged from 2 to 90 years in age.

62. (A)

This question tests understanding of evidence-based assessments that are effective and appropriate. Answer option A is correct because a "diagnostic test" is used to obtain further information about a specific skill.

63. (A)

This question tests understanding of evidence-based assessments that are effective and appropriate. Answer option A is correct because the "Test of Mathematical Abilities—Second Edition" is a test that assesses areas of math functioning typically not addressed by other instruments.

64. (B)

This question tests understanding of evidence-based assessments that are effective and appropriate. Answer option B is correct because the Peabody Picture Vocabulary Test—4 uses visual stimuli to measure students' receptive vocabulary.

65. (C)

This question tests understanding of evidence-based assessments that are effective and appropriate. Answer option C is correct because "functional behavior assessment" seeks to find why a student's inappropriate behavior is occurring.

66. (A)

This question tests the ability to define and use various assessments. Answer option A is the correct answer because "ecological assessment" analyzes the student's total learning environment.

67. (D)

This question tests understanding of effective and appropriate evidence-based assessments. Answer option D is correct because research suggests the "Connors rating scales—revised" are most often used to help assess students' problem behaviors and determine whether they are related to ADHD.

68. (A)

This question tests the ability to define and use various assessments. Answer option A is correct because it is an ongoing assessment that is completed during the acquisition skill.

69. (C)

This question tests the ability to define and use various assessments. Answer option C is correct because it is an example of a summative assessment that is completed at the conclusion of an instructional period.

70. (C)

This question tests understanding of evidence-based assessments that are effective and appropriate. Answer option C is correct because "arena assessment" is a technique that places the child and facilitator in the center of multidisciplinary team members during evaluation.

71. (A)

This question tests understanding of evidence-based assessments that are effective and appropriate. Answer option A is correct because "multiple measures, multiple examiners, and multiple situations" represent the best practice in assessing infants and toddlers as well as preschool-age children.

72. (A)

This question tests understanding of evidence-based assessments that are effective and appropriate. Answer option A is correct because this assessment is most often used to evaluate students' emotions and feelings.

73. (B)

This question tests the understanding of how to interpret test results. Answer option B is correct because "measures of central tendency" describes a way to organize data to see how the data cluster or are distributed around a numerical representation of the average score.

74. (B)

This question tests understanding of federal definitions. Answer option B is correct because, as defined in IDEA, special education is the "specifically designed instruction, provided by the school, to meet the unique needs of the student."

75. (A)

This question tests understanding of federal definitions. Answer option A is correct because, as defined in IDEA, "related services" are those that are necessary for the child to benefit from special education services.

76. (C)

This question tests understanding of federal definitions. Answer option C is correct because the "Individualized education program," or IEP, is the document that provides a written plan of special education and related services that a student will receive.

77. (D)

This question tests understanding of federal safeguards of the rights of stakeholders. Answer option D is correct because the "least restrictive environment" provision in IDEA guarantees a student's right to be educated in the setting most like that of his or her peers without disabilities.

78. (A)

This question tests understanding of federal definitions. Answer option A is correct because this is the federal definition of an assistive technology device, according to IDEA.

79. (D)

This question tests understanding of major legislation. Answer option D is correct because Public Law 94–142, Education for All Handicapped Children Act was passed in 1975 and laid the foundation on which current special education practice rests.

80. (B)

This question tests understanding of major legislation. Answer option B is the correct answer because the Individuals with Disabilities Education Improvement Act (IDEIA 2004) is the most recent authorization of IDEA.

81. (B)

This question tests understanding of federal definitions. Answer option B is correct because this group is not directly addressed in IDEA as it is not a disability category, per se. However, some students with ADHD may receive special education services when identified as Other Health Impaired.

82. (A)

This question tests understanding of federal definitions. Answer option A is correct because students with "specific learning disabilities" have dysfunctions in processing information typically found in language-based activities.

83. (D)

This question tests the understanding of the role and responsibilities of the special education teacher. Answer option D is correct because "design interventions to address speech needs" is the role of the speech/language pathologist.

84. (C)

This question tests understanding of the roles of other professionals who deliver special education services. Answer option C is the correct answer because the "school principal" is not involved in delivering special education services.

85. (D)

This question tests understanding of the federal requirements for prereferral, referral, and identification. Answer option D is the correct answer because the "multidisciplinary team" convenes to complete a full assessment on students who have not been responsive to interventions.

86. (C)

This question tests understanding of the components of a legally defensible individualized education program. Answer option C is correct because "intervention assistance" is not a component that IDEA states must be addressed on the IEP.

87. (D)

This question tests understanding of federal safeguards of the rights of stakeholders. Answer option D is correct because IDEA requires that all states offer "mediation" at no cost to parents as another early formal step in resolving differences.

88. (A)

This question tests understanding of potential bias issues that may impact teaching and interactions with students and their families. Answer option A is the correct answer because research suggests "high-quality instruction" may decrease the likelihood of CLD students being disproportionately represented.

89. (B)

This question tests understanding of potential bias issues that may impact teaching and interactions with students and their families. Answer option B is correct because a standardized test is a traditional assessment procedure and this is not an example of an alternative assessment strategy.

90. (B)

This question tests understanding of preventative strategies and intervention strategies for at-risk learners. Answer option B is correct because Tier 2 interventions are appropriate for students who are not responding to the interventions given in Tier 1. Furthermore, students eligible for Tier 2 interventions have performance that is markedly discrepant from that of their peers.

In this section, you will find three samples of constructed-response questions similar to those you are likely to encounter on the Special Education: Core Knowledge and Mild to Moderate Applications test.

CAREFULLY READ AND FOLLOW THE SPECIFIC DIRECTIONS FOR THE QUESTIONS. If the question has more than one part, be sure to answer each part.

At the test administration, you will write your responses in your test booklet. These sample responses are less polished than if they were written at home, edited and carefully presented. As an examinee you will not know the questions in advance and will have to decide, on the spot, how to respond. **To review the constructed response scoring guide refer to Chapter 1, page 17.**

QUESTION 1: CONSTRUCTED-RESPONSE SAMPLE

Learning environment and classroom management

Juanita was diagnosed with developmental delays with suspected learning disabilities at the age of five. She is in a general education classroom and her special education teacher, Ms. Caterina offers her support in preacademic skills (prereading and prenumeration), and she also receives extra help from her classroom teacher, Ms. Tootle. While Juanita does seem to be supported appropriately for her academics, she displays numerous behavior problems including biting and hitting other children, refusal to share toys, and an inability to take turns during preferred activities. These behavioral issues are making her continued placement in a large general ed classroom difficult and unmanageable for Ms. Tootle, who has eighteen other five-year-olds in the classroom.

Task

1. Design a plan for Juanita that includes input from both teachers to address the behaviors while in the general education classroom.
2. In your plan, explain the importance of maintaining Juanita's placement with her nondisabled peers as appropriate.

Sample Response with a Grade of 3

Since her skill deficits seem to be in age-appropriate peer relationships, it is important that Juanita remain in an environment where she can see appropriate behavior modeled for her, so staying in the general education classroom is the best place for that.

First, it must be determined what positive reinforcement will work with Juanita so that the teachers may consistently reinforce her when she is interacting appropriately. If this behavior is occurring infrequently, it may be necessary for her special education teacher to provide instruction in appropriate behaviors, along with her academic remediation.

Once a reinforcer is determined, Juanita should be placed on a behavioral contract in the general ed classroom with immediate reinforcement of appropriate interactions in sharing, taking turns, and voicing her anger rather than biting and hitting. Some punishment may be included, but this should be designed around a "time out" from a preferred activities with her peers, as it is important to build the relationship with her peers. Do not exclude her unless absolutely necessary.

Ms. Tootle and Ms. Caterina may decide that a group contingency would be appropriate for Juanita, in which Juanita would earn the class a preferred activity for meeting weekly goals. This type of group reward may help Juanita build friendships and relationships with her same-age peers while being socially reinforced for appropriate interactions.

Sample Response with a Grade of 1

1. While her IEP may say that the appropriate placement is in the general ed classroom, the

best behavior plan would be one where Juanita was moved, even temporarily, to the special ed classroom where she could be taught how to behave appropriately through role-playing with Ms. Tootle. She could be moved back to the general ed classroom when she learns how to behave. Ms. Caterina might want to prepare the rest of the class by telling them that Juanita is learning how to play with her classmates if they ask where she is.

2. Once she demonstrates that she knows how to take turns and share, Juanita can be moved back to the general ed classroom, with the understanding that if she misbehaves, she will be sent back to Ms. Tootle's room.

QUESTION 2: CONSTRUCTED-RESPONSE SAMPLE

Instruction and Assessment

While Judith is reading at grade level according to the annual reading evaluation, she has trouble completing assignments that require reading from her fifth-grade social studies text. She seems to be unable to find key words in the passages that will lead her to answers for the end of chapter questions. When Ms. Harris asked Judith to read a passage from the social studies text, Judith was able to identify only 65–70% of the words. Judith was able to read the word problems from the math text, but exhibited similar low mastery of vocabulary when Ms. Harris asked her to read from the curriculum reading series. When Ms. Harris had Judith read passages from lower levels of the curriculum reading series, Judith was able to answer the comprehension questions.

Task

Identify further areas of evaluation and assessment methods that will help Ms. Harris design accommodations for Judith across all content areas.

Explain how curriculum-based assessments are informative in determining student skill sets.

Response grade of 3

1. Ms. Harris should continue to use the classroom texts as evaluation tools, and have Judith read more texts from the curriculum reading series at lower levels to verify that Judith does not have a comprehension problem when the material is written at Judith's performance level. Judith needs additional evaluation to determine the match between her skills and the classroom materials. More information needs to be gathered about her word analysis and word recognition skills. Further testing specific to word analysis would clarify Judith's deficits in this area.

2. Curriculum-based reading assessments, such as Ms. Harris' use of the grade-level texts, can pinpoint specific problems that the students may demonstrate in word analysis, word recognition, and normative assessments. Some assessments such as the annual reading tests may only provide the range that the student falls within, not the skill deficits.

Sample Response with a Grade of 1

1. Ms. Harris should revisit the reading probe first, and then test Judith again to determine if there was a mistake. She could also give Judith a normative test at the grade level where she was successful in answering comprehension questions. This may provide more information about her true reading level

2. Curriculum-based assessments are helpful in between normative testing and when the teacher needs to test individually. Curriculum-based assessments are created from classroom materials so the teacher can give them at any time.

QUESTION 3: CONSTRUCTED-RESPONSE SAMPLE

Collaboration

Mr. Beck prides himself that his class is the only science classroom that is inclusive, and contributes his ability to run a "tight ship" as a reason why his class was selected as the one in which to place students with disabilities. While it is true that Mr. Beck's organization is helpful in providing structure to the students, and he is willing to modify and accommodate his lessons, he is unwilling to allow his co-teacher, Ms. Lu, the special education teacher, to do any more than grade papers, read tests aloud, and remove students who are disruptive. Ms. Lu views Mr. Beck as somewhat tyrannical, and while she appreciates his willingness to include "her students," she feels disempowered and little more than a teaching aide in the classroom. In an upcoming unit, Ms. Lu identifies a specific topic in which she is interested, but Mr. Beck is reluctant to allow her to "take over" the class. He is unsure about her knowledge of content and isn't confident that she will cover the necessary information included on the end of course test.

Task

Identify the barriers to a collaborative teaching partnership that are present in this coteaching setting. What support can be provided by other teachers and administration to assist in the development of this partnership?

Sample Response with a Grade of 3

Several barriers are evident in this collaborative teaching relationship; the most obvious is a lack of communication compounded by ignorance of each of the teacher's strengths. Another barrier is the lack of parity between the two teachers, as the classroom is seen as being Mr. Beck's domain, and Ms. Lu views the students with disabilities as "her students." Mr. Beck is unwilling to support Ms. Lu's desire to teach,

because he feels solely responsible for the students' test scores, and there is no shared accountability for the students' learning outcomes. There does not seem to be a common goal that is identified by the two teachers that will assist them in participating in a truly collaborative partnership.

Other teachers in the school can provide support by modeling their own collaborative partnerships as well as provide observations of the classroom to identify areas for improvement. Other teachers may offer some release time to enable Mr. Beck and Ms. Lu more planning time, and provide their own ideas for shared lesson planning, assessment, and classroom management. Administration at the school can reconfirm that this collaborative teaching assignment is voluntary, and provide professional development to support a working relationship where each teacher is respectful of the other's contribution to the learning of all the students.

Sample Response with a Grade of 1

It seems clear that the two teachers do not agree on how to teach the students and there isn't any common ground that they can stand on. One of the barriers is Ms. Lu's lack of knowledge of the science content and her desire to teach science when her specialty is special education. Another barrier is Mr. Beck's lack of respect for the special skills that Ms. Lu can bring to the classroom, instead of being treated like a teacher's aide.

The other teachers can help Ms. Lu learn a science unit and ask Mr. Beck if he will allow her to teach it. They can provide her with the science standards so she can be sure she covers the content for the test. The administration can give the two teachers release time so they can get to know each other and have a better relationship in the classroom. The administration can also tell the teachers that a good relationship between the two of them is what is best for the students.

Practice Test 4

Special Education: Core Knowledge and Severe to Profound Applications (0545)

1. Ⓐ Ⓑ Ⓒ Ⓓ
2. Ⓐ Ⓑ Ⓒ Ⓓ
3. Ⓐ Ⓑ Ⓒ Ⓓ
4. Ⓐ Ⓑ Ⓒ Ⓓ
5. Ⓐ Ⓑ Ⓒ Ⓓ
6. Ⓐ Ⓑ Ⓒ Ⓓ
7. Ⓐ Ⓑ Ⓒ Ⓓ
8. Ⓐ Ⓑ Ⓒ Ⓓ
9. Ⓐ Ⓑ Ⓒ Ⓓ
10. Ⓐ Ⓑ Ⓒ Ⓓ
11. Ⓐ Ⓑ Ⓒ Ⓓ
12. Ⓐ Ⓑ Ⓒ Ⓓ
13. Ⓐ Ⓑ Ⓒ Ⓓ
14. Ⓐ Ⓑ Ⓒ Ⓓ
15. Ⓐ Ⓑ Ⓒ Ⓓ
16. Ⓐ Ⓑ Ⓒ Ⓓ
17. Ⓐ Ⓑ Ⓒ Ⓓ
18. Ⓐ Ⓑ Ⓒ Ⓓ
19. Ⓐ Ⓑ Ⓒ Ⓓ
20. Ⓐ Ⓑ Ⓒ Ⓓ
21. Ⓐ Ⓑ Ⓒ Ⓓ
22. Ⓐ Ⓑ Ⓒ Ⓓ
23. Ⓐ Ⓑ Ⓒ Ⓓ

24. Ⓐ Ⓑ Ⓒ Ⓓ
25. Ⓐ Ⓑ Ⓒ Ⓓ
26. Ⓐ Ⓑ Ⓒ Ⓓ
27. Ⓐ Ⓑ Ⓒ Ⓓ
28. Ⓐ Ⓑ Ⓒ Ⓓ
29. Ⓐ Ⓑ Ⓒ Ⓓ
30. Ⓐ Ⓑ Ⓒ Ⓓ
31. Ⓐ Ⓑ Ⓒ Ⓓ
32. Ⓐ Ⓑ Ⓒ Ⓓ
33. Ⓐ Ⓑ Ⓒ Ⓓ
34. Ⓐ Ⓑ Ⓒ Ⓓ
35. Ⓐ Ⓑ Ⓒ Ⓓ
36. Ⓐ Ⓑ Ⓒ Ⓓ
37. Ⓐ Ⓑ Ⓒ Ⓓ
38. Ⓐ Ⓑ Ⓒ Ⓓ
39. Ⓐ Ⓑ Ⓒ Ⓓ
40. Ⓐ Ⓑ Ⓒ Ⓓ
41. Ⓐ Ⓑ Ⓒ Ⓓ
42. Ⓐ Ⓑ Ⓒ Ⓓ
43. Ⓐ Ⓑ Ⓒ Ⓓ
44. Ⓐ Ⓑ Ⓒ Ⓓ
45. Ⓐ Ⓑ Ⓒ Ⓓ
46. Ⓐ Ⓑ Ⓒ Ⓓ

47. Ⓐ Ⓑ Ⓒ Ⓓ
48. Ⓐ Ⓑ Ⓒ Ⓓ
49. Ⓐ Ⓑ Ⓒ Ⓓ
50. Ⓐ Ⓑ Ⓒ Ⓓ
51. Ⓐ Ⓑ Ⓒ Ⓓ
52. Ⓐ Ⓑ Ⓒ Ⓓ
53. Ⓐ Ⓑ Ⓒ Ⓓ
54. Ⓐ Ⓑ Ⓒ Ⓓ
55. Ⓐ Ⓑ Ⓒ Ⓓ
56. Ⓐ Ⓑ Ⓒ Ⓓ
57. Ⓐ Ⓑ Ⓒ Ⓓ
58. Ⓐ Ⓑ Ⓒ Ⓓ
59. Ⓐ Ⓑ Ⓒ Ⓓ
60. Ⓐ Ⓑ Ⓒ Ⓓ
61. Ⓐ Ⓑ Ⓒ Ⓓ
62. Ⓐ Ⓑ Ⓒ Ⓓ
63. Ⓐ Ⓑ Ⓒ Ⓓ
64. Ⓐ Ⓑ Ⓒ Ⓓ
65. Ⓐ Ⓑ Ⓒ Ⓓ
66. Ⓐ Ⓑ Ⓒ Ⓓ
67. Ⓐ Ⓑ Ⓒ Ⓓ
68. Ⓐ Ⓑ Ⓒ Ⓓ
69. Ⓐ Ⓑ Ⓒ Ⓓ

70. Ⓐ Ⓑ Ⓒ Ⓓ
71. Ⓐ Ⓑ Ⓒ Ⓓ
72. Ⓐ Ⓑ Ⓒ Ⓓ
73. Ⓐ Ⓑ Ⓒ Ⓓ
74. Ⓐ Ⓑ Ⓒ Ⓓ
75. Ⓐ Ⓑ Ⓒ Ⓓ
76. Ⓐ Ⓑ Ⓒ Ⓓ
77. Ⓐ Ⓑ Ⓒ Ⓓ
78. Ⓐ Ⓑ Ⓒ Ⓓ
79. Ⓐ Ⓑ Ⓒ Ⓓ
80. Ⓐ Ⓑ Ⓒ Ⓓ
81. Ⓐ Ⓑ Ⓒ Ⓓ
82. Ⓐ Ⓑ Ⓒ Ⓓ
83. Ⓐ Ⓑ Ⓒ Ⓓ
84. Ⓐ Ⓑ Ⓒ Ⓓ
85. Ⓐ Ⓑ Ⓒ Ⓓ
86. Ⓐ Ⓑ Ⓒ Ⓓ
87. Ⓐ Ⓑ Ⓒ Ⓓ
88. Ⓐ Ⓑ Ⓒ Ⓓ
89. Ⓐ Ⓑ Ⓒ Ⓓ
90. Ⓐ Ⓑ Ⓒ Ⓓ

PRACTICE TEST 4

Special Education: Core Knowledge and Severe to Profound Applications (0545)

TIME: 2 hours
         90 Multiple-choice questions
         3 Integrated Constructed-Response Questions

In this section, you will find examples of test questions similar to those you are likely to encounter on the Special Education: Core Knowledge and Severe to Profound Applications (0545) test.

1. "Concomitant impairment" describes children who exhibit

   (A) deafness.
   (B) blindness.
   (C) physical disability.
   (D) several coexisting impairments.

2. Failure of the spinal column to close properly during fetal development refers to which of the following?

   (A) Cerebral palsy
   (B) Spina bifida
   (C) Hydrocephaly
   (D) Scoliosis

3. The cause of cognitive impairments (formerly known as mental retardation) is more readily known among individuals who need

   (A) intermittent supports.
   (B) limited supports.
   (C) no support.
   (D) extensive supports.

4. Considering the discussion of terminology, which of the following phrases is the MOST acceptable?

   (A) Retarded children
   (B) Mentally handicapped children
   (C) Children with mental retardation
   (D) Mentally retarded children

5. The 2002 AAMR definition does not use which of the following terms?

   (A) Measured intelligence
   (B) Adaptive skills
   (C) Individual's background
   (D) Levels of retardation

6. Which of the following factors would be considered on an Apgar test for a newborn?

   I. Activity and muscle tone
   II. Rh factor
   III. Birth weight and length of gestation
   IV. Grimace response

   (A) I only
   (B) I, II, and III
   (C) III only
   (D) I and IV

7. The Bayley Scales of Infant Development assessment is NOT typically useful for which of the following?

   (A) Predicting intellectual function of children with intellectual disabilities
   (B) Predicting intellectual functioning of non-high risk populations
   (C) Screening of children with intellectual disabilities
   (D) Screening of a non-high-risk population

8. Intelligence tests can be considered generally strong in which of these areas?

   (A) Consideration of intra- and inter-individual differences
   (B) Measurement of behavior
   (C) Recognition of emotional disturbance

217

(D) Taking into account the student's attention while taking the test

9. In reference to the phrase "severe disabilities," which of the following statements is/are MOST accurate?

   I. Severe disabilities is one of the 13 IDEA disability categories.
   II. There is no single authoritative definition of severe disabilities.
   III. Some, but not all, students identified in the categories of autism, deaf-blindness, intellectual disabilities, multiple disabilities, traumatic brain injury, may have severe disabilities.

   (A) I and II
   (B) II and III
   (C) II only
   (D) I, II, and III

10. The IEP team must provide for transition services to plan for the child's postsecondary future by the time the child turns age

   (A) 12.
   (B) 14.
   (C) 16.
   (D) 18.

11. Which of the following is the MOST important element of parenting support when a family has a child with a disability and other children who do not have disabilities?

   (A) Access to specialized care for the child
   (B) Access to sibling support networks
   (C) Access to information, advice, and resources about the disability
   (D) Access to financial support

12. Alternate assessments should align with

   (A) developmental assessment tests.
   (B) state academic content standards.
   (C) environmental inventories.
   (D) Alternative Achievement Standards.

13. Which of the following is NOT an example of adaptive behavior?

   (A) Brushing teeth
   (B) Eating with utensils
   (C) Object permanence
   (D) Telling time

14. According to the Pyramid of Support model for inclusive education, efforts to include students with severe disabilities initially focus on

   (A) implementing individualized adaptations to curricular and instructional practices.
   (B) building an inclusive culture in the school and classroom, and using curricular and instructional practices known to be effective in enhancing achievement for most students.
   (C) assessing students with disabilities to determine their prerequisite skills.
   (D) securing additional funding to ensure each classroom has a general educator and a special educator.

15. Which of the following is true of appropriate learning goals for a student with severe disabilities?

   (A) They should be identical to the learning standards provided in the general curriculum, but suited to the student's mental age.
   (B) They should emphasize doing simple, repetitive tasks, such as folding paper, sorting by color, and grasping preferred objects.
   (C) They should include selected academic goals, plus skills needed to participate in school and community activities that are appropriate for the student's age, gender, and culture.
   (D) They should not deviate from the functional curriculum guide.

16. What general guideline should be followed when modifying lessons and assignments for students with severe disabilities who are served in general education classes?

   (A) Use peer tutoring
   (B) Use collaborative teaming

(C) Be sure modifications address both social and instructional participation

(D) Conduct ecological assessment, complete matrices, and then write the IEP

17. Shear or friction (two surfaces rubbing against each other) can result in skin breakdown. Shear is MOST likely to occur in the classroom when a student is

(A) sitting in a wheelchair.
(B) being repositioned or transferred.
(C) sitting for extended periods of time.
(D) being toileted.

18. When a student has a seizure in the classroom or on the playground, it is important to

(A) restrain the student's movements.
(B) place a tongue depressor in the student's mouth.
(C) immediately give him/her oral medication.
(D) keep the student comfortable and safe.

19. A simple tool that allows us to detect growth abnormalities, monitor nutritional status, and/or evaluate the effects of nutritional or medical interventions is

(A) repeated growth (height and weight) measurements.
(B) a food journal.
(C) increasing caloric intake.
(D) assessing physical activity.

20. A student with hydrocephalus may have a shunt that drains excess cerebrospinal fluid from the brain into another part of the body. Signs that the shunt may be malfunctioning include

(A) lethargy, nausea, and vomiting.
(B) increased activity level.
(C) increase in body temperature.
(D) increase in fluid consumption.

21. Students with physical disabilities may not be able to complete self-care routines independently. It is the adults' responsibility to

(A) dress, toilet, or feed these students since they are unable to be independent.
(B) provide instructional programs to teach students to do all self-care routines without adult assistance.
(C) assess students' participation in these routines and identify adaptations or assistive technology (AT) to help them participate to whatever extent possible.
(D) complete a task analysis to determine who is responsible for instruction.

22. Instructional programs for students with motor disabilities are designed to

(A) teach students to perform individually identified skills (e.g., learn to grasp objects) without using adult assistance or adaptations or assistive technology (AT).
(B) teach students to perform individually identified skills (e.g., learn to walk) using adaptations/assistive technology (AT) or whatever types of supports that allow the student to perform the skill as independently as possible.
(C) teach students to remediate areas in deficit (e.g., remediate gross-motor skill deficiencies).
(D) be developed by physical or occupational therapists and taught to teachers so that teachers can practice with and teach motor skills to students.

23. Physical therapists should interview teachers to learn about classroom activities that are successful or unsuccessful. This interview provides information about a teacher's perspective about these situations. Which statement below is true?

(A) Teachers' perspectives may not agree with the perspective of the therapist(s), thus releasing the teacher from the responsibility of instruction in routines.
(B) Activities or routines that are not going well offer opportunities to provide more direct assistance as the student will probably not learn this activity.
(C) Activities and routines that are not completed satisfactorily should be identified so that

both a student's participation is improved and the activity/routine becomes one that is identified as successful.

(D) Nothing needs to be done when an activity/routine is identified as mastered because there are more pressing activities to complete.

24. The goal of proper physical management is to

(A) directly increase muscle tone.
(B) teach students how to move around safely.
(C) maintain normal body alignment.
(D) carry the student to another place in the classroom.

25. Under which of the following instructional formats are peer interactions among students with and without severe disabilities often LEAST likely to occur in secondary school?

(A) Large-group instruction
(B) Same-age group instruction
(C) Independent practice
(D) When receiving direct assistance from an adult

26. For which of the following impairments would the DynaVox device NOT meet a student's communication needs?

(A) Autism
(B) Cerebral Palsy
(C) Traumatic Brain Injury
(D) Spinal Bifida

27. Which statement BEST describes the standards-referenced approach to developing academic goals and objectives for students with severe disabilities?

(A) The IEP team identifies a skill based on an ecological curriculum guide and aligns the skills with an appropriate state content standard.
(B) The IEP team identifies a content skill from a criterion-referenced test based on the student's grade-level score.
(C) The IEP team adapts a state academic content standard in reading, math, or science so that it accommodates the student's learning needs and symbol use.

(D) The IEP team uses the appropriate state content standard and uses only the adaptive skill content.

28. What can a teacher do to encourage self-determination during instruction?

I. Teach the student goal setting and problem-solving.
II. Offer the student opportunities for choice making.
III. Follow the student's desired tasks.
IV. Have the student work in a group

(A) I only
(B) II, III, and IV
(C) IV only
(D) I, II, and III

29. Which of the following is NOT a person-centered planning approach?

(A) Making Action Plans, known as MAPS
(B) Group Action Planning, known as GAP
(C) Planning Alternative Tomorrows with Hope, known as PATH
(D) Individualized Education Program, known as IEP

30. A fifth-grader who has dyspraxia needs support in a language arts class. Which of the following accommodations would be appropriate for this child?

I. Give him more time on written assignments.
II. Give him clear and simple instructions and make sure he understands what to do.
III. Let him opt-out of difficult assignments.
IV. Create handouts in Braille.

(A) I only
(B) I and III
(C) III and IV
(D) I and II

31. A teacher who creates an effective lesson plan relies on a clear objective for each lesson, presents a logical sequence of tasks, gives simple and clear directions, models the task, and engages the student in guided practice. The teacher is using which of the following approaches?

(A) Metacognitive

(B) Diagnostic-prescriptive

(C) Cooperative learning

(D) Direct instruction

32. Which of the following is NOT essential when planning instruction of leisure activities?

(A) Assessing and honoring individual preferences for activities

(B) Providing instruction or support for participation in inclusive settings

(C) Teaching a leisure activity to mastery level to ensure the individual will be able to fully participate in the activity

(D) Teaching individuals to self-initiate leisure activities

33. Someone with the chronological age of 40 and the mental age of 6 should be approached as approximately

(A) between 6 and 7 years old.

(B) 34 years old.

(C) 23 years old.

(D) 40 years old.

34. Developmental milestones may be reached more slowly by students with medical or severe disabilities because

(A) of a chromosomal defect.

(B) of their inability to grow properly.

(C) they have had fewer opportunities to interact with the environment and peers.

(D) their developmental milestones are different from those of nondisabled peers.

35. Students who are medically fragile have intellectual levels

(A) only within the moderate, severe, profound intellectual disabilities range.

(B) from profound intellectual disabilities to gifted and talented.

(C) equal to their motor development disability.

(D) have no intellectual disability.

36. A students with physical and health disabilities may have a diminished ability to focus on school work as a result of

(A) lack of vitamins.

(B) fatigue.

(C) a substitute teacher.

(D) absenteeism.

37. Learned helplessness may result from

(A) laziness.

(B) the parent or teacher performing tasks for the student.

(C) a discrepancy between chronological age and mental age.

(D) planned ignoring.

38. Students with severe intellectual disabilities have an IQ score within the range of

(A) −55.

(B) 25 and below.

(C) 85–100.

(D) 25–40.

39. Students with severe intellectual disabilities have trouble using the information they have learned in one setting to another setting. The inability to apply skills to new settings is known as a deficit in

(A) rehearsal.

(B) generalization.

(C) observational learning.

(D) acquisition.

40. Cerebral palsy is defined as

(A) most often caused by accidents, sports injuries and violence-related injuries.

(B) a progressive disorder resulting in decreased movement over time.

(C) a nonprogressive disorder characterized by impaired movement that occurs during the developmental period.

(D) a neurological impairment usually caused by an accident that may adversely affect development, daily functional living and, if severe/profound, may further affect short- or long-term educational performance.

41. Causes of cerebral palsy include

    (A) a seizure characterized by tonic-clonic movements.
    (B) meningitis and ingestion of toxins.
    (C) Down syndrome, PKU, and maternal malnutrition.
    (D) head trauma after birth.

42. The MOST common cause of spinal cord injury in children under the age of 16 is

    (A) car accidents.
    (B) gymnastics.
    (C) child abuse.
    (D) tumors.

43. The MOST common cognitive deficits following a traumatic brain injury in children and youth include

    (A) memory impairments and disorders in attention.
    (B) ataxia.
    (C) articulation deficits.
    (D) poor motor skills.

44. In order to meet the criteria for federal eligibility as a student with a traumatic brain injury (TBI), the student must have sustained the injury from which of the following sources?

    (A) An infection
    (B) A stroke
    (C) Trauma due to an external physical force
    (D) A congenital brain defect

45. Assessment of a student following a traumatic brain injury is

    (A) identical to assessment of students with other disabilities.
    (B) conducted only by medical personnel.
    (C) challenging because it is difficult to determine how much retention the students had at the previous level of functioning, as well as his or her current ability to learn and retain new information.
    (D) always required for students with a significant medical disability.

46. Which of the following is the MOST appropriate placement for a student with a traumatic brain injury upon return to school?

    (A) A self-contained class
    (B) A resource class for students with orthopedic impairments
    (C) A class for students with cognitive impairments
    (D) Can vary due to the student's level of functioning, as deficits may change over time

47. When considering assistive technology for a student, a thorough assessment is necessary to

    I. ensure that the device provides a good match for the setting, the individual, and the features of the technology.
    II. compare the student's use of assistive technology to the assistive technology use of peers.
    III. reduce the possibility of device abandonment.
    IV. recommend a placement.

    (A) I only
    (B) I, II, III, and IV
    (C) III only
    (D) I and III

48. Why is it important NOT to assume that discrepancies in performance for students with physical or multiple disabilities are always related to motor issues?

    (A) Two students with the same disability may have different performance on the same task, with one being due to motor issues and one due to cognition.
    (B) Performance difficulties are more likely to be a result of assistive technology.
    (C) Performance rates due to motor issues may cause discrepancies, but they will usually be minor.
    (D) It is not important.

49. Training on the use of an AT device is important

    (A) when the device is complicated.
    (B) no matter how simple and seemingly self-explanatory the device may be.

(C) if the teacher or the student has no experience with assistive technology.

(D) when the teacher wants to ensure more of the same devices are purchased.

50. Augmentative and alternative communication would NOT include which of the following?

(A) Gestures
(B) Pointing to pictures to convey needs
(C) Listening to a story on tape
(D) Vocalizations

51. Which of the following provides students with the ability to move about and interact with their social and physical environment?

(A) AAC devices
(B) Mobility devices
(C) Life management devices
(D) Computer access devices

52. Most computers come with built-in options that make it easier for people with disabilities to use them, such as changes to the display, mouse, or keyboard functions. These are called

(A) accommodation features.
(B) multi-key features.
(C) accessibility features.
(D) disability features.

53. Word-prediction software can help with

(A) decreasing keystrokes and increasing typing speed.
(B) predicting the next event that will occur in the reading passage.
(C) recognizing that the writing content is not making sense.
(D) increasing comprehension.

54. When considering what assistive technology to use or purchase, it is important to

(A) quickly decide on devices.
(B) know which technology will help the students work more efficiently.
(C) know a few devices well and use them with all students.
(D) use commercially available equipment.

55. What is the MOST common form of muscular dystrophy in children?

(A) Facioscapulohumeral
(B) Limb-girdle muscular dystrophy
(C) Becker's
(D) Duchenne's

56. The MOST common symptoms that are evidenced in people with cystic fibrosis are

(A) coughing, sneezing, watery eyes, and diarrhea.
(B) bloating, weight gain, and coughing.
(C) weight loss, excessive mucus, and coughing.
(D) broken bones, chronic bruising, and diarrhea.

57. In *Timothy W. v. Rochester School District* (1989), a student with severe, multiple disabilities had been denied admission to his local public school because school officials deemed him too severely disabled to benefit from education. What important principle of the IDEA was challenged and affirmed?

(A) Every child, even the most severely disabled, is entitled to a free and appropriate public education under IDEA.
(B) School districts are required to locate even those children with severe disabilities under Child Find.
(C) Public school classrooms represent the least restrictive environment for all students.
(D) Parents must be involved in the development of a child's IEP.

58. When a student with a disability and peers without disabilities participate together in a shared activity (e.g., science lab experiment) and each student has individually appropriate learning outcomes at different levels within the same curriculum area, it is known as

(A) multi-level curriculum/instruction.
(B) curriculum overlapping.
(C) universal instruction.
(D) understanding by design.

59. Which of the following terms has been suggested to replace the term "mental retardation"?

(A) Mental disability
(B) Mental handicap
(C) Intellectual disability
(D) Cognitively impaired

60. The court case that used test scores to inappropriately label minority students and place them into classrooms for students with mental retardation was

(A) *Daniel R.R. v. State BOE* (1989).
(B) *Larry P. v. Riles* (1972).
(C) *Honig v. Doe.* (1988).
(D) *PARC v. Commonwealth of Pennsylvania* (1972).

61. According to the *Mills v. Board of Education* (1972) court case, school systems cannot deny access to the public schools because of the degree of disability or

(A) ethnicity.
(B) cost of educating the individual.
(C) age of the individual.
(D) location of the neighborhood school.

62. The differences between augmentative communication systems and alternative communication systems are

(A) augmentative systems use common technology such as speech recognition whereas alternative systems are individual-based and rely on programming for the individual.
(B) augmentative systems are used to assist the individual to communicate in a way similar to those without communication difficulties, and alternative systems allow the individual to communicate with those who are familiar with the alternative system.
(C) alternative systems are used primarily within a family setting, and augmentative systems must be used in an environment that is supported by technology.
(D) alternative systems require an interpreter, while augmentative systems need an information manager.

63. All low-incidence, severe, and multiple disabilities combined probably affect what percentage of the population?

(A) About 2%
(B) Less than 1%
(C) About 0.2%
(D) About 0.1%

64. Effective education and treatment for students with TBI often requires each of the following EXCEPT

(A) avoiding trying to develop a personal relationship.
(B) practicing classroom behavior management techniques.
(C) engaging in family therapy.
(D) arranging communication training.

65. Each of the following statements about the outcomes for individuals with deaf-blindness is true EXCEPT:

(A) All interactions with adults and the environment should be viewed as learning opportunities.
(B) The quality and intensity of instruction the person receives is critical.
(C) The more severe the impairments, the greater the impact on a person's ability to adapt.
(D) Additional disabilities do not tend to increase the impact on a person's ability to adapt.

66. Any manual or electronic means by which a person who is unable to communicate through normal speech can express wants and needs, share information, engage in social closeness, or manage social etiquette is

(A) facilitated communication.
(B) augmentative or alternative communication.
(C) manual communication.
(D) applied functional communication.

67. The process of identifying alternative, acceptable ways to communicate through teaching more appropriate behaviors and/or changing the environment to reduce the likelihood of prompting the undesirable behavior is

(A) positive behavioral support.
(B) functional behavioral assessment.

(C) functional behavior analysis.

(D) positive behavior management.

68. Kitty is an early intervention specialist who works with families who have children with severe disabilities. She knows that she needs to provide individualized practices for each family, communicate with family members in a respectful manner, and ensure that any placement she recommends be safe. These are examples of

(A) multiculturally-based practices.

(B) cross-disciplinary collaboration.

(C) family-centered practices.

(D) values-based practices.

69. A change in philosophy regarding transition programming for individuals with severe or multiple disabilities is represented by the current emphasis on which of the following concepts?

(A) Self-determination and natural supports

(B) Sheltered workshops and competitive employment

(C) Person-centered plans and self-determination

(D) Self-determination and facilitated supports

70. Which of the following components is part of the most recent American Association on Intellectual and Developmental Disabilities (AAIDD) definition of intellectual disabilities?

(A) Significant limitations in intellectual functioning

(B) Discrepancy between intellectual ability and achievement

(C) Deficits in vocational skills

(D) Manifest before age 10

71. The American Association on Intellectual and Developmental Disabilities (AAIDD) recommends that professionals classify individuals with intellectual disabilities according to

(A) IQ score.

(B) adaptive level.

(C) intensity of support needed.

(D) estimate of educability.

72. The classification system that most school systems use to describe levels of intellectual disabilities is based on

(A) an estimate of educability.

(B) IQ score.

(C) the intensity of support needed.

(D) adaptive level.

73. In recent years, the percentage of cases in which the cause of intellectual disabilities is known has dramatically increased due to

(A) better assessment practices by teachers.

(B) the mapping of the human genetic code.

(C) better assessment practices by medical doctors.

(D) advances in microscopic technology.

74. The MOST common known hereditary cause of intellectual disabilities is

(A) Fragile X syndrome.

(B) Down syndrome.

(C) Williams syndrome.

(D) Prader-Willi syndrome.

75. Craig, a 15-year-old boy, performs about as well on an intelligence test as an average 6-year-old. His IQ is about

(A) 25.

(B) 40.

(C) 60.

(D) 90.

76. In functional academics, academics are taught in the context of

(A) daily living skills.

(B) vocational settings.

(C) community living.

(D) simplified curricula.

77. Virtually all special educators agree that full-time placement in a self-contained program with no opportunity for interaction with students without disabilities is

(A) better for the students without disabilities.

(B) necessary to teach students with severe or profound intellectual disabilities functional skills.

(C) often the least restrictive environment regardless of the level of intellectual disabilities.

(D) inappropriate.

78. In person-centered planning, professionals are seen as

(A) working for individuals with intellectual disabilities.

(B) collaborating with individuals with intellectual disabilities.

(C) advising individuals with intellectual disabilities.

(D) planning everything for individuals with intellectual disabilities.

79. What effect have advances in medicine had on the need for special education due to physical disabilities?

(A) The need for special education for the majority of students with physical disabilities has been almost eliminated.

(B) The need for special education for students with severe disabilities has increased.

(C) It has become more difficult to identify students with physical disabilities.

(D) The number of students needing services has been unaffected by medical advances.

80. The intelligence of children with cerebral palsy is

(A) almost always in the range of intellectual disabilities.

(B) clearly higher than the average for the general population.

(C) nearly the same as for the general population.

(D) difficult to assess due to difficulties in perception, movement, or response speed.

81. The primary goal of adapted physical education is to

(A) eliminate physical education as a requirement for students with physical disabilities.

(B) provide physical education in a separate setting for students with physical disabilities.

(C) give students with physical disabilities more time in physical education to catch up to their peers.

(D) allow access to activities that support physical, recreational, and leisure goals.

82. Providing support for the child's body and arranging instructional or play materials in certain ways is known as

(A) positioning.
(B) handling.
(C) assisting.
(D) adapting.

83. Which of the following statements about intelligence and autism is true?

(A) Intelligence does not appear to be affected by autism.

(B) About 20% of individuals with autism have mental retardation as well.

(C) People with autism are unusually intelligent as a group.

(D) It is difficult to determine the IQ of a child with autism because of his or her typically low engagement when assessed.

84. Student-Centered Individualized Education Planning encourages families to consider which of the following?

(A) The child's social disabilities
(B) Family involvement in the school
(C) The child's weaknesses and preferences
(D) The family's goals for the child

85. The fastest growing population needing foster care in the United States is

(A) infants and young children with physical, cognitive, and health-related disabilities.

(B) homeless infants and young children.

(C) homeless teenagers (13–18).

(D) male teenagers (14–18) with mental illness.

86. Students with disabilities can be placed in separate or segregated settings if

(A) the setting has been determined to provide an appropriate education for the student.

(B) the student's family submits a request in writing.

(C) a professional submits a request in writing.

(D) the student has limited bowel control.

87. The approach that teaches professionals to be more culturally competent and responsive in interactions with families from culturally diverse backgrounds is referred to as

(A) multiple dialogue.
(B) reality dialogue.
(C) skilled dialogue.
(D) positive dialogue.

88. Predisposing factors for low birth weight that result in intellectual disabilities include

I. Gestational age
II. Mother's age and pregnancy history
III. Fetal alcohol effect
IV. Smoking during pregnancy
(A) I and IV
(B) I only
(C) III and IV
(D) I, II, III, and IV

89. The concept of "seamless transition" involves

(A) handing over documents of a student to a case manager.
(B) discussing what the student will do after graduation.
(C) a collaboration process between the school, student, and the provider system.
(D) transition to an institutional program.

90. One outcome common to all of the person-centered planning models is

(A) the teacher/facilitator is the key figure to the process.
(B) written materials are a key communication component.
(C) the development of a key group of people who will be the beginning of a network of support for the individual.
(D) the lack of a structured support mechanism.

Answer Explanations for Practice Test 4

Special Education: Core Knowledge and Severe to Profound Applications (0545)

1. (D)	19. (A)	37. (B)	55. (D)	73. (B)
2. (B)	20. (A)	38. (D)	56. (C)	74. (A)
3. (D)	21. (C)	39. (B)	57. (A)	75. (B)
4. (C)	22. (B)	40. (C)	58. (B)	76. (A)
5. (D)	23. (C)	41. (B)	59. (C)	77. (D)
6. (D)	24. (C)	42. (A)	60. (D)	78. (B)
7. (B)	25. (D)	43. (A)	61. (B)	79. (B)
8. (C)	26. (D)	44. (C)	62. (B)	80. (D)
9. (D)	27. (A)	45. (C)	63. (B)	81. (D)
10. (C)	28. (D)	46. (D)	64. (A)	82. (A)
11. (C)	29. (D)	47. (D)	65. (D)	83. (D)
12. (B)	30. (D)	48. (A)	66. (B)	84. (D)
13. (C)	31. (D)	49. (B)	67. (A)	85. (A)
14. (B)	32. (C)	50. (C)	68. (D)	86. (A)
15. (C)	33. (D)	51. (B)	69. (A)	87. (C)
16. (C)	34. (D)	52. (C)	70. (A)	88. (D)
17. (B)	35. (B)	53. (A)	71. (C)	89. (C)
18. (D)	36. (B)	54. (B)	72. (B)	90. (C)

ANSWER KEY ALIGNED TO CONTENT CATEGORIES

Question	Answer	Content Category
1	D	IV. Assessment
2	B	I. Development and Characteristics of Learners
3	D	IV. Assessment
4	C	I. Development and Characteristics of Learners
5	D	IV. Assessment
6	D	IV. Assessment
7	B	IV. Assessment
8	C	IV. Assessment
9	D	V. Foundations and Professional Responsibilities
10	C	II. Planning and the Environment
11	C	V. Foundations and Professional Responsibilities
12	B	IV. Assessment
13	C	V. Foundations and Professional Responsibilities
14	B	III. Instruction
15	C	III. Instruction
16	C	III. Instruction
17	B	IV. Assessment
18	D	V. Foundations and Professional Responsibilities
19	A	IV. Assessment
20	A	V. Foundations and Professional Responsibilities
21	C	II. Planning and the Environment
22	B	III. Instruction
23	C	V. Foundations and Professional Responsibilities
24	C	II. Planning and the Environment
25	D	II. Planning and the Environment
26	D	III. Instruction
27	A	II. Planning and the Environment
28	D	III. Instruction
29	D	III. Instruction
30	D	II. Planning and the Environment

(continued)

Question	Answer	Content Category
31	D	III. Instruction
32	C	II. Planning and the Environment
33	D	V. Foundations and Professional Responsibilities
34	D	IV. Assessment
35	B	I. Development and Characteristics of Learners
36	B	III. Instruction
37	B	II. Planning and the Environment
38	D	IV. Assessment
39	B	III. Instruction
40	C	I. Development and Characteristics of Learners
41	B	IV. Assessment
42	A	I. Development and Characteristics of Learners
43	A	I. Development and Characteristics of Learners
44	C	I. Development and Characteristics of Learners
45	C	III. Instruction
46	D	III. Instruction
47	D	III. Instruction
48	A	I. Development and Characteristics of Learners
49	B	III. Instruction
50	C	III. Instruction
51	B	III. Instruction
52	C	III. Instruction
53	A	III. Instruction
54	B	III. Instruction
55	D	I. Development and Characteristics of Learners
56	C	I. Development and Characteristics of Learners
57	A	V. Foundations and Professional Responsibilities
58	B	III. Instruction
59	C	I. Development and Characteristics of Learners
60	D	V. Foundations and Professional Responsibilities
61	B	V. Foundations and Professional Responsibilities
62	B	III. Instruction
63	B	I. Development and Characteristics of Learners

(*continued*)

Question	Answer	Content Category
64	A	II. Planning and the Environment
65	D	I. Development and Characteristics of Learners
66	B	III. Instruction
67	A	II. Planning and the Environment
68	D	V. Foundations and Professional Responsibilities
69	A	V. Foundations and Professional Responsibilities
70	A	V. Foundations and Professional Responsibilities
71	C	I. Development and Characteristics of Learners
72	B	V. Foundations and Professional Responsibilities
73	B	I. Development and Characteristics of Learners
74	A	I. Development and Characteristics of Learners
75	B	IV. Assessment
76	A	II. Planning and the Environment
77	D	III. Instruction
78	B	V. Foundations and Professional Responsibilities
79	B	I. Development and Characteristics of Learners
80	D	IV. Assessment
81	D	III. Instruction
82	A	II. Planning and the Environment
83	D	II. Planning and the Environment
84	D	V. Foundations and Professional Responsibilities
85	A	I. Development and Characteristics of Learners
86	A	V. Foundations and Professional Responsibilities
87	C	V. Foundations and Professional Responsibilities
88	D	I. Development and Characteristics of Learners
89	C	V. Foundations and Professional Responsibilities
90	C	V. Foundations and Professional Responsibilities

1. (D)

Children who have severe or profound disabilities are often said to have concomitant impairment, meaning having several different impairments including cognitive and physical.

2. (B)

Children with spina bifida are most commonly severely and profoundly disabled.

3. (D)

The more severe the cognitive impairment, the more likely the cause can be determined through genetic or biomedical factors.

4. (C)

The correct terminology is referred to as "people-first" language and promotes the consideration of the individual before his or her disability.

5. (D)

The current definition accepted by the AAMR does not refer to differing levels of cognitive impairment as related to IQ.

6. (D)

The Apgar test, which includes testing for activity and muscle tone, and the grimace response, is used to determine a newborn's health and whether there is a need for medical attention.

7. (B)

The Bayley's Scales are useful in describing the current developmental functioning of infants and to assist in diagnosis and treatment planning for infants with developmental delays or disabilities, but are not predictive for typically developing infants.

8. (C)

In general, intelligence tests measure a wide variety of human behaviors better than any other measure that has been developed.

9. (D)

People with severe disabilities are those who traditionally have been labeled as having severe to profound mental retardation, though this cognitive issue may occur concomitantly with a wide range of other disabilities.

10. (C)

IDEA requires transition at age 16, though typically for students with severe and profound disabilities, transition planning begins much earlier. Many states also require transition planning earlier than the federal guidelines.

11. (C)

When supporting a family, all information regarding the disability and all available resources are the most important materials to provide.

12. (B)

According to NCLB, any alternative assessment must be aligned with the existing state content standards.

13. (C)

Object permanence is the ability of a child to know that an object still exists even though it is no longer visible. This skill is not considered an adaptive behavior.

14. (B)

Universal support is the first step in the Pyramid of Support (or Pyramid of Interventions) and it consists of teaching practices that are used effectively to teach all students.

15. (C)

Learning goals for students with severe disabilities should include all components of the learning environment: academics, social skills, and community skills are written with the consideration of the students' age, gender, and culture.

16. (C)

Modifications in the general education classroom for students with severe disabilities should promote student participation in the classroom both as a peer and as a member of the learning community.

17. (B)

Students who experience skin breakdown have this condition occur as a result of repositioning and transferring. Care should be taken to ensure the student's correct positioning to reduce the needs for repositioning and correct adaptive equipment to reduce the need for transferring from chair to chair, chair to toilet, etc.

18. (D)

Teachers and paraprofessionals have the primary responsibility to make sure a student experiencing a seizure is in a safe location where no undue harm can occur. This may involve removing objects, loosening tight clothing, or rolling the student onto his or her side.

19. (A)

The easiest way to detect growth abnormalities is to take height and weight measurements on a scheduled weekly basis.

20. (A)

Teachers of a child with hydrocephalus should monitor the child closely to determine that the shunt, which is often used to drain fluid, is operating correctly.

21. (C)

The goal of all assistance to students with severe disabilities is to increase their independence, thus it is essential to analyze how to maximize participation in self-care routines.

22. (B)

Students with motor disabilities are taught that using the AT will assist in promoting independence.

23. (C)

Physical therapists can assist in providing supports for instruction in those activities that are difficult to do successfully.

24. (C)

Physical management of the student is designed to ensure that body alignment is correct.

25. (D)

Students are less likely to interact with age-appropriate peers when they are instructed in a tutorial one-on-one with an adult.

26. (D)

The answer is option D, spinal bifida, which most often does not affect the ability to communicate by speech. Depending on the severity of the impairment,

DynaVox could help those students impaired by cerebral palsy, TBI, or autism.

27. (A)

The student's abilities are identified within the setting, and then goals in those skills are aligned with the state content standards.

28. (D)

Teaching a student problem-solving and setting goals, how to make choices, and allowing the student to follow their desired tasks all help a student with self-determination. Thus option D is the best answer.

29. (D)

Person-centered planning goes beyond the traditional individualized planning processes that occur in the development of individualized educational programs (IEP). The person-centered approach relies much less on the service system by organizing truly individualized, natural, and creative supports to achieve meaningful goals based on the individual's strengths and preferences. Planning is no longer based on "the services available at the present time."

30. (D)

This question tests your knowledge of dyspraxia, a learning disability which can affect up to six out of ten people and is much more common in boys. While it is not linked to ability and many dyspraxics are very bright, they may appear immature. Severe cases of dyspraxia include the inability to speak clearly, copy information from the board, organize information or materials, and the child may have trouble with concentration making reading and mathematics difficult. Giving a student more time on writing assignments, making sure they understand clear and simple instructions, and giving a helping hand in organization are all acceptable accommodations for children with dyspraxis—letting them opt out of difficult assignments is not.

31. (D)

This question is testing your knowledge of instructional approaches and their purpose. The major component of an effective lesson plan is direct instruction, which is teacher-centered. The teacher ensures student learning by following the steps of the direct instruction approach, in part, because the student demonstrates that the learning outcome, as set by the teacher, has been mastered.

32. (C)

It is not essential that any leisure activity be taught to mastery, as the intent is for the individual with severe disabilities to be an active participant.

33. (D)

It is appropriate to address individuals with severe cognitive impairments according to their chronological age.

34. (D)

Students who are more severely involved have different developmental milestones from typically developing individuals.

35. (B)

Students with medical issues can range in cognitive abilities, from gifted to profoundly cognitively impaired.

36. (B)

Many students with physical and health disabilities tire very easily, and may lose interest in instruction.

37. (B)

Students learn that if they express inadequacy in completing tasks, often parents or teachers will complete the task for them.

38. (D)

Students who fall into the severe range of intellectual impairments have an IQ at or below 40. Students who are profoundly intellectually impaired have an IQ below 25.

39. (B)

The ability to take information learned in one setting and use it in another is known as generalization.

40. (C)

Cerebral palsy is a disorder of muscle control or conditions resulting from injury to the brain during early stages of development.

41. (B)

Apart from causing cerebral palsy and meningitis, the ingestion of toxins can also result in differing levels of cognitive impairments.

42. (A)

The most common cause of spinal cord injuries to children adventitiously is automobile accidents.

43. (A)

The impact of a moderate to severe brain injury on cognition depends on the severity of the injury and the rehabilitation of the individual.

44. (C)

TBI must be an adventitious occurrence.

45. (C)

Many students retain some learning from instruction prior to the TBI, but it is difficult to determine how much is retained, and how the other functioning skills including memory and attention are affected.

46. (D)

Many times the student may be most appropriately placed in a resource class or self-contained setting and then moved into more inclusive classrooms.

47. (D)

The introduction of assistive technology is best done after an assessment to determine if the technology is necessary and easy to use.

48. (A)

Just as all students without disabilities are different, those students who may have similar disabilities are also different. Students with multiple disabilities may have performance issues that are related to cognition and not modality.

49. (B)

Training with all assistive technology is necessary to ensure full command of the tool.

50. (C)

Listening to a story on tape is not a form of communication.

51. (B)

Mobility devices, like wheelchairs, are intended to assist with navigating the physical environment.

52. (C)

Accessibility features are available to all computer users, but are especially helpful to students with disabilities.

53. (A)

Word-recognition and word-correction software fill in words that are used often, thus decreasing the number of keystrokes required and increasing typing speed.

54. (B)

The decision to purchase technology should be made with the students in mind.

55. (D)

Duchenne's is the most common type of muscular dystrophy in children, affecting only males.

56. (C)

Cystic fibrosis causes a thick fluid to build up in the lungs and digestive track, thus causing people with the disease to lose weight and experience excessive mucus, which promotes difficulty in breathing and increased occurrences of pneumonia.

57. (A)

Timothy set forth the standard that no child is "too disabled" to receive a free and appropriate public education.

58. (B)

Curriculum overlapping is a type of modification to the curriculum that creates common goals within a singular curriculum for students with and without disabilities.

59. (C)

"Intellectual disability" is now the preferred term for the disability of mental retardation.

60. (D)

In the *Larry P* case, the Supreme Court ruled that IQ tests were being used inappropriately to label students as MR and that test bias against minorities was causing an inordinate number of black males to be identified as MR.

61. (B)

In the *Mills* case, the Supreme Court ruled that the expense of educating a student with severe disabilities would be the responsibility of the school district, and that students could not be excluded based on their disability or the cost of educating them.

62. (B)

An augmented system is used to assist a person in communicating (e.g., DynaVox) and for both parties to communicate, the receiver must know an alternative system (sign language).

63. (B)

Students who are severely involved cognitively, physically, and medically represent less than 1%.

64. (A)

It is just as important for students who have had a TBI to develop relationships as it is for any other student, regardless of the severity of the disability.

65. (D)

Additional disabilities tend to increase a person's ability to adapt. The more extensive the disability, the more likely it is that the student will experience multiple challenges.

66. (B)

Augmented or alternative communication considers all possible means of assisting a person who cannot communicate through normal speech to make his or her needs known.

67. (A)

Positive behavior support promotes the positive reinforcement of appropriate behavior through modeling, practice, and reinforcement.

68. (D)

Values-based practices are used to ensure that the considerations on the personal level of the individual and family (values, commitment) are paired with the abilities of the professionals (knowledge, best practice, competence).

69. (A)

By emphasizing the worth of all human beings to live the lives they choose for themselves, the current shift in the philosophy of transition planning has been to encourage individual decision making, supported by those services that occur within the environment (churches, family, friends) rather than artificial and forced goals.

70. (A)

Significant limitation in intellectual functioning is the only component that is contained in the most current definition.

71. (C)

The classification by level of support as suggested by AAIDD is much more useful in helping individuals plan for their education and life goals.

72. (B)

Schools continue to use IQ scores as cut scores for eligibility and levels of support when planning for students with intellectual disabilities.

73. (B)

As the genetic code is revealed to researchers, more anomalies are recognized in the genetic code that identify specific disabilities, especially those that are rare and severe.

74. (A)

Fragile X syndrome is the most common cause of inherited intellectual disabilities in boys.

75. (B)

IQ is a function of mental age, over chronological age, so $6/15 = 40$ IQ. Mental age is determined by standardized tests measuring intelligence.

76. (A)

Functional academics seek to provide authentic learning experiences for success in day-to-day living.

77. (D)

It is essential that all students have the opportunity to engage and interact with peers who are both like them and not like them.

78. (B)

Person-centered planning promotes the action of individuals to advocate for others who may not have the cognitive abilities to self-advocate.

79. (B)

Medical advances have led to an increased rate in survival in low-birth-weight babies, severely disabled infants, children exposed to toxins, abuse, and injury, and as such, are now placed in public schools and are appropriate for special education services.

80. (D)

Children with cerebral palsy are difficult to assess because their spastic motor movements often interfere with their ability to respond to IQ tests, and as such, the outcomes may belie their actual intelligence.

81. (D)

Adaptive PE is intended to help students with disabilities achieve the same type of satisfaction with physical, recreational, and leisure activities that individuals without disabilities achieve.

82. (A)

Positioning enables children to more fully participate in instructional and play activities.

83. (D)

Due to the nature of autism and the way intelligence is measured (through standardized testing) it is more challenging to assess a child with moderate to severe autism. Since young autistic children are often nonverbal or have significant problems processing language and responding verbally, some research notes that verbal responses may not be a good measure of IQ. Neither is a a child's ability to manage interpersonal relationships, sensory input or motor skills. Therefore, non-verbal skills become more significant as a measure of intelligence.

84. (D)

Families should be encouraged to express their own goals for the child when considering long-term care and quality of life.

85. (A)

It is reported that approximately one-third of all children in foster care have physical, cognitive, and health-related disabilities, and this number is growing.

86. (A)

The first consideration for all placements is the least restrictive environment. For some students, this is a separate classroom.

87. (C)

Skilled dialogue promotes respect for the differences that exist in different cultures and the desire to communicate with parents with responsive interactions is key to demonstrating respect for that culture.

88. (D)

Many factors may result in low birth weight, which is a condition that can lead to intellectual disabilities in children at less than 2 lb.

89. (C)

When all agencies work together to promote postsecondary outcomes, the student with severe disabilities is more likely to be successful.

90. (C)

A person-centered model is primarily focused on support systems, with specific individuals in mind, who will act as the entry point into a more expansive network.

In this section, you will find three samples of constructed-response questions similar to those you are likely to encounter on the Special Education: Core Knowledge and Severe to Profound Applications test.

CAREFULLY READ AND FOLLOW THE SPECIFIC DIRECTIONS FOR THE QUESTIONS. If the question has more than one part, be sure to answer each part.

At the test administration, you will write your rsponses in your test booklet. These sample responses are less polished than if they were written at home, edited and carefully presented. As an examinee you will not know the questions in advance and will have to decide, on the spot, how to respond. **To review the constructed response scoring guide refer to Chapter 1, page 17.**

QUESTION 1: CONSTRUCTED-RESPONSE SAMPLE

Ms. Nelson teaches an inclusive fourth-grade English/Language Arts class that has students with a wide range of cognitive abilities, including two students, Eric and Angie, who are eligible for special education services under severe intellectual disabilities. Eric is nonverbal while Angie has some communication with intentionality. Ms. Nelson has decided to design a story-based lesson to teach literature, in which she uses read-aloud techniques and takes advantage of the read-aloud event to model reading strategies and lead a discussion of themes, vocabulary, and events of the story.

Task:

Describe three activities that Ms. Nelson can embed in her lesson plan when she introduces the book that will engage Eric and Angie in the story-based lesson. Detail the activities in such a way that the student's specific disability is taken into consideration in the instructional model.

Response with a Grade of 3

Activity 1: When introducing the book to Eric, provide concrete objects such as stuffed animals or other representations to identify the main characters of the story. When introducing the book to Angie, show pictures of the main characters that include their written names. Allow each student to interact with materials.

Activity 2: When presenting the title of the book to Eric, help him discriminate the title from the author's name by helping him (hand over hand or other physical prompt) to touch the title of the book and move his finger along the title as you read it. When presenting the title to Angie, ask her to repeat the title and point to it after you read it.

Activity 3: When asking Eric to predict what the story will be about, present one of the objects represented in the story and an object that is unrelated and ask, "What is the story about?" When Eric looks at the object from the story, reinforce him with praise. For Angie, do the same activity, only use the pictures and short phrases for her choices.

Sample Response with a Grade of 1

Activity 1: For Eric, show him the book and let him hold it while introducing the story. For Angie, let her sit next to you while you introduce the book to the rest of the class.

Activity 2: For Eric, show him the pictures in the book while explaining what the pictures are. For Angie, ask her to look at the pictures and pick out her favorite one.

Activity 3: Allow Eric to watch the movie of the story before the read-aloud. For Angie, ask her to draw one of the characters in the story.

QUESTION 2: CONSTRUCTED-RESPONSE SAMPLE

Lorraine and her family have recently moved into her school district and her teacher, Ms. Robbins, will have only two years to help Lorraine transition into postsecondary options. Lorraine has severe intellectual disabilities and is confined to a wheelchair as a result of her physical disability. When she joined Ms. Robbins' class, she was still in need of extensive support, including toileting and supervision while eating. Lorraine's parents seem to be at a loss regarding what Lorraine will do when she exits the school system. Ms. Robbins has expressed to the parents that Lorraine is not entitled to adult services, and has encouraged them to determine their interest for Lorraine as they prepare for the transition team meeting.

Task:

Describe the initial steps that Ms. Robbins should encourage Lorraine's parents to discuss as they prepare for transition planning for Lorraine's postsecondary opportunities. Clearly outline the focus of the transition planning that will include Lorraine, her parents, and Ms. Robbins.

Sample Response with a Grade of 3

Step 1: Assessments of Lorraine's independent living skills should be conducted to determine what skills Lorraine currently has mastery of and what skills she will need to acquire in order to live as independently as possible. Ms. Robbins should plan with the family what personal care and daily living skills have priority based on the cultural values of the family.

Step 2: In alignment with the person-centered IEP and transition plan, Lorraine's parents should brainstorm what they believe to be Lorraine's preferences from past experience and offer Lorraine the opportunity to choose from those preferences. These preferences should be honored in the transition planning.

Step 3: Ms. Robbins will need to incorporate the skills and preferences into the school routine for Lor-

raine. These trainings will provide the transition team members information on what the possible independent living options are relative to Lorraine's current skills and preferences.

Sample Response with a Grade of 1

Step 1: Determine if Lorraine can perform necessary hygiene. Teach her how to communicate that she needs to use the restroom.

Step 2: Ask Lorraine's parents what their future plans are and how Lorraine fits into those plans to determine if Lorraine will be living with the family or in a group home.

Step 3: Involve Lorraine in the transition planning by determining her preferences and using them to create the transition plan.

QUESTION 3: CONSTRUCTED-RESPONSE SAMPLE

Chuck is one of the more challenging students in your middle school class, though he enjoys interaction with his nondisabled peers. Chuck is 13 years old, has severe intellectual disabilities, and engages in screaming during independent seatwork, when he is transitioning from one activity to another, and in settings other than the classroom—like the gymnasium. You have completed a functional behavior assessment and your hypothesis is that his screaming is a function of attention-seeking, particularly attention-seeking from adults.

Task:

Design a plan of support to reduce Chuck's screaming during seatwork, transition, and in the lunchroom. Include reinforcements that occur naturally in the environment.

Sample Response with a Grade of 3

1. During seatwork, provide teacher attention to hold Chuck's attention, academic engagement, and work completion. When the student screams, redirect the student to work completion, and reiterate that doing work is what results in teacher attention.

2. Prior to transition, precorrect Chuck with an outline of the expected behaviors, and pair each of the behaviors with teacher reinforcement. During transition, provide attention only when Chuck is behaving appropriately (no screaming).

3. In the gym, again state the behavioral objectives to Chuck prior to transitioning, and allow Chuck to scream or yell when appropriate during physical activity. Since he may scream for teacher attention because he is excited or engaged in a physical activity, teach him a signal to indicate he would like the teacher to attend to him, but reinforce Chuck only when he signals for attention with the signal prompt.

Sample Response with a Grade of 1

1. If Chuck has independent seatwork, seat him next to the teacher so the teacher can provide immediate attention to him if he starts screaming.

2. Let Chuck move to the next activity prior to the rest of the class so that he can receive teacher-directed instruction and prevent him from screaming.

3. Send a paraprofessional with Chuck to other settings like the gym so that he can receive attention from an adult and not interfere with the activities of others.

Glossary of Terms[1]

ABC model
A behavioral method through which to select interventions by analyzing events that occur antecedent to, concurrent with, or consequent to a target behavior.

Ability grouping
To place students with comparable achievement and skill levels in the same classes or courses; an approach often used in gifted education.

Above-level testing
The use of assessment instruments designed for older students as a means to evaluate the academic ability of a student thought to be gifted.

Absence seizure; petit mal seizure
An epileptic seizure involving brief loss of consciousness (usually less than 30 seconds).

academic English
Mode of English, a grasp of which is required to understand abstract concepts in highly structured academic settings; the abstract language abilities required for academic work; also called Cognitive Academic Language Proficiency (CALP).

academic vocabulary
Terms and expressions used across academic subject areas that are considered crucial for student comprehension and learning.

Acceleration
The practice of advancing learners through levels of curriculum according to individual achievement and performance.

Acceleration Phase
The fourth stage of the behavior cycle (acting-out behavior cycle), during which a student exhibits an increase in the frequency of a problem behavior; although the Acceleration Phase falls in the middle of the behavior cycle, it is often when many teachers first recognize that a problem is occurring.

accessibility
An optimal state in which barrier-free environments allow maximum participation and access by individuals with disabilities

accommodation
Service or support related to a student's disability that allows her or him to fully access a given subject matter and to accurately demonstrate knowledge without requiring a fundamental alteration to the assignment's or test's standard or expectation.

acquired hearing loss
Hearing loss that occurs through illness or accident in an individual born with normal hearing, also called adventitious hearing loss.

acquired immune deficiency syndrome (AIDS)
A virus-borne illness that results in a breakdown of the immune system; caused by an infection from the human immunodeficiency virus (HIV).

acting-out behavior cycle
The seven-stage process often enacted by students who exhibit behavioral problems: Calm Phase, Trigger Phase, Agitation Phase, Acceleration Phase, Peak Phase, De-escalation Phase, and Recovery Phase. Acting-out behavior is that characterized as inappropriate, aggressive, or destructive.

action plan
A strategy designed to support the implementation of the comprehensive behavior management (CBM) system.

adapted physical education teacher
Professional whose role it is to assist physical education teachers in the development of appropriate accommodations and modifications so that students with disabilities can participate in physical education activities; adapted physical education teachers may also provide an individualized program of physical education for students with disabilities.

adapting instruction
To make changes to classroom instruction in order to allow students equal access to the curriculum and to give students the opportunity to both process and demonstrate what has been taught; instructional adaptations can include both accommodations and modifications.

---

1 These definitions have been compiled from a variety of sources, including projects funded by the U.S. Department of Education.

adaptive behavior
The performance of the everyday life skills expected of adults, including communication, self-care, social skills, home living, leisure, and self-direction.

adaptive skill area
Any one of numerous instructional targets that focus on an individual's ability to function in a typical environment and on successful adult outcomes (independent living, employment, and community participation).

Adderall
A psycho-stimulant drug used primarily to treat Attention Deficit Hyperactivity Disorder (ADHD).

adult service
Any one of a variety of services available to individuals with disabilities who meet certain eligibility requirements and that typically falls into one of three categories: employment services, social security and health services, and community living and support services. In some cases, adult services are provided through agencies that also serve persons without disabilities (e.g., Medicaid).

advance organizer
A preview or organizational guide used to acquaint students with the content, structure, or importance of written material or a lecture.

adventitious blindness
A visual disability that is acquired after the age of two.

adventitious hearing loss
Hearing loss that occurs through illness or accident in an individual born with normal hearing; also called acquired hearing loss.

advocacy training
Process through which school counselors prepare families to become advocates for their children and children to become self-advocates. In advocacy training, school counselors work with families to help the child to become as independent as possible, make mistakes and learn from them, and gain more responsibilities throughout the transition process.

affective disorder
A mental disorder characterized by dramatic changes or extremes of mood; may involve manic or depressive episodes.

aggression
A state of hostility in which combative or violent behavior, which can include oral communication, is directed toward the student's own self, at others, or toward the physical environment.

Agitation Phase
The third part of the behavior cycle (acting-out behavior cycle), during which students manifests a variety of sometimes contradictory seeming behaviors. Some students might dart their eyes, tap their fingers, or start and stop their activities, whereas others disengage, stare off into space, or diminish their involvement in the classroom.

alerting device
Any one of numerous devices that employ a visual cue, sound, or vibration to make individuals who are deaf or hard-of-hearing aware of an important sound in their environment (e.g., a flashing light, loud gong, or vibration might signal a fire alarm, doorbell, clock alarm, or ringing telephone).

alphabetic principle
The phonic relationship between sounds and written letters.

alternate form
A variant assessment test that measures the same skills and has the same format as the standard version but that features different content. Not to be confused with an alternative format, which may assess skills differently or utilize different content.

alternative and augmentative communication (AAC)
The clinical practice that attempts to compensate for the impairment and disability patterns of people with severe expressive communication disorders.

alternative portfolio
A collection of a student's work; often used to evaluate students' school performance through authentic assessments.

amblyopia
Dimness in vision not attributable to eye structure

or injury; can lead to blindness if not addressed.

American Sign Language (ASL)
A form of sign language or manual communication system used by the deaf.

Americans with Disabilities Act (ADA)
Federal disability antidiscrimination legislation passed in 1990 to guarantee basic civil rights to people with disabilities; similar to those provided to individuals on the basis of race, sex, national origin, and religion, ADA guarantees equal opportunities for individuals with disabilities in areas of employment, transportation, government services, telecommunications, and public accommodations.

anchored instruction
An instructional strategy that attempts to make learning relevant and meaningful by 'anchoring' tasks and assignments to examples from students' culture or from real-life situations.

annual goals
Statements in a student's IEP that outline the major expectations for that student during the upcoming twelve months; must be objective and measurable.

annual review
Required meeting of the IEP team, including parents and school professionals, to review the student's goals for the next year.

anorexia
An eating disorder characterized by a fear of weight gain, disturbed body image, and chronic absence or refusal of appetite for food, resulting in severe weight loss.

anoxia
A severe deficiency of oxygen; can result in brain injury.

antecedent
Any situation, action, or event that immediately precedes a behavior.

anxiety disorder
Any one of a family of conditions characterized by an irrational dread of ordinary circumstances and everyday occurrences; the condition causes painful uneasiness and emotional tension or con-

fusion.

aphasia
The loss or impairment of language ability due to brain injury.

applied behavior analysis
Research methodology that employs single subject designs (e.g., reversal, multiple baseline); paradigms that describe human behavior in terms of events that stimulate behavior, maintain behavior, and increase its likelihood.

apraxia
The inability to perform purposive actions, such as moving the muscles in speech or other voluntary acts.

array of services
A constellation of special education services, personnel, and educational placements.

articulation disorder
The abnormal production of speech sounds or an inability to speak fluently or coherently.

Asperger syndrome
A disorder that is part of the autism spectrum disorders (ASD) in which cognition is usually in the average or above-average range.

assessment
The process of gathering information, both formal and informal, and identifying a student's strengths and needs through a variety of instruments and products; the data used in making decisions.

assessment results interpretation
The process through which school counselors or other qualified professionals offer analysis of assessment test results in order to identify areas of strength and need, and to assist in the development of appropriate goals for students.

assistance
Help offered to a teacher by an aid or other staff member during the administration of a universal screening assessment (e.g., a teacher's aid or other staff member supervises a class so that the teacher is able to assess students).

assistance card
A small card containing a message that alerts the

public that the user is deaf-blind and needs assistance crossing the street.

assistive device
Any piece of equipment or technology that facilitates people's work, communication, mobility, or other aspect of daily life.

assistive listening device (ALD)
Any piece of equipment or technology (e.g., hearing aids, audio loops, FM transmission devices) that helps deaf and hard-of-hearing individuals to use their residual hearing.

assistive technology
Any item, service, equipment, or product system, whether acquired commercially, specially designed, or created via modifications to an existing product, that is used to increase, maintain, or improve the functional capabilities in the daily life of an individual with a disability; comes in two forms, devices and services.

assistive technology specialist
Specialist who collaborates with teachers, other professionals, and families to ensure that all of the assistive technological needs of a student are met in order to reduce the barriers to the physical and learning environments.

association
The ability to recognize the relationships among different concepts or knowledge bases; made up of memory and the executive control.

at-risk
Term used to describe students whose condition or situation makes it probable for them to develop disabilities.

ataxia
A type of cerebral palsy characterized by a difficulty in coordinating the muscles in voluntary movement.

athetosis
A type of cerebral palsy that involves almost constant uncontrolled movement and writhing, particularly in the wrist, fingers, and face, and occasionally the toes and feet.

atresia
An absence or closure of a part of the body that is normally open.

attention deficit
A characteristic often associated with learning disabilities characterized by an inhibited ability to pay attention to or focus on relevant tasks.

attention deficit (ADD)/ hyperactivity disorder (ADHD)
Any of a range of behavioral disorders in children characterized by symptoms that include poor concentration, an inability to focus on tasks, difficulty in paying attention, and impulsivity.

Attribute Treatment Interaction Approach
An instructional strategy in which learning methods are matched to a student's modality strength (e.g., visual learners are taught primarily through visual modes).

attribution
The explanation that an individual uses to make sense of his or her successes or failures.

audiogram
A graphic record produced by audiometry through which an individual's ability to hear pitches (frequencies) and different volumes (intensities) is quantified.

audiologist
A professional trained to diagnose hearing losses and auditory problems.

auditory accomodation
Any audio material offered to students with visual impairments.

auditory habituation
Part of the auditory-verbal approach for students with hearing loss in which students attempt to develop their residual hearing to its greatest possible extent.

auditory-verbal approach
Part of the oral approach to teaching students with hearing loss in which students attempt to make use of their remaining hearing to the greatest possible extent; emphasis is placed on amplification and the teaching of speech.

augumentative communication system
One of a family of alternative methods of communication, which includes communication boards, communication books, sign language, and com-

puterized voices; used by individuals unable to communicate readily through speech.

auricle
The visible part of the ear, composed of cartilage, that collects sounds and funnels them through an external auditory canal to the eardrum.

authentic assessment
An ongoing assessment process that occurs in the individual's natural environment and includes a student's performance as well as the necessary supports; also includes student work samples.

autism
A pervasive developmental disorder considered to be part of the autistic spectrum disorders (ASD) characterized by problems in communication and social interaction, and repetitive or manneristic behaviors; generally evident by age three.

autistic disorder
An autistic spectrum disorder (ASD) character-ized by problems in communication and social in-teraction, and repetitive or manneristic behaviors.

autistic savant
A person with autism whose social language skills are delayed but who demonstrates advanced skills in a particular area such as mathematics or graphic arts.

autistic spectrum disorder (ASD)
Any one of a family of disorders characterized by a pronounced difficulty with communication, inhibited social interaction, and manneristic be-haviors.

autosomal recessive disorder
A genetically transmitted disorder which can only be passed down when both parents carry the gene (e.g., Usher syndrome).

background knowledge
The personal characteristics and experiences of students that teachers can use in the classroom to help build connections with new information and concepts.

baclofen pump
A surgically implanted pump designed to deliver small amounts of baclofen, a medication to re-lieve spasticity, into the spinal fluid; allows those

with certain spasticity related disabilities, such as cerebral palsy, to have more flexibility.

barrier game
A drill-and-practice activity in a game format that requires the application of verbal skills to solve problems.

basal ganglia
The interconnected gray masses within the ce-rebral hemisphere and brain stem; generally re-sponsible for the coordination and control of movement.

basal reader
A textbook, often an anthology, that contains sto-ries and lessons for reading instruction.

baseline
The level at which students, school personnel, or other individuals are performing before a new practice or program is implemented.

baseline data
The level at which the behavior occurs before an intervention is implemented. This information is gathered at the beginning of an assessment period for later comparative use.

Basic Interpersonal Communicative Skills (BICS)
Term refering to a student's ability to understand basic conversational English, sometimes called social language. See also: second language ac-quisition.

Beacons of Excellence school
A school selected through a national search for its excellent results for students with disabilities, including collective responsibility among school leadership, staff, and the community at large.

behavior
An observable or measurable act.

behavior analyst
An expert in behavioral support. Professionals who have undergone rigorous credentialing re-quirements will have the initials BCBA (Board Certified Behavior Analyst) after their name.

behavior management
A combination of strategies and techniques used to increase desirable behaviors and decrease un-

desirable ones.

behavior modification
Systematic control of environmental events, especially of consequences, designed to produce specific changes in observable responses. May include reinforcement, punishment, modeling, self-instruction, desensitization, guided practice, or any other technique for either strengthening or eliminating a particular response.

behavior recording sheet
Log sheet used to collect data on a student's observed behavior, especially its frequency, latency, or duration.

behavior-specific praise
Reward and feedback issued in response to a correct academic or behavioral performance.

behavioral
Of, describing, or having to do with behavior itself and the observable conditions and events that cause it, rather than on unconscious motivations.

behavioral inhibition
A tendency among young children to avoid or withdraw from unfamiliar circumstances or individuals; the ability to regulate one's attention, as well as the behavior that accompanies this ability.

behavioral intervention plan (BIP)
A set of strategies designed to address the function of a student's behavior as a means through which to alter it; requires a functional behavioral assessment and an associated plan that describes individually determined procedures for both prevention and intervention.

behavioral phenotype
A collection of behaviors, including cognitive, language, and social behaviors as well as psychopathological symptoms, that tend to occur together in persons with specific genetic syndrome.

behavioral support
The organization and arrangement of environments (e.g., schools, homes, workplaces) as an attempt to lessen the frequency of problem behaviors.

benchmark
An indicator used to identify the expected understandings and skills needed for content standards by grade level; benchmarks are tracked during predetermined intervals (e.g., a mid-year benchmark).

Best Buddies
A program that pairs college students with people with mental retardation as a means through which to build relationships, friendships, and opportunities for support.

best practice
Term used to describe any instructional technique, scientifically based practice, or method proven through research to be effective or valid.

best-evidence information
Recommendations that, because no large-scale studies exist to confirm their validity, are instead based on the best available evidence.

bicultural-bilingual approach
An approach to instructing students with hearing impairment that stresses teaching American Sign Language as a first language and English as a second language in order to promote a student's ability to function in both hearing and deaf culture.

bilateral hearing loss
Deafness or hearing loss in both ears.

bilingual education
Instructional approach in which a non-English-speaking student's native language is used in primary instruction until he or she has developed sufficient command of English.

bilingual special education
Instructional approach in which students' home language and culture, along with English, are used as the means through which to deliver individualized instruction to English language learners with disabilities.

blindness
Disability or condition in which an individual has no vision or possesses only the ability to detect the presence or absence of light.

booster session
A method of follow-up support in which a trainer provides an additional training session to review

previously covered skills, present new skills, elaborate on and refine skills, or troubleshoot problems.

Braille
A system of reading and writing that uses dot codes embossed on paper; the concept of tactile reading was promoted by Louis Braille in 1824, whose method is a precursor to the one used today.

Braille bills
Legislation passed in several states to increase the availability of braille to students with visual impairments.

Braille notetakers
Portable devices that can be used to take notes in braille, which are then converted to speech, braille, or text.

Braille transcribers
Individuals who prepare braille versions of textbooks, which in turn allow students with visual impairments to access the general education curriculum.

bulimia
An eating disorder characterized by periods of binge eating followed by compulsive purging (i.e., vomiting, refusing to eat).

C-Print
A real-time, speech-to-text, computer-aided service designed to help students to understand lectures through the use of special word processing software, a trained typist, and a computer display.

Calm Phase
The first phase of the behavior cycle (acting-out behavior cycle), during which student behavior is characterized as goal-directed, compliant, cooperative, and academically engaged. Students are responsive to teacher praise and are willing to work with peers.

captions
Subtitles that print the words spoken in film or video; can be either 'closed' (so that only those who want to can see them) or 'open' (so that everyone always sees them).

career exploration
Process during which students with disabilities begin to explore their career options. Ideally, they should begin to do so as early as middle school. In high school, students may job shadow, participate in vocational assessments, and explore employment options. Counselors can help students and families to process these experiences and to use them to influence further decisions.

cataract
A condition in which the lens of the eye becomes cloudy to the effect that light rays are not properly transmitted to the retina.

categorical approach
A system of classifying disabilities (e.g., learning disabilities, mental retardation).

catheter
A tube that is inserted into the body in order to either introduce or remove fluid.

center school
Separate school (sometimes residential), typically dedicated to serving students with a particular disability (e.g., a school for the deaf).

cerebral palsy
A nonprogressive, neuromotor impairment that affects body movements and muscle coordination.

certified vision rehabilitation therapist (CVRT)
A specialized therapist who works with students with visual impairments to ensure that they have the necessary skills to succeed in post-secondary settings.

changing expectations
Term sometimes used to describe an emerging attitude in American society regarding what is expected for students with disabilities: An increasing number of parents now expect schools to assume responsibility for their children's overall health.

choice making
Process through which students are given increased control over their own learning.

choral responding
Instructional activity in which all of the students in a group say a response together.

ClassWide Peer Tutoring (CWPT)
Instructional program in which pairs of students take turns acting as the tutor; originally designed to address developmental goals among students, with or without disabilities, from low socioeconomic backgrounds.

coaching
A method of ongoing support in which an individual (often of similar position or age) guides, instructs, and trains another person or group to develop specific skills.

cognates
Words that sound similar in two languages and have the same meaning.

Cognitive Academic Language Proficiency (CALP)
Term referring to a student's ability to effectively understand and use the more advanced and complex language necessary for success in academic endeavors, sometimes referred to as academic language; See also: second language acquisition.

collaboration
Any collective action in which two or more individuals work together towards a common goal of planning, implementing, or evaluating a specific aspect of an educational program for a student or group of students.

Collaborative Strategic Reading (CSR)
A multi-component approach to reading improvement in which students apply comprehension strategies while reading expository text in small cooperative learning groups.

college exploration
In the context of special education, the activities of school counselors to help students with disabilities, an increasing number of whom are attending post-secondary schools, and their families to prepare for and select an institution of higher learning.

communication
The organized transfer of knowledge, ideas, opinions, or feelings. It comprises both speech and language.

communication access real-time translation (CART)
A method of communication for students who are deaf or hard of hearing involving a trained professional transcribing spoken language as it is happening (i.e., in real-time) through the use of a keyboard; also known as open captioning.

community participation
In the context of special education, the efforts of clergy, youth ministry personnel, recreational staff, or others to help students with disabilities to become and remain more fully active in their communities.

community transition team
Group composed of education and agency staff, families, employers, and students with the purpose of developing linkages, accessing and monitoring services, and constructing a means for ongoing communication and collaboration.

community-centered learning environment
Used to describe an environment in which explicit values or norms that promote lifelong learning are fostered.

compensation
The use of technology or strategies to make up for a student's difficulty in performing specific tasks, with an emphasis on functional performance rather than instruction.

comprehensible input
Instructional method by which teachers, using sheltered instruction, teach at a level that is just beyond the students' current level of language competence, while also providing the scaffolded supports necessary to understand the information.

comprehensive behavior management (CBM)
A method of behavioral management that entails viewing a classroom not as a conglomeration of discrete parts, but rather as an organized, consistent, and integrated setting in which instructors, school leaders, students, and parents are all active participants.

computation
In student assessment, a test in which a student is presented with a number of computational

problems sampled from the year's curriculum and given a short amount of time (based on the child's grade level) in which to complete as many of them as possible. The student's score is the number of correctly placed digits. This test can be administered to a group.

concept development
The construction of ideas or mental images through a process of classifying or grouping similar things (e.g., beagles, poodles, and golden retrievers are all dogs) and through discriminating categories or concepts (e.g., dogs are different from cats).

concepts and applications
In student assessment, a test in which a student is presented with 25 problems selected from the year's curriculum dealing with concepts and application and given a short amount of time (based on the child's grade level) to finish as many as possible. The student's score is the number of correct answers. This test can be administered to a group.

connected text
The reading material in a textbook.

consequence-based intervention
A systematized means of negating certain undesirable behaviors through the use of negative and positive consequences.

consequences
In behavior management and modification, the stimulus that follows a behavior that may serve either to increase or decrease its future incidence.

consultation
Process through which a professional assists or interacts with other professionals and the families of students with disabilities in order to acquire information that facilitates the learning of such students.

content scaffolding
Instructional strategy in which educators teach material that is not too difficult or unfamiliar to students learning a new skill.

content standards
An instructional outline delineating what students should know, understand, and be able to do in specified content areas throughout the course of their K-12 education; a definition of the breadth and depth of knowledge, skills, and processes that are to be taught in a given domain.

contextual supports
Sheltered instructional method in which teachers use their students' unique or personal experiences or characteristics as a means to facilitate greater learning and comprehension.

conversational English
Variety of English-language exchange that occurs when students use the context or contextual clues around them to receive social communication and information (e.g., playing on the playground, socializing in the classroom); also known as Basic Interpersonal Language Skills (BICS).

cooperation
Collaborative process requiring interaction and mutual agreement among multiple entities working toward a common goal.

cooperative learning
Instructional arrangement in which heterogeneous (mixed ability) groups are employed as a method of maxmizing the learning of everyone in those groups; also helps students to develop social skills and has been demonstrated to yield especially favorable results for students in at-risk groups, such as those with learning disabilities.

cooperative teaching
An approach in which general educators and special educators teach together in the general classroom.

cornea
The transparent, convex front of the eye; responsible for most of the refraction of light rays in focusing on an object.

corrective feedback
Constructive comments provided as soon as possible following the implementation of an activity in order to help an individual improve his or her performance.

cortical visual impairment
Any damage to the part of the brain dealing with sight resulting in the incorrect interpretation of images received by the eye.

course of study
The courses and educational experiences that

help a student to achieve his or her post-school goals.

creativity
A form of intelligence characterized by advanced divergent thought, the production of original concepts, and an ability to develop flexible and detailed responses and ideas.

criterion-referenced measure
A benchmark used to identify the expected skill levels for students at each grade level.

criterion-referenced testing
An assessment wherein an individual's performance is compared to a goal or standard of mastery, as opposed to a comparison to the performance of other students.

cross-cultural dissonance
Situation created when the home and school cultures are in conflict.

cued speech
A method to aid speech and reading in people with hearing impairment in which an interpreter uses hand signals near his or her mouth to supplement or clarify lip reading by helping to distinguish sounds.

cued-language transliterators
Professionals who provide a verbatim translation of communication for a student who is deaf or hard of hearing through means of speech "cued speech." Cued speech transliterators use hand shapes and placements of hand shapes, along with mouth movements representing phonemes of spoken language, to assist students with speech reading; also known as cued-speech transliterators

cultural competence
Refers to the ability to learn from and relate respectfully to other cultural backgrounds, heritages, and traditions.

cultural pluralism
Social or cultural organization in which distinct cultural groups are seen as valued components of the society, and the language and traditions of each group are maintained.

cultural responsiveness
The process through which educators and others broaden their awareness of the cultural and racial issues facing diverse students, families, and communities by reflecting on their own cultures and learning about those of others.

cultural-familial mental retardation
Mild mental retardation due to an unstimulating environment or hereditary factors.

culturally and linguistically diverse (CLD)
Term sometimes used to describe students from diverse cultural or linguistic backgrounds.

culturally responsive instruction
Instructional modifications or adjustments made by culturally responsive educators to meet the individual needs of their diverse classrooms and students.

culture
The complex system of underlying beliefs and attitudes that shape the thoughts and behaviors of a group of people.

curricular materials
Any of a variety of resources, items, or tools, including textbooks, supplemental materials, and activities, used by teachers to engage students in the learning process.

curriculum based assessment (CBA)
A method of evaluating student performance by directly and frequently collecting data on their academic progress.

curriculum based measurement (CBM)
A type of progress monitoring conducted on a regular basis to assess student performance throughout an entire year's curriculum; teachers can use CBM to evaluate not only student progress but also the effectiveness of their instructional methods.

curriculum compacting
The act of reducing the instructional time spent on typical academic subjects so that enrichment activities can be included in the curriculum; used in gifted education.

curriculum mapping
A method used to gather information about what

has been taught in a classroom over a specific period of time.

curriculum ommission
Information consciously excluded from the curriculum, often occurring due to an erroneous belief of some teachers that certain topics will be taught at a later time or within another subject area.

curriculum overload
Situation that occurs when the range of taught content is too broad and the instructional time offered to students to learn it too short.

cystic fibrosis
An inherited disease affecting most of the organs and bodily functions; characterized by thick, sticky mucous that often interferes with breathing or digestion; generally does not affect intellectual functioning but is increasingly debilitating.

cytomegalovirus (CMV)
A herpes virus that usually produces only mild symptoms but that can cause severe neurological damage in newborns or persons with weakened immune systems.

De-escalation Phase
The sixth part of the behavior cycle (acting-out behavior cycle) in which a student exits the Peak Phase confused, disoriented, and at a reduced level of agitation. Many students will withdraw, deny any responsibility or involvement, attempt to blame others, and even try to reconcile with those they harmed or offended. Although students will most likely not want to discuss the incident, they are often responsive to directions.

deaf
Hearing loss severe enough that speech and most other sounds cannot be perceived without the use of a hearing aid.

Deaf culture
The structures of social relationships, language, dance, theater, and other cultural activities that characterize the deaf community.

deafblindness
A dual disability wherein an individual has both vision and hearing problems but might not be both profoundly deaf and also blind.

deafness
The inability to usefully perceive sounds in the environment with or without the use of a hearing aid; the inability to use hearing as a means of processing information.

debriefing
Process through which a teacher deals not only with a misbehaving student but also with the emotions and expectations of the entire class. In addition, the teacher must deal honestly with his or her own mistakes and feelings surrounding a behavior-related incident. The goal of debriefing is to create a healthier learning environment.

decibel (dB)
A unit of measure for the intensity of sounds; commonly expressed as dB.

decodable text
Text that contains previously taught letter-sound correspondences and patterns.

decreased visual acuity
A reduction in one's ability to visually perceive fine details.

deinstitutionalization
Process of decreasing the number of individuals with disabilities (e.g., mental retardation) who live in large congregate facilities with a goal of closing all institutions and segregated settings.

demographics
Term used to denote any of a variety of pre-selected population characteristics (e.g., racial, ethnic, gender) that are collected and analyzed usually for the purpose (either scientific or commercial) of studying group action dynamics; not to be conufsed with demography.

demography
The study of populations and their defining characteristics.

depression
A continued and sustained state of despair and dejection.

descriptive video service
A service for use by people with visual impairment that provides audio narrative of the key visual elements of television programs and movies.

developmental bilingual education
Method of language instruction in which cademic content is provided to ELLs in their native language; also referred to as late-exit bilingual program or maintenance bilingual programs.

developmental delay
Term used to encompass a variety of disabilities in infants and young children indicating that they are significantly behind the norm for development in one or more areas, including motor development, socialization, independent functioning, cognitive development, or communication.

developmentally appropriate practice (DAP)
Educational methods for young children that are compatible with their developmental levels and that meet their individual needs; coined by the National Association for the Education of Young Children (NAEYC).

diabetic retinopathy
A leading cause of blindness; results from a complication of diabetes, occurring when diabetes damages blood vessels inside the retina.

dialect
Variety within a language involving variations in pronunciation and word usage; a particular form of a language associated with a specific region or social group.

differential reinforcement
A behavioral management technique designed to decrease instances of problem behaviors by either giving (in the case of desirable behavior) or withholding (in the case of undesirable behavior) reinforcement.

differential reinforcement of incompatible behavior (DRI)
A behavior management technique in which a teacher reinforces a positive behavior in order to prevent a student from engaging in another, problematic one.

differential reinforcement of low rates of behavior (DRL)
A behavior management technique through which a teacher can keep a given student behavior at a manageable level without fully suppressing it.

differential reinforcement of other behaviors (DRO)
A behavior management technique through which a teacher reinforces the absence of a problem behavior.

differentiated curriculum
The flexible application of curriculum targets to ensure content mastery, in-depth and independent learning, and the exploration of issues and themes; often used in gifted education.

differentiated instruction
The use of flexible teaching approaches in order to accommodate the individual learning needs of all students.

diplegia
Weakness or paralysis in the legs and arms caused by disease or injury to the nerves of the brain or the spinal cord.

direct instruction
Instructional approach through which specific skills or concepts are taught in highly structured environments using clear, direct language; focused on producing specific learning outcomes and sometimes achieved through the use of scripted lessons. See also: explicit instruction.

direct vocabulary instruction
An instructional method in which a focus is placed on words and their meanings in order to help students to directly learn new vocabulary.

disabilities studies
A college course of studies about people with disabilities, their history, culture, and rights.

disability
Any of a wide variety of conditions characterized by limitations in typical function (e.g., seeing, hearing, speaking, or learning) or development resulting from a physical or sensory impairment.

discalculia
A severely impaired ability to calculate or perform mathematical functions; presumed to be caused by central nervous system dysfunction.

discrepancy formula
Any one of a variety of formulas developed by state educational agencies or local districts to determine the difference between a child's actual

achievement and, using the student's IQ scores, expected achievement; used to identify students with learning disabilities.

discrepancy score
The score used in some states to determine eligibility for services designed for students with learning disabilities; calculated by applying one of several different discrepancy formulas.

disgraphia
A severely impaired ability to write; presumed to be caused by central nervous system dysfunction.

disproportionate representation
Situation wherein a particular group is represented significantly more or less than would be predicted by the percentage that group represents in the general population.

doctor's office effect
The observation that children with ADHD often do not exhibit their symptoms when examined by a clinician during a brief office visit.

Down syndrome
A disorder arising from chromosome defect (i.e., an extra chromosome on the twenty-first pair) that often results in identifiable physical characteristics (e.g., short stature, broad facial profile) and that usually causes delays in physical and intellectual development.

drift
In implementation fidelity, the inadvertent modification or omission over time of the recommended procedures or activities that make up a practice or program; usually occurs gradually and is considered a threat to fidelity.

dual-discrepancy approach
The use of twin criteria, performance level and rate of growth, to evaluate student progress.

due process hearing
A noncourt proceeding before an impartial hearing officer that can be used if parents and school personnel disagree on a special education issue.

duration
In behavior intervention, the length of time that a student engages in a behavior.

dysfluencies
Any break, interruption, or aberration in the normal flow of speech; typical of normal speech development in young children, but considered to be speech impairments in older children (e.g., stuttering).

dyslexia
A severely impaired ability to read; presumed to be caused by a central nervous system dysfunction.

early childhood special education
The provision of customized services crafted to meet the individual needs of young children with disabilities; generally used among children from birth to five years old.

early expressive language delay (EELD)
A significant interruption in the development of expressive language that is apparent by age two.

early intervening
Instructional intervention in which assistance or services are offered to students as soon as they begin to struggle academically and before they fall too far behind their peers.

early intervention
Specialized services provided to very young children at risk for or showing signs of developmental delay.

ecological assessment
A procedure that includes observational data collected in the student's natural environments to identify specific events that cause a problem behavior or consequent events that maintain or increase the target behavior; ABC analysis is an example.

Education for All Handicapped Children Act (EHA) or PL (Public Law) 94-142
Act of Congress passed in 1975 with many provisions for assuring free appropriate public education for all students with disabilities; later renamed the Individuals with Disabilities Education Act (IDEA).

educational interpreter
Related service provider who translates or converts spoken messages to the mode of manual communication prefered by a student who is deaf.

effective instruction
The use of research-based instruction in the classroom.

effective teaching behaviors
Instructional methods that engage students in learning and increase their on-task behavior as a means through which to their increase academic achievement.

Emotional/Behavioral Disorder
An educational or school-based term and not a specific diagnosis. It generally refers to a situation in which the student has significant or prominent problems adhering to the expected behavioral standards and/or in regulating their emotional state.

Emotional Disturbance or Emotionally Disturbed
1. A specific category/classification under IDEA.
2. In general, dysregulation or inability to maintain emotional state and behavior within "normal" or accepted range of variation.

empirically validated
Condition or characteristic of having been proven through high-quality research to be accurate or to produce positive results.

encephalitis
An inflammation of the brain often brought on by a viral infection; can affect the child's mental development adversely and may result in seizures, brain damage, and partial paralysis.

encopresis
Bowel incontinence; soiling oneself.

endogenous
Of or having come from within the body; used to describe an inherited disability.

English as a second language (ESL)
Instructional approach in which non-native speakers are instructed in English until a level of proficiency is achieved; does not provide support in the student's native or primary language; also referred to as English for speakers of other languages (ESOL).

English language development
An instructional method used with English Language Learners (ELL) that focuses on learning the formal structures of language (grammar);

English language learner (ELL)
The preferred term for a student engaged in learning English as his or her second language; sometimes called limited English proficient (LEP) students.

enrichment
To add topics or skills to the traditional curriculum or to present a particular topic in more depth; an approach used in gifted education.

enuresis
Urinary incontinence; wetting oneself.

environmental restructuring
Classroom behavior approach in which a student's peers are instructed and reinforced for encouraging appropriate behavior in a classmate who exhibits disruptive behavior.

epidemiological studies
The scientific and medical study of the causes, transmission, and characteristics of disease or disorders within a population.

epilepsy
A neurological disorder characterized by recurrent seizures.

error analysis
The process by which instructors identify the types of errors made by students when working mathematical problems.

error correction procedure
A method of corrective feedback in which a student who has made an error is immediately prompted to say or write the correct response.

ESL/bilingual paraprofessional
Professional who provides instruction or support under the supervision of an ESL or bilingual teacher.

ethnocentrism
A tendency to see one's own culture as natural and correct, while viewing other cultures as unnatural or inferior; the tendency to evaluate other cultures according to one's own cultural standards or assumptions.

etiology
The causes of a disability, including genetic, physiological, environmental, or psychological factors.

eugenics
A pseudoscientific social study characterized by its belief in the 'perfectibility' of human beings through directed breeding; supports improving the human race through selective reproduction and protecting society by not allowing people with disabilities to reproduce, reside in mainstream society, or, in some cases, live.

evaluation
Assessment or judgment of special characteristics such as intelligence, physical abilities, sensory abilities, learning preferences, and achievement.

event
In behavior intervention, the number of times a behavior occurs; also called frequency.

evidence-based practice
Skills, techniques, and strategies that have been proven to work through experimental research studies or large-scale research field studies. Examples include the Good Behavior Game and peer tutoring.

evidence-based program
A collection of practices that has been proven to work through experimental research studies or large-scale research field studies. Examples include Peer Assisted Learning Strategies (PALS).

evoked response audiometry
The use of a electroencephalograph to measure changes in brain-wave activity in response to sounds; can be used with newborns, who do not need to voluntarily respond to sound.

exceptional learning needs (ELN)
The exhibition of variations in behavior or performance sufficient to warrant a special educational intervention.

excess cost
Additional expenses, beyond those for typical learners in the general education program, incurred to educate students with disabilities.

exclusionary clause
The omission of possible etiological factors to explain a student's learning disabilities.

expanded core curriculum
Curriculum encompassing the range of skills that address the disability-specific needs of students who have visual impairments, including communication skills, daily living skills, social skills, and orientation and mobility skills.

explicit instruction
Instructional approach in which teachers clearly identify the expectations for learning, highlight important details of the concept or skill, offer precise instruction, and connect new learning to earlier lessons and materials.

expository text
Written text that is informational, descriptive, persuasive, or explanatory in nature.

expressive language
The ability to communicate thoughts and feelings through gestures, sign language, verbalization, or the written word.

externalizing behavior
Any behavior, especially aggressive ones, that are directed toward others.

extinction
In behavior intervention, means through which teachers attempt to eliminate the likelihood that a behavior will reoccur by withholding something pleasant; can be thought of as 'planned ignoring.'

extinction burst
In behavior intervention, an elevation or increase in the rate of an undesirable behavior in response to a teacher's use of the extinction consequence.

facilitated communication
Augmentative technique in which a facilitator assists a person with a communication disorder to express himself or herself through either written or manual communication.

family system of supports
Potential sources of support for people with disabilities, including sons and daughters, spouses, parents, siblings, in-laws, aunts and uncles, grandparents, extended family members, stepfamily members, and legal guardians; might also include close friends or others outside the family.

feedback
Constructive feedback offered by an observer (e.g., a coach, principal, or fellow teacher) to a teacher about a specific lesson or instructional technique.

fetal alcohol syndrome (FAS)
A condition that can result in congenital cognitive disabilities, behavior problems, and physical disability in the children of women who drink alcohol during pregnancy.

fidelity of implementation
The degree to which an intervention is implemented accurately, following the guidelines or restrictions of its developers.

field of vision
The range of physical space that is visible to a person looking straight ahead; 180 degrees is considered normal.

financial planning workshop
An instructional or advisory session during which appropriate personnel can communicate and collaborate with the families of students with special needs on such topics as guardianship and financial planning.

finger spelling
A form of manual communication that assigns each letter of the alphabet a sign; one form of sign language used by people who are deaf.

five core reading components
The five essential building blocks of reading ability: phonemic awareness, phonics and word study, vocabulary, fluency, and comprehension.

fluctuating hearing loss
Hearing loss that varies from day to day.

fluency problems
Hesitations or repetitions of sounds or words that interrupt a person's flow of speech; a speech impairment.

FM system
An assistive listening device that brings sound to a student's ears so that he or she can hear better. An FM system allows teachers to talk into a microphone and transmit the sound of their voices to a student. An FM system consists of three parts: a microphone, a receiver, and a transmitter.

follow-up study
The provision of an evaluation, diagnosis, or treatment of a condition.

formative assessment
A system of providing continual feedback about preconceptions and performances to both learners and instructors; an ongoing evaluation of student learning.

four-tiered RTI model
An RTI model in which the fourth level of intervention is provided by the special education program. Tiers 1 through 3 are provided by the general education program and are increasingly intensive.

fragile X syndrome (FXS)
An inherited genetic disorder associated with disabilities and particularly linked to mental retardation; some children with fragile X have average intelligence with or without learning disabilities; other symptoms include a large head and prominent forehead, nose, ears, and jaw, ADHD, heart murmurs, and some incidence of autism-like behaviors.

free appropriate public education (FAPE)
A provision of IDEA ensuring that students with disabilities receive necessary education and services without cost to the child or family.

frequency
In behavior intervention, the number of times a behavior occurs; also called event.

frequent progress monitoring
A type of formative assessment in which student learning is evaluated often and on a regular basis in order to provide useful feedback about performance to both learners and instructors.

full inclusion
An interpretation of the least restrictive environment concept that all students with disabilities should receive their instruction in the general education classroom; the act of facilitating the full participation of an individual in an activity, lesson, or course of study.

function
In behavior assessment, term used to describe the motive for particular behaviors.

function-based intervention
A systematized means of negating certain undesirable behaviors, often by replacing them with behaviors that serve the same function.

functional academics
Category of instruction in which an emphasis is placed on the skills needed for daily living.

functional assessment
Method used to determine special education eligibility, the nature of the needed instructional program, and long-term goals for individuals with severe disabilities; evaluations focus on independent living and are conducted in natural settings.

functional behavioral assessment
A behavioral evaluation technique that determines the exact nature of problem behaviors, the reasons why they occur, and under what conditions the likelihood of their occurrence is reduced.

functional magnetic resonance imaging (fMRI)
Adaptation of the MRI used to detect changes in the brain while it is in an active state; unlike a PET scan, it does not involve using radioactive materials.

functional vision
A quality in which a person possesses enough useable vision to employ sight as a primary channel for learning.

functional vision assessment (FVA)
An assessment, required in most states, to determine a student's eligibility for educational vision services. Conducted in the student's natural learning environment by a teacher of students with visual impairments, an FVA describes the ways in which the student's visual impairment affects his or her development and learning.

functionally equivalent behavior
Any appropriate behavior that serves similar purposes to, and can be used to replace, an inappropriate one.

gait training
The analysis of and instruction in walking as a means of locomotion.

general education
A typical (regular education) classroom and curriculum designed to serve students without disabilities.

generalization
The transfer of learned information from particular instances to other environments, people, times, and events.

genetic counseling
Discussions between medical personnel and prospective parents for the purpose of determining the parents' genetic history and their likelihood of bearing children with disabilities.

genetic hearing loss
Hearing loss caused by the presence of an abnormal gene within one or more chromosomes.

genius
Term sometimes used to indicate a particular aptitude or capacity in any area; rare intellectual talents.

gifted
Used to describe individuals with high levels of intelligence, outstanding abilities, and the capacity for high performance.

glaucoma
A family of diseases characterized by excessive pressure in the eyeball that results in damage to the optic nerve; if untreated, blindness results.

globus pallidus
Structure in the basal ganglia of the brain; site of abnormal development in persons with ADHD.

goal line
On a chart of a student's academic progress, the indicator that connects a student's initial CBM probe scores to an expected short-term goal or benchmark.

Good Behavior Game
A game-like situation that uses the principles of positive reinforcement and group contingencies and divides students into teams, competing against each other, to encourage improved classroom deportment.

graphic organizer
Any visual aid designed to help students to organize and comprehend substantial amounts of text and content information.

group contingency
Any of a number of reinforcement systems that involves an entire class and in which rewards are contingent upon a group's performance.

guardianship
A legal authority that grants one person the right to make decisions for another.

guided example
A step-by-step instructional guide for how to apply a strategy or how to complete a task.

guided practice
A method of practice that involves working with students on activities that focus on a previously modeled or taught skill.

hard-of-hearing
Hearing loss significant enough to adversely affect education and communication but sufficient, with the assistance of a hearing aid, to comprehend others' speech and oral communication.

hearing aid
An electronic device worn by those with hearing loss to help to amplify received sounds.

hearing impairment
A term referring to any degree of hearing loss, either permanent or fluctuating, mild or profound, that adversely affects an individual's education and that requires special training or adaptations.

hearing loss
A general term used to loosely describe a variety of hearing impairments.

hearing threshold
The point at which a person can perceive the softest sound at each frequency level.

hemiplegia
A condition in which one half of the body (right or left) is paralyzed.

heritability studies
Method of determining the degree to which a condition is inherited.

herpes simplex
A viral infection caused by a group of herpes viruses that may result in cold sores and, if contracted late in pregnancy, can cause mental abnormalities in the child.

heterogeneous grouping
To place students of varying abilities (i.e., lower achieving, typically achieving, and higher achieving) together in a small instructional group.

high achiever
Label applied to those students who consistently perform at a high academic level.

high-frequency word
Any of those words that commonly appear in reading materials and are often times not easily decodable (e.g., the, and, of, a, to).

high-probability request (high-p request)
In behavior management, a request based on the assumption that students are more likely to obey teacher directives if they are already actively engaged in compliant classroom behavior.

high-quality instruction
Effective instruction (i.e., research-based instruction) provided to all students in the general education setting using a standards-based curriculum and research-validated practices.

high-stakes testing
A term frequently used to describe the significant consequences tied to the performance of students on a test; tests that involve incentives and disincentives on teachers, schools, and school districts.

HIV infection
The human immunodeficiency virus; a microorganism that infects the immune system, impairing the body's ability to fight infections.

home or hospital teacher
An educator who teaches in a child's home or hospital when the child must be absent from school due to health problems.

home-based
Term used to describe instruction delivered primarily in a student's home rather than in a school or center.

homogeneous grouping
To place students of similar abilities together into groups; can be used by teachers to provide more intensive instruction to students who are working at a similar level and who can benefit from instruction that is designed for their specific learning needs.

Hoover cane
A long, white cane used in the mobility and orientation system developed in 1944 by Richard Hoover to help people with visual disabilities to move with a greater degree of independence through their environment.

hydrocephaly
Condition characterized by enlargement of the head due to an excess build-up of cerebrospinal fluid; can result in brain damage.

hyperactivity
Term used to describe the impaired ability to sit or concentrate for long periods of time.

hyperopia
Farsightedness.

I Can Read (ICARE)
Instructional approach in which teachers work with and track the progress of small groups of reading students in order to focus more on students' individual needs.

identification
The process of seeking out and designating students with disabilities who require special education and related services.

idioms
Words and phrases that have meanings different from the literal one.

IEP Team
The multidisciplinary team of education and related services professionals that develops and evaluates, along with the students and their parents, the individualized education program plan for each student with a disability.

impaired vision field
A limitation in one's ability to perceive the average visual field (generally speaking, an area one can see when looking straight ahead, typically 160 to 180 degrees wide).

impulsive
Term used to describe an impaired ability to control one's own behavior.

inactive learner
Term applied to students who do not become involved in learning situations, do not approach the learning task purposefully, do not ask questions, do not seek assistance, or do not initiate learning.

incidence
Frequency of occurrence, such as the number of children identified with autism and receiving early intervention services.

incidental learning
The acquisition of knowledge and skills without being directly taught.

incidental teaching
Instructional technique in which information and skills are taught through the reinforcement of behaviors and activities performed naturally by students.

inclusion
In education, a state of inclusivity in which all students are educated so as to reach their fullest potentials, regardless of ability or disability.

independent practice
Instructional method in which students are encouraged to work on their own or to work separately from the teacher on activities that they are capable of performing without significant assistance.

indirect vocabulary instruction
Instructional method through which students learn words and their meanings via daily conversations and independent reading.

individualized education program (IEP)
A written plan used to delineate an individual student's current level of development and his or her learning goals, as well as to specify any accommodations, modifications, and related services that a student might need to attend school and maximize his or her learning.

individualized family service plan (IFSP)
A written document used to record and guide the early intervention process for young children with disabilities and their families; designed to reflect

individual concerns, priorities, and resources.

individualized transition plan (ITP)
A statement, included in a high-school student's IEP, outlining the transition services required for coordination and delivery of services as the student nears adulthood.

Individuals with Disabilities Education Act (IDEA)
Name given in 1990 to the Education for All Handicapped Children Act (EHA) and used for all reauthorizations of the law that guarantees students with disabilities the right to a free appropriate education in the least restrictive environment.

informal reading inventory (IRI)
Method of reading assessment in which a student is asked to read progressively more difficult material, while his or her teacher notes any errors.

infused
Term used to describe a general education curriculum that has been enhanced with any of a number of enrichment activities.

inner ear
The portion of the ear that contains the cochlea and the vestibular apparatus.

input
Any of the numerous ways that a learner can receive information.

instructional scaffolding
A process in which a teacher adds supports for students to enhance learning and aid in the mastery of tasks; the teacher accomplishes this by systematically building on students' experiences and knowledge while they are learning new skills.

instructional support
Element added to an instructional routine in order to accommodate the different learning needs of students with disabilities.

instructional technology
Any device or instrument that exists in a classroom and that teachers use for the purpose of day-to-day instruction; such devices, when assigned to an individual student through an IEP, are known as assistive technology.

insulin pump
A surgically implanted medical device used to administer insulin medication and help those with diabetes to keep their blood-sugar levels within a prescribed range.

integrated (or supported) employment
An employment setting in which an individual with a disability receives the support necessary to learn and maintain his or her job.

integration
The process by which people of different backgrounds, abilities, social classes, religious persuasions, genders, etc., are permitted full and equal access to social institutions, services, and legal protections.

intellectual functioning
The actual performance of tasks believed to represent intelligence, such as observing, problem solving, and communicating.

inter-observer reliability
The extent to which two or more observers agree in their rating or coding of the same behavior or action.

interdisciplinary instruction
Instructional technique in which students study a topic and its related issues in the context of several different disciplines.

interdisciplinary team
Group of professionals from different disciplines who work together to plan and manage a student's IEP.

interim alternative setting
A temporary (no more than 45 days) educational placement for a student with disabilities who is violent, brings a gun to school, or is involved with drugs; not considered a change in educational placement and does not require a new IEP.

internalizing behavior
Behavior that is withdrawn, directed inward, or focused on oneself.

interpreter
Individual who helps people who are deaf or hard-of-hearing to communicate by translating

what a hearing person says into signs or some other means of transmitting information.

interval
In behavior intervention, an indication of whether or not the behavior occurs within a given period of time.

intervener
Professional who facilitates communication between a person who is deaf and another individual by translating spoken language into a manual one, such as American Sign Language.

intervening
In behavior management, to interrupt the acting-out cycle when behavior problems are less serious and when students are more amenable to intervention efforts.

intervention
An instructional technique designed to improve or remediate a certain set of skills.

Intervention Ladder
A hierarchy of disciplinary tactics organized from the least intrusive and least complex to the most intrusive and most complicated.

IQ-achievement discrepancy model
The traditional assessment vehicle used to determine whether a student has a learning disability and requires special education services.

iris
The clear tissue of the eye, under which are pigment cells that give the eye its color.

itinerant teacher
Educator who teaches students or who consults with others in more than one setting.

job coach
Individual who works alongside people with disabilities in order to help them to learn all the parts of a job.

joint attention deficit
A deficiency or inability to mutually interact or to share interest in events or objects.

judicial hearing
A hearing before a judge in court of law.

juvenile arthritis
A chronic and painful muscular condition seen in children.

knowledge-centered learning environment
Instructional environment in which facts, ideas, concepts, and principles are introduced when a need for their introduction becomes apparent.

Kurzweil Reader
One of the first computerized systems designed for people with visual disabilities; translates print into synthesized speech.

language
Rule-based method of communication, typically defined through social systems.

language delay
Circumstance in which a child's language development occurs at a slower rate or over a longer period of time than is usually seen.

language difference
Natural variations or anomalies that occur in the language development of non-native English speakers or of those who speak nonstandard English.

language impairment
A pronounced difficulty or inability to master the various systems of rules in language.

latency
In behavior intervention, the length of time it takes for a behavior to occur.

learned curriculum
All of the information that students learn as a result of being in the classroom and by interacting with the taught curriculum; can include information that may not be a part of the standards-based or taught curriculum.

learned helplessness
A phenomenon in which individuals, usually as a result of repeated failure or control by others, gradually become less willing to attempt tasks.

learner-centered learning environment
Instructional environment in which a teacher designs lessons to uncover the knowledge, skills, interests, attitudes, and beliefs of each learner.

learning disability (LD)
Any one of a variety of disorders characterized by a difficulty or delay in the development of the ability to learn or use information.

learning media assessment
Evaluation process in which a variety of information is used to determine the primary and secondary learning media and literacy needs of students with visual impairments; often addresses a student's use of sensory channels and needs for general learning media.

learning strategies
Instructional methods employed to help students to read, comprehend, and study better by helping them to strategically organize and collect information.

least restrictive environment (LRE)
One of the principles outlined in the Individuals with Disabilities Education Act requiring that students with disabilities be educated with their non-disabled peers to the greatest appropriate extent.

legal mandates
In reference to education policy, the laws or legislative changes that outline the required guidelines for serving students with disabilities.

legally blind
Visual acuity measured as 20/200 or worse in the better eye with correction, or peripheral vision no greater than 20 degrees.

legislation
Law or laws passed by a state or federal representative entity or other governing agency and signed by a governor or the president.

lens
The part of the eye that functions to focus on image on the retina.

lesson plan
The most detailed standards-based plan that a teacher will develop; outlines the purpose and activities of what will be done on a specific day or across several days.

letter naming fluency
Test in which a student is given a sheet of randomized letters and asked to name as many letters as possible in one minute; this test must be administered to each student individually.

letter sound fluency
Test in which a student is given a sheet of randomized letters and asked to say as many sounds corresponding to the letters as possible in one minute; this test must be administered to each student individually.

letter-sound correspondence
Method of learning language in which students associate a letter or group of letters with its spoken sound.

life skill
Generally speaking, any of those skills used to manage a home, cook, shop, manage finances, and organize personal living environments.

limited English proficient (LEP)
Term used to describe non-native English speakers whose ability to read, write, or speak may be limited or developing more slowly than that of their peers; English language learners is the preferred term.

litigation
A lawsuit or legal proceeding.

long cane
A variety of white cane used to facilitate the independent mobility of people who are blind; developed during World War II by Dr. Richard Hoover and so sometimes referred to as a Hoover cane.

low achievers
Students who experience school failure and poor academic achievement, come to expect failure, and develop an attitude that expending effort to learn will not produce results.

low birth weight (LBW)
Condition in which babies are born weighing less than 5.5 pounds; usually a result of premature birth or intrauterine growth retardation.

low incidence disability
Term used describe a disability whose occurrence in a general population is relative uncommon (e.g., deafness, deafblindness).

low vision
A level of visual disability in which vision is still useful for learning or for the execution of a task.

low-stakes testing
State- and district-wide testing that does not entail negative consequences for schools or teachers that perform poorly.

macroculture
A nation or other large social entity whose culture, beliefs, and assumptions are shared by a majority of its inhabitants.

macular degeneration
Medical condition in which the deterioration of the central part of the retina results in an inability to clearly perceive fine details.

mainstreaming
Process through which students with special needs are placed in an educational setting that is as close to what is considered the norm for most students for some or all of their school day; the term is now somewhat outdated.

maintenance
In behavior assessment, term used to describe the extent to which a student's behavior is self-sustaining over time.

malleus
The hammer-shaped bone in the ossicular chain of the middle ear.

manifestation determination
The result of a process used to determine whether a student's disciplinary problems are the result of a disability.

manipulatives
Concrete objects, for example, an abacus or popsicle sticks, that students can use to develop a conceptual understanding of math topics.

manual communication
Form of organized expression in which the hands are used as a means of communication (e.g., sign language, finger spelling).

mastery measurement (MM)
A form of classroom assessment conducted on a regular basis; once a teacher has determined the instructional sequence for the year, each skill in the sequence is assessed until mastery has been achieved, after which the next skill is introduced and assessed.

material scaffolding
The use of written prompts and cues to help students to perform a task or to use a given strategy.

mathematics disability
Condition characterized by significant difficulty in the area of mathematics.

Maze Fluency
Test during which the student is given two and a half minutes to read a passage in which every seventh word has been deleted and three choices offered to fill the blank; the student's score is the number of correct replacements that he or she makes; can be administered to a group.

mediation
Process through which a neutral party facilitates a meeting between parents and school officials to resolve disagreements about a student's individualized education program and questions about his or her placement and services.

medical advances
In the context of special education, improvements in medical care and technology that allow students who are medically fragile to participate in school with their non-disabled peers.

medically fragile
Term used to describe children whose medical conditions are subject to sudden change or that place them at risk for developmental delays.

melting pot
Idiomatic metaphor used to describe a homogenized society in which the cultural traditions and home languages of non-native citizens are largely abandoned in favor of the dominant culture.

meningitis
An inflammation of the coverings of the brain and spinal cord that affects the central nervous system and characterized by intense headaches, fever, sensitivity to light, and muscular rigidity.

mental age (MA)
An age estimate of an individual's mental ability, derived from an artificial comparison of the individual's IQ score and chronological age; not

a preferred means of describing an individual's abilities.

mental retardation
A disability characterized by significant intellectual impairment and deficits in adaptive functioning that occurs in the developmental period (before the age of eighteen) and has adverse effects on education.

mentoring
A method of ongoing support in which a more-experienced or more-knowledgeable person helps a less-experienced or less-knowledgeable person to learn or refine skills.

mentorship
A program in which a student is paired with a qualified adult for the purpose of learning to apply knowledge in real-life situations.

meta-analysis
A research methodology that allows for the synthesis of many individual research studies to determine the power or effectiveness of an educational practice.

metacognition
Process through which one comes to understand one's own learning, to organize one's thinking before acting, or to relate information just learned to information already stored in the brain; thinking about thinking.

microcephaly
A neurological condition characterized by the occurrence of a small, conical-shaped head and an underdeveloped brain.

middle ear
The air-filled central cavity of the ear that contains the eardrum, the Eustachian tube, and the three little bones (hammer, anvil, and stirrup) that together are called the ossicles.

milieu teaching strategy
Any of a number of naturalistic approaches to language intervention in which the goal is to teach functional language skills in a natural environment.

mixed hearing loss
Hearing loss that results from a combination of conductive and sensorineural hearing impairments and is characterized by a difficulty in hearing faint or muffled sounds.

mnemonics
A learning strategy in which a verbal device is employed to help promote the memorization of names or other information (e.g., the mnemonic device 'HOMES' for lakes Huron, Ontario, Michigan, Erie, and Superior, is sometimes used to help students remember the names of the Great Lakes).

mobility
The ability to travel safely and efficiently from one location to another; a topic of instruction for students with severe visual problems; also used to describe any of the means through which an individual with a motor impairment ambulates (e.g., walking, using a wheelchair or cane).

modeling
The act of providing an example as a means through which to encourage the imitation of a skill, process, characteristic, or style; process whereby a teacher observes a colleague as he or she provides instruction in order to see the process in action and to see its benefits firsthand.

modification
Any of a wide variety of services or support related to a child's disability that help a student to access the subject matter and demonstrate knowledge; such services and supports fundamentally alter the standard or expectation of the assignment or test.

morpheme
The smallest element of language that still carries meaning.

motivation
The inner drive to work hard, achieve, and master skills and learn concepts; internal incentives that are often influenced by previous success or failure.

multi-tiered systems of support
A model or approach to instruction that provides increasingly intensive and individualized levels of support for academics (e.g., response to intervention or RTI) and for behavior (e.g., Positive Behavioral Interventions and Supports or PBIS).

multicultural education
An instructional principle that employs concepts of culture, differences, equality, and democracy to develop effective classroom instruction and school environments.

multidisciplinary team
A team of teachers, educational professionals (e.g., related services personnel, school psychologist), administrators, specialists, and parents or guardians who assess the individual needs of students to determine eligibility for special education and develop individualized education programs (IEP); often called IEP teams.

multiple disabilities
Circumstance in which an individual has more than one disability.

multiple intelligences (MI)
A theory originally developed by the psychologist Howard Gardner in which human intelligence is viewed as multidimensional.

multiple opportunities to respond
Instructional technique in which teachers offer their students several chances to practice a response and to attain mastery in a targeted skill.

multiple-severe disability
Term used to describe any of a number of especially challenging disabilities in which more than one condition combine to affect learning, independence, and the range of intensive and pervasive supports required by individuals and their families.

muscular dystrophy
Hereditary disease characterized by progressive weakness caused by the degeneration of muscle fibers.

muscular/ skeletal condition
Any of a number of conditions that affect the muscles or bones and that result in limited motor functioning.

myopia
Nearsightedness.

natural supports
System of supports that are available to all individuals as a natural result of typical family and community living (e.g., through their family and friends).

negative consequence
Any of a variety of reinforcements used to decrease a student's problem behavior; negative consequences are functional and should be applied in an educative rather than vindictive fashion.

negative punishment
Means by which teachers can decrease the probability that a behavior will reoccur; negative punishment removes something that is pleasant.

negative reinforcement
Means by which teachers can increase the probability that a behavior will reoccur; negative reinforcement removes something that is unpleasant.

networking
Level of cooperation in which inter-connected professionals or agencies coexist, work together, and communicate.

neural tube disorder
Any congenital defect of the brain and spinal cord caused by failure of the neural tube to close (e.g., spina bifida).

neuromotor impairment
Condition that affects the central nervous system, limiting an individual's ability to move or to control the operation of his or her muscles.

No Child Left Behind Act of 2001 (NCLB)
Federal school reform legislation that aimed to increase school accountability for student learning, offer more choices for parents and students, create greater flexibility for schools in the use of funds, and emphasize early-reading intervention.

non-verbal learning disabilities
Term used to describe a subgroup of learning impairments that hinders an individual's ability to decipher non-verbal communication (e.g., facial expressions, eye contact) due to a dysfunction in the part of the brain that controls non-verbal reasoning.

nondiscriminatory testing
Term used to describe any assessment that properly takes into account a student's cultural and linguistic diversity.

nonexample
In instruction, a concept used to define a topic, idea, or material object by referencing its disqualifying attributes (e.g., a sphere lacks the vertices of a triangle).

nonoptical device
Any device or instructional strategy used to improve the performance of tasks linked to visual ability among individuals with low vision that does not involve direct optical enhancement (e.g., book stands, writing guides, lighting, and large-type materials).

nonpaid supports
Assistance of a kind available in one's natural environment, such as that offered by friends and neighbors.

nonrepresentative norming samples
A systemic deficiency in which a test is developed without a sufficient number of students from linguistically diverse cultures in the norming group; such a test is unlikely to yield valid results when administered to English language learners (ELLs).

nonsense word fluency
Test in which a student is given one minute to read as many nonsense words (or separate sounds in each word) as possible; must be administered to each student individually.

norm-referenced measure
A standardized assessment tool that compares a student's test scores to the average score of a representative group.

normal curve
A bell-shaped, theoretical construct used to illustrate the normal distribution of human traits such as intelligence.

normalization
An underlying philosophy of special education holding that every individual, regardless of disability or severity thereof, should have available to them the ordinary patterns and conventions of everyday living.

nystagmus
Condition characterized by rapid involuntary movements of the eyes; may affect fine-motor skills and cause difficulty in reading.

obstacle sense
Skill possessed by some people who are blind, whereby they are able to detect the presence of obstacles in their environments.

occupational therapist (OT)
Professional who directs activities to help improve fine-motor muscular control and develop self-help skills and adaptive behavior in conjunction with services for persons with disabilities.

off-level testing
The use of assessment instruments designed for older students in the academic evaluation of a student believed to be gifted.

open-head injury
Physical trauma in which the skull is fractured to the extent that the membrane surrounding the brain is penetrated; an open wound to the head.

ophthalmologist
Medical doctor who specializes in diagnosing and treating disorders of the eye; also performs surgery and evaluates visual acuity, visual fields, and the need for glasses.

optic nerve
The nerve that carries messages from the eye to the visual center of the brain.

optometrist
A non-medical professional who tests vision, evaluates the need for glasses and low vision devices, and prescribes corrective lenses.

oral language proficiency
The knowledge of or use of vocabulary, grammar, and sentence structure, as well as strong comprehension skills. Research has shown that students with poor oral language proficiency struggle with academic skills such as reading fluency and reading comprehension.

oral transliterators
Professionals trained to facilitate spoken language for students who are deaf or hard of hearing by silently repeating what the speaker has said so that the student can easily read his or her lips. These people also sometimes serve as the 'voice' of the person who is deaf or hard of hearing; also known as oral interpreters.

oral-only approach
Instructional approach to educating children with deafness or hearing loss that stresses learning to speak in order to communicate in the hearing world.

organizing routine
Any one of a variety of activities, including question-and-answer sessions, that precede instruction and are used to focus students' attention on the information to be presented.

orientation
The process of using vision and other senses to establish one's position and relationship to other significant objects in the environment; the mental 'map' the people use to navigate their environments; a topic of instruction for people with severe visual deficits.

orientation and mobility (O&M)
The sense of where one's physical position in relation to other people, objects, and landmarks.

orientation and mobility (O&M) specialist
A professional who specializes in teaching travel skills to visually impaired persons, including the use of a cane, dog guide, or sophisticated electronic travel aids, as well as the sighted guide technique.

orthopedic impairment
A condition related to a physical deformity or disability of the skeletal system and associated motor function.

ossicles
The collective name for the tiny bones (malleus, incus, and stapes) that assist in the transfer of sound waves.

otitis media
An infection of the middle ear, usually caused by an upper-respiratory tract infection that affects the Eustachian tube, that can result in hearing loss, communication impairments, or learning disabilities.

otoacoustic emission (OAE)
The low level of sound produced when the hair cells inside the inner ear vibrate; testing for OAEs allows for newborn hearing assessment.

outcomes
The results of decisions and actions; a term used to describe students' achievements.

outer ear
The part of the ear composed of the pinna, what most people call the ear, and the auditory canal.

outreach program
Specialized program offered in communities or in students' homes by local schools or agencies that serve students with special needs.

overrepresentation
Circumstance in which the number of students from a cultural or ethnic group found to be participating in a special education category is above the level one might expect based upon that group's proportion of the overall school population.

pacing
Instructional consideration through which teachers attempt to provide instruction quickly enough to keep students engaged but not so fast that those students get lost.

PALS set-up procedures
Any or all of the steps necessary to ensure the successful execution of a PALS session, including but not limited to moving to a partner quickly and quietly, working cooperatively, gathering materials, and following the rules of PALS.

paradigm shift
A fundamental change in the conceptual framework, orientation, or belief system that underlies a field of study.

paraplegia
Paralysis of the lower body, typically caused by a spinal injury or disease; term used to describe a type of cerebral palsy that affects both of the legs.

paraprofessional
An individual trained to assist a professional.

partial participation
Educational approach in which students with disabilities in general education classrooms engage in the same learning activities as students without disabilities, but on an appropriately modified basis.

passage reading fluency (teacher copy) or passage reading fluency (student copy)
A form of curriculum based measurement (CBM) in which the student reads a passage for one minute; the passage's difficulty is based on his or her expected end-of-year reading competence; the student's score is the number of words read correctly, this test must be administered to each student individually.

passage reading fluency probe (PRF)
A form of curriculum based measurement (CBM) in which the student reads a passage for one minute; the student's score is the number of words read correctly; this probe is appropriate for students in second through sixth grade and should be administered to each student individually.

Peak Phase
The fifth stage in the behavior cycle (acting-out behavior cycle) during which a student's behavior is clearly out of control; students may physically assault others, hurt themselves, cry hysterically, and destroy property, any of which may produce devastating outcomes.

Peer Assisted Learning Strategies (PALS)
Instructional approach in which teachers pair a high-performing reader with a low-performing one in order to complete activities designed to promote the development of reading skills; complements the existing reading curriculum by providing research-validated learning strategies through a course of peer-mediated instruction (i.e., peer pairing, peer tutoring); grade-appropriate versions of PALS (e.g., K-PALS, PALS-High School) address specific reading issues.

peer tutoring
In special education, a cooperative learning strategy that pairs a student with disabilities with a non-disabled student; either student may adopt the role of teacher or learner.

performance level
An indication of a student's academic skills, usually denoted by a score on a given test or probe.

performance or achievement standards
The level of mastery in a given content area that a student is expected to attain.

perinatal
Of or having to do with the period just before and just after birth.

peripheral vision
The outer area of a person's visual field.

perseveration
The tendency to repeat behaviors; may be found in persons with brain injuries or ADHD.

personal reader
A person who reads text orally to those who cannot read print.

personality disorder
A deeply ingrained and maladaptive pattern of behavior, such as anxiety, depression, guilt, shyness, or feelings of inferiority, that typically manifests by the time of adolescence and causes long-term difficulties in personal relationships or in one's ability to function normally in society.

pervasive developmental disorder-not otherwise specified (PDD-NOS)
A disorder included in the autistic spectrum disorder (ASD) characterized by problems in communication and social interaction, and repetitive or manneristic behaviors.

petit mal seizure (absence seizure)
A form of generalized seizure that causes a brief clouding or loss of consciousness.

phenylketonuria (PKU)
A hereditary condition in which the amino acid phenylalanine is not properly metabolized; can cause mental retardation if not diagnosed and regulated through diet shortly after birth.

phoneme
The smallest unit of sound that can be identified in spoken language.

phonemic awareness
The ability to listen to, identify, and manipulate phonemes,the smallest units of sounds that are combined to create words.

phonics
A method of reading instruction in which students are taught the relationship between sounds and written letters.

phonics and word study
Instruction designed to teach students about the relationship between sounds and written letters (known as the alphabetic principle) so that they learn how to decode and read words; the combination of phonics and word study helps students to improve their word recognition, reading, and spelling.

phonological awareness
An understanding of the relationship between sounds and the corresponding words or word parts that they represent; facilitates the abilities to rhyme and to understand sound-symbol relationships; an oral language skill that enables children to understand that words can be represented in print.

phonology
The rules within a language used to govern the combination of speech sounds to form words and sentences.

physical therapist (PT)
A professional who treats movement dysfunctions through a variety of nonmedical means in a program tailored to the individual's needs; provides a special education related service.

picture exchange communication system (PECS)
A technique used to provide individuals who are nonverbal, particularly children with autism, where pictures are used to make requests

planning
In the context of writing instruction, a deliberate and organized approach to tackle a writing task that includes a writer's first thoughts or basic ideas about a given topic.

Play Audiometry
A game-like format used to test the hearing of young and hard-to-test children during which the examiner teaches the child to respond to sounds.

portfolio assessment
An alternative form of individualized evaluation that includes numerous samples of the student's work across all curriculum targets and reports of teachers and parents about that individual's social skills.

positive behavior intervention plan (PBIP)
Instructional strategy which deploys positive reinforcement procedures as a means through which to support a student's appropriate or desirable behavior.

positive behavior support
An approach to behavior management in which scientifically validated practices are applied across a number of settings, such as the home, school, place of work, and community.

positive consequences
Reinforcement used to recognize and, ideally, to increase the frequency with which students engage in prescribed behaviors.

positive punishment
Means by which teachers can decrease the probability that a behavior will reoccur in the future; positive punishment provides something that is unpleasant.

positive reinforcement
Means by which teachers can increase the probability that a behavior will reoccur in the future; positive reinforcement provides something that is pleasant.

Positron Emission Tomography (PET scans)
Computerized method for studying the metabolic and chemical activities of tissue, mainly that of the brain.

postlingual hearing loss
Hearing Loss that occurs after the development of speech and language.

postnatal
Of or having to do with the period after birth.

Prader-Willi syndrome
A form of genetic disorder caused by a mutation of chromosome 15; a leading genetic cause of obesity often related to some degree of mental retardation.

pragmatics
The study within psycholinguistics of how people employ language in social situations; emphasizes the functional use of language, rather than its mechanics.

preference
Of or having to do with an individual's values and based on informed personal choices among interest-related options.

prelingually deaf
Total hearing loss that occurs before the development of speech and language.

prenatal
Of or having to do with the period before birth.

prereferral
Term used to describe a set of procedures designed to assist students experiencing academic or behavior difficulties prior to any consideration of special education services.

present level of educational performance
Information pertaining to a student's current level of academic achievement and other areas of development, such as social, behavior, and communication skills; a required component of a student's IEP.

prevalence
The total number of cases of a disease in a given population at any particular time.

primary prevention
Intervention designed to eliminate or counteract risk factors so that a disability is never acquired.

problem behavior
In behavior intervention, the behavior that a teacher wishes to reduce or eliminate; also called the target behavior.

problem solving
The process through which an individual finds answers or solutions to situations for which a resolution is not immediately obvious.

procedural safeguards
In the context of IDEA, the guarantee of a free appropriate public education in the least restrictive environment possible through a process of resolving disagreements and disputes beginning with mediation and ending with civil action.

procedure
The accepted process for carrying out a specific activity, such as walking in the hallway, using lockers, sharpening pencils, attending an assembly, or going to the lavatory.

progress monitoring
A form of assessment in which student learning is evaluated on a regular basis in order to provide useful feedback about performance to both learners and instructors.

progressive time delay
Instructional technique in which the amount of time given to a student to provide correct answers is gradually decreased.

prosthesis
An artificial body part (e.g., teeth, an arm) designed to replace, either partially or completely, a part of the body.

psychoeducational evaluation
An evaluative measure that usually includes intelligence testing, achievement testing, and an assessment of adaptive behavior skills for the purpose of designing an educational program appropriate to the needs of the student.

Public Law (PL) 94-142
The first special education law, passed by Congress in 1975 as the Education of All Handicapped Children Act and later updated as IDEA.

pull-in program
Educational program in which instruction and related services are delivered to students with disabilities within the general education classroom.

pull-out program
Educational program in which instruction and related services are delivered to students with disabilities outside the general education classroom.

punishment
Any of a spectrum of prescribed penalties used either to discourage or encourage certain behaviors.

pupil
The contractile opening in the middle of the iris of the eye; admits light into the eye.

pure-tone audiometry
A test whereby tones of various intensities and frequencies are presented as a means through which to determine a person's hearing loss.

quadriplegia
A condition in which all four limbs are paralyzed.

quality-of-life issue
A subjective and individual-specific concept dependent on a number of life-dimensions, including social relationships, personal satisfaction, employment, choice, leisure, and community adjustment.

rate of growth
An indication of how much a student's academic skills have improved; represented by the slope on a graph of the student's scores.

reading coach
A professional who provides teachers and other school personnel with support and supervision in the areas of instruction, assessment, and professional development; also offers support and supervision toward the effective implementation of the RTI approach.

reading comprehension
The ability to understand written text.

reading disability
Any condition in which a student's learning disability in reading is significant or unusually pronounced.

reading fluency
The ability to read text with accuracy, speed, and intonation.

real-time captioning (RTC)
The practically instantaneous translation of speech into print; an accommodation for deaf students attending lectures.

realia
Any concrete item or device used in the classroom to teach vocabulary or aid in comprehension.

reauthorization
The act of amending and renewing a law.

receptive language
The ability to understand what is being expressed either verbally or nonverbally.

reciprocal peer tutoring
A method of instruction in which students take turns acting as tutor. In the Peer Assisted Learning Strategies method, the student in the role of tutor is referred to as the Coach, while the student being tutored is referred to as the Reader. Typi-

cally, the Coach provides constructive feedback (i.e., corrective feedback) to the Reader regarding his or her performance.

reciprocal teaching
An instructional tactic wherein teachers and students switch roles in predicting, summarizing, questioning, and clarifying reading passages.

Recovery Phase
Some teachers will want to avoid talking about the Peak incident. Teachers often incorrectly think that they will re-trigger the misbehavior if they try to debrief the student. Not only is this erroneous but it is also the case that not talking about the situation with the student can unintentionally reinforce the behavior.

recursive
In the context of classroom instruction, a reference to a 'test-teach-test-teach' process through which a teacher uses student performance data to fine-tune his or her instruction; this instruction often changes in order to determine the most effective way of accelerating student performance.

recursive (2)
Term used to describe the way in which school personnel continually improve implementation of a new practice or program through the cyclical process of implementation, evaluation, and refinement.

referents
Words that are used to represent other words.

referral
Process through which a student is sent to another professional for services to support his or her academic, social, or behavioral needs.

refraction
The bending of light rays as they pass through the structures of the eye.

Regular Education Initiative (REI)
An instructional philosophy holding that general education, rather than special education, should be primarily responsible for the education of students with disabilities.

rehabilitation
Program designed to teach persons with recently

acquired disabilities the basic skills needed for independence.

related services
A part of special education that includes services from professionals (e.g., occupational therapist [OT], physical therapist [PT], Speech-Language Pathologist [SLP]) from a wide range of disciplines typically outside of education, all designed to meet the learning needs of individual children with disabilities.

remediation
Educative program designed to teach individuals to overcome the effects of disabilities on functioning.

replacement behavior
In behavior intervention, the behavior that a teacher uses to replace a problem or target behavior.

research-validated practice
A strategy or practice has been proven to work through experimental research studies or large-scale research field studies. Also called research-validated strategy.

research-validated strategy
A strategy or practice has been proven to work through experimental research studies or large-scale research field studies. Also called: research-validated practice.

residual vision
The amount and degree of vision of which one has functional use despite a visual disability.

resistant to treatment
A newly emerging and defining characteristic of learning disabilities in which, despite systematic instruction efforts, a student fails to learn the targeted skill or task.

resource room
Classroom in which students with exceptional learning needs receive individualized services for part of the school day.

response cards
Cards, signs, or items that are simultaneously held up by all students to display their response to a question or problem presented by the teacher.

response cost
Method of behavior management in which reinforcement is withdrawn when an objectionable behavior occurs.

response to intervention (RTI)
A multi-tiered method for delivering instruction to learners through increasingly intensive and individualized interventions.

retina
The back portion of the eye, containing nerve fibers connected to the optic nerve, upon which images from cornea and lens are focused and transmitted to the brain.

retinitis pigmentosa
A condition, usually hereditary, resulting in the degeneration of the retinas of both eyes that causes a narrowing of the field of vision and increased difficulty seeing at night.

retinopathy of prematurity (ROP)
An eye disorder that can develop in premature infants (often seen in those who exposed to high concentrations of oxygen at birth as a treatment for respiratory distress); causes scar tissue to form behind the lens of the eye.

Rett's disorder
One of the disorders included in the autistic spectrum disorders (ASD) characterized by difficulties with communication and social interaction as well as in repetitive or manneristic behaviors; genetic in nature.

Reye's syndrome
Rare disease (possibly related to a virus or to the use of aspirin) that occurs in children over the age of six; can be fatal or lead to neurological damage or mental retardation.

rigidity
A type of cerebral palsy characterized by increased muscle tone or spasticity, with little muscle elasticity.

Ritalin
The most commonly prescribed psychostimulant for ADHD or ADD; its generic name is methylphenidate.

rocket words
In the Peer Assisted Learning Strategies (PALS)

method, vocabulary words embedded in first-grade stories as a means of enhancing student interest. Examples of rocket words for first-graders are 'fuzzy' (beginning of the year), 'birthday party' (mid-year), and 'marshmallows' (end of the year).

rods
In the anatomy of the eye, the receptors located on the periphery of the retina, needed for peripheral vision, detection of movement, and vision in dim light.

round of intervention
A set period of time, determined by the school or district, during which an intervention is implemented.

RTI (response to intervention)
A multi-tiered method for delivering instruction to learners through increasingly intensive and individualized interventions.

RTI coach
Professional who has specific expertise in instructional techniques, interventions, and the RTI approach; hired to provide professional support to school personnel implementing RTI.

rubella (German measles)
A contagious viral infection whose symptoms include rash, fever, and enlarged lymph nodes; if it occurs in the first trimester of pregnancy it is likely to result in fetal abnormalities, including mental retardation.

scaffolded instruction
Instructional technique in which teachers offer support for students learning new skills by systematically building on their experiences and knowledge.

scaffolding
The process of using scaffolded instruction.

scaled model
Any model, either larger or smaller than the original object, the parts of which are in equal proportion to their actual size.

schizophrenia
A rare disorder in children that sometimes is characterized by bizarre delusions, hallucinations, and flat (or blunted) affect dissociation from reality; usually appears during adolescence or early childhood.

school counselor
Professional whose job it is to advise students in matters related to school success and planning, including academics, attendance, social issues, and post-secondary transitions.

school nurse
Professional who participates in delivering services to students with disabilities by assisting with medical services at school and designing accommodations for students with special health-care needs.

school psychologist
A professional trained to test and evaluate individual students' abilities.

scientifically validated interventions
Instructional procedures or methods proven by careful and systematic research.

scoliosis
A c-shaped or s-shaped curvature of the spine; may occur as a result of neuromuscular disease, of one leg being shorter than the other, or of a congenital abnormality of the vertebrae.

screening
Procedure in which groups of children are examined or tested in an effort to identify those most likely to have a disability; the first step in the assessment process that helps identify the need for further testing.

scripted lessons
Written scripts that guide teachers through instructional lessons for the purpose of enhancing fidelity of implementation and increasing the likelihood of positive student outcomes.

second language acquisition
The process whereby non-native speakers learn a new language; second language acquisition is divided into stages and the speed of the process is determined by the type and purpose of the language being acquired. See also: BICS, CALP.

secondary prevention
Intervention directed at reducing or eliminating the effects of existing risk factors.

Section 504 of the Rehabilitation Act of 1973
Federal law that set the stage for both the Individuals with Disabilities Education Act, passed in 1975, and the Americans with Disabilities Act, passed in 1990, by outlining basic civil rights for people with disabilities.

seizure
Involuntary movement or changes in consciousness or behavior brought on by abnormal bursts of electricity in the brain. See also: epilepsy.

seizure disorder
A spontaneous abnormal discharge of the electrical impulses of the brain; sometimes referred to as a convulsive disorder.

selective attention
The ability to attend to the crucial features of a task.

selective listening
Focusing attention on only one sound in the environment, such as on a speaker's voice in a lecture.

selective mutism
A form of communication disorder in which an individual, usually a child, is unable to speak in certain situations despite the ability to do so in others.

self-advocacy movement
A social and political movement started by and for people with mental retardation to speak for themselves on important issues such as housing, employment, legal rights, and personal relationships.

self-contained class
A special classroom, usually located within a regular public school building, that exists only for students with exceptional learning needs.

self-determination
A set of behaviors that includes making decisions, choosing preferences, and practicing self-advocacy; a curriculum target for many students with disabilities, particularly those with mental retardation.

self-injurious behavior (SIB)
Behavior that results in self-inflicted injuries (e.g., intentionally hitting one's head with or against an object, poking oneself in the eye).

self-instruction
A cognitive training technique that requires individuals to speak aloud and then to themselves as they solve problems.

self-management techniques
A set of instructional procedures whereby an individual uses self-instruction, self-monitoring, or self-reinforcement to modify his or her behavior.

self-monitoring
A cognitive training technique that requires individuals to keep track of their own behavior and record it in writing.

self-regulation
Generally refers to a person's ability to regulate his or her own behavior.

semantic feature analysis (SFA)
An instructional strategy designed to increase students' vocabulary by using a grid to show relationships and common features among known and unknown concepts.

semantic map
An instructional device in which a series of connected circles illustrates relationships among word meanings.

semantics
The system within a language that governs the content, intent, and meaning of spoken and written language; the study of same.

sensorineural hearing loss
Hearing loss caused by damage to the inner ear or the auditory nerve.

sequencing
Mentally categorizing and arranging items, facts, or ideas according to various dimensions; a thinking skill.

service coordination
The process of facilitating students' access to services, and coordinating the services, supports, and resources as identified on the IFSP or IEP; assures that services will be provided in an inte-

grated way and that they will not be needlessly duplicated.

service coordinator
The case manager who oversees the implementation and evaluation of an Individualized Family Service Plan (IFSP).

service delivery option
Any one of numerous means through which special education services are provided to students with disabilities (e.g., full inclusion programs, pull out programs, special classes, center schools).

setting demands
The behavioral requirements, both obvious and subtle, that characterize a given environment.

severe disorder/ disability
Term generally understood to describe disorders or disabilities that compromise an individual's functional skills to the extent that substantial assistance with daily living activities and ongoing supervision is required.

sheltered instruction
Educational strategy in which English language learners are taught knowledge in specific subject areas while also attaining a higher level of proficiency in the English language.

sheltered workshop
Facility that provides a structured environment for persons with disabilities in which they can learn skills, either on a transitional or permanent basis.

shunt
A tube used in a medical procedure that draws excess fluid from the brain and head area and disposes of it in a safe area in the body, such as the stomach; used to prevent cognitive disabilities resulting from hydrocephaly.

sickle-cell anemia
A hereditary blood disorder that inhibits blood flow; African Americans are most at risk for this health impairment.

side-by-side teaching
Instructional collaboration in which a teacher works with a colleague to practice a new lesson or technique.

sign language
An organized system of manual gestures used as a means of communication; used by some people with severe cognitive disabilities and by people who are deaf.

sign-language tranliterators
Trained professionals who facilitate voice-to-sign and sign-to-voice communication for students who are deaf or hard of hearing.

Snellen chart
A chart used to determine visual acuity; consists of rows of letters corresponding to the distances at which normally sighted persons can see them; developed in 1862 by the Dutch ophthalmologist Hermann Snellen.

social competence
The ability to understand social situations, respond to others appropriately, and interact with other people.

social maladjustment
In connection with determining the eligibility for special education, a term applied to children who do not act within society's norms but who are excluded from the definition of children with emotional or behavioral disorders.

social validity
In behavior assessment, the extent to which the intervention and desired replacement behavior represent socially accepted practices.

socioeconomic status (SES)
The relative measurement of an individual's or family's status in a given society, usually determined by professional attainment, level of education, and income.

sound blending
Process of vocalization through which the sounds of individual letters are combined into a spoken word.

spastic
A type of cerebral palsy characterized by the uncontrolled tightening or pulling of muscles.

special education
Individualized education for children and youth with exceptional learning needs.

specialized support
Any of a variety of disability-specific benefits used to help people with disabilities to participate in their communities.

specific language impairment (SLI)
Language disorder with no identifiable cause and not attributable to another disability.

speech
Vocal production of language requiring the coordination of oral movement to make sounds.

speech audiometry
Technique that tests an individual's ability to detect and to understand speech; an alternative to using pure tones to detect hearing loss.

speech impairment
Any one of several disorders that interferes with an individual's ability to communicate clearly and articulately; used to refer to speech and language disorders.

speech reception threshold (SRT)
The decibel level at which an individual is able to understand spoken language.

speech/ language pathologist (SLP)
A professional who diagnoses and treats problems in the area of speech and language development; a related services provider.

speechreading
Instructional method in which children are taught to use visual information from a number of sources to understand what is being said to them, rather than relying on their ability to interpret lip and facial movements to understand speech.

spina bifida
A developmental defect whereby the spinal column fails to close properly.

spinal cord disorder
Any injury or disease of the spinal column, usually one affecting both the nerves and muscles.

spontaneous recovery
In behavior management, instance or instances in which a previously extinguished behavior unexpectedly reappears.

squaring off
A method of positioning the body so that it is perpendicular to an object, wall surface, or sound in order to establish a perpendicular line of direction to cross an open space.

standard deviation (SD)
In connection with standardized assessments, a statistical measure that expresses the variability and the distribution from the mean of a set of scores.

standard protocol
A validated intervention, selected by the school (often for the secondary intervention level), to improve the academic skills of its struggling students.

standard protocol approach
An approach to RTI that uses a intervention (selected by the school at the secondary intervention level) to improve the academic skills of its struggling students; an alternative to the problem solving approach, which individualizes instruction at Tier 2. Sometimes also referred to as the standard treatment protocol approach.

standard scores
In connection with norm-referenced tests, scores resulting from statistical operations on raw scores; converted test scores that equalize those from different tests as a means of comparison.

standards-based curriculum
The content and skills believed to be important for students to learn.

standards-based reform
A process of school improvement or reform that is tied to the achievement of verifiable goals.

stapes
The stirrup-shaped bone in the ossicular chain of the middle ear.

Star Legacy model
A formalized inquiry cycle constructed around the basic principles of the How People Learn

(HPL) framework; the structural basis for all IRIS Modules.

statewide and districtwide assessments
Part of the national education reform movement that includes the annual achievement testing of all schoolchildren for the purpose of increasing school accountability.

stay-put provision
The legal mandate that prohibited the expulsion of students with disabilities due to behaviors associated with their disabilities.

stereotypic behaviors
Nonproductive motor behaviors (such as twirling, flapping hands, rocking) that an individual repeats at a high rate; commonly observed in youngsters with autistic spectrum disorders.

stimulus
Any condition or input that evokes a response from an individual.

stimulus control
Process of reinforcing a desired response in the presence of a specific stimuli, while not reinforcing undesired responses in the presence of other stimuli.

story maps
Simple diagrams that help students to organize and recall important elements and features of the stories they have heard or read.

strabismus
A condition that prevents the eyes from aiming in the same direction at the same time; a misalignment of the eyes.

strategies instruction
Instruction designed to teach students the elements or steps for implementing successful strategies.

strategy
A coordinated series of steps designed to help an individual to use preskills (i.e., his or her pre-existing knowledge) to perform a task.

structured teaching
A feature of TEACCH (Treatment and Education of Autistic and Related Communication-handi-capped CHildren), an instructional program in which visual aids are used to help students with autism to comprehend their environments.

student accountability
A system of accountability in which primary responsibility is assigned to the student; designed to motivate students to achieve their best.

stuttering
The lack of fluency in an individual's speech pattern, often characterized by hesitations or repetitions of sounds or words.

summative assessment
An evaluation administered to measure student learning outcomes, typically at the end of a unit or chapter. Often used to evaluate whether a student has mastered the content or skill.

supported employment
An approach to job training whereby students with disabilities are placed in paying jobs for which they receive significant assistance and support.

survival period
Period of time during which a teacher's early-career optimism often gives way to discouragement and disillusionment.

syntax
The way words are joined together to structure meaningful sentences; grammar.

syphilis
A venereal disease that can cause mental abnormality in a child, especially if it is contracted by the mother during the latter stages of pregnancy.

system accountability
Program of assigning responsibility for the performance of an educational system to individuals within that system; designed to improve educational programs.

systemic bias
Favoritism toward a particular group that occurs at multiple levels within a society or institution.

systems of supports
The network of supports that all individuals develop in order to function optimally in life.

tactile accomodation
A modification that allows for access to print materials and that enables students who are blind to learn about their environment through the sense of touch.

tactile map
A map on which information is perceptible to the touch; used by people with severe visual disabilities.

tactile material
Any material, object, model, or learning tool designed to be manipulated digitally or through the sense of touch.

talent development
The process of translating ability into achievement; another name for the education of the gifted.

talking book
A version of a book made available in auditory format.

target behavior
In behavior intervention, the behavior that a teacher wishes to reduce or eliminate; also called the problem behavior.

targeted intervention
Strategy of intervention in which a teacher offers a standard, validated instructional program to students in a group, typically consisting of no more than five students; may be implemented by general education teachers, paraprofessionals, reading specialists, or other qualified individuals.

task analysis
Process of breaking down problems and tasks into smaller, sequenced components.

task scaffolding
Method of instruction whereby a teacher begins by specifying the steps in a task or instructional strategy and then goes on to model those steps for his or her class while verbalizing his or her thought process.

taught curriculum
The daily events that occur in the school community, including all lessons and activities, social gatherings among peers, techniques used by teachers during instruction such as lectures and discussions, and the teacher's style of instruction.

Tay-Sachs disease
An autosomal recessive brain disorder characterized by a failure to thrive, mental retardation, deafness, blindness, paralysis, and seizures; usually fatal by age five; symptoms present by the time an infant is six months old.

teacher of students with visual impairments (TVI)
A specially trained and certified teacher who provides direct or consultative special education services related to the effects of vision loss.

teacher-reflection
An on-going practice that occurs when teachers identify their own thoughts, values, and behaviors about other cultures in order to gain deeper levels of self-knowledge and recognize how their personal worldviews can influence their teaching and shape their students' concepts of self.

technology-dependent children
Term used to describe children whose survival is heavily dependent on the use of high-tech devices such as ventilators.

telecommunications relay service (TRS)
A telephone system required by federal law wherein an operator at a relay center converts a print-telephone message to a voice-telephone message.

teratogen
Any of a number of chemical agents that can disrupt the normal development of the fetus.

tertiary prevention
Intervention designed to minimize the effect of a specific condition or disability.

test item bias
Bias that occurs when tests rely on concepts, shared assumptions, or events that are by definition outside the experience or understanding of English language learners (ELL).

text telephone (TTY)
Communication equipment (formerly called the telecommunication device for the deaf [TDD]) that allows people to make and receive telephone calls by typing messages over the phone lines.

the 504 Plan
A plan that specifies the accommodations and modifications necessary for a student with a disability to attend school with her or his peers; named for Section 504 of the federal Rehabilitation Act of 1973, which prohibits discrimination against individuals with disabilities, ensuring that children with disabilities have equal access to public education; students with 504 plans do not meet the eligibility requirements for special education under IDEA.

theoretical construct
A model based on theory, rather than on practice or experience.

three-year re-evaluation
Triannual process, conducted by a multidisciplinary team, to reassess the needs of students with disabilities.

Tier 1: class- or school-wide interventions (primary prevention)
Program of reading instruction that includes all students, whether struggling in reading or not.

Tier 2 service provider
Any individual who has been trained in the appropriate Tier 2 instruction: classroom teacher, reading specialist, special education teacher, supervised paraprofessional, tutor, or trained volunteer.

Tier 2: targeted interventions (secondary prevention)
Program of reading instruction that offers more focused instruction than is usually offered in the typical classroom.

Tier 3: intensive, individualized interventions (tertiary preventions)
Program of increasingly intensive, specialized services designed to help students to become successful readers.

time delay
An instructional procedure in which a student is given a set period of time (e.g., 20 seconds) in which to answer to a question, read a sight word, or spell a word, after which the correct answer is given.

time of onset
The moment in time during which a disability first occurs.

tonic-clonic seizures
Seizures characterized by a stiff (tonic) phase in which the muscles become rigid, followed by a jerking (clonic) phase in which the arms and legs snap; formerly referred to as grand mal seizures.

topic association
Style of oral communication characterized by free association and the frequent omission of explanations about the relationships between topics or ideas; also called topic chaining.

topic chaining
Style of oral communication characterized by free association and the frequent omission of explanations about the relationships between topics or ideas; also called topic association.

total communication approach
A system of instruction for deaf students that employs any and all methods of communication (oral speech, manual communication, ASL, gestures) that are easy, efficient, and preferred by the student for communication.

total immersion
An instructional strategy wherein a student is taught entirely in English in a classroom in which all the other students are likewise non-native English speakers, and the teacher can speak the students' home language.

Tourette's syndrome
A low incidence disability characterized by multiple and uncontrollable motor or verbal tics.

toxoplasmosis
An infection caused by a parasite carried by more than 60 million individuals; usually dangerous only to expectant women, who can pass it on to their unborn children, causing them to develop mental retardation or blindness.

trailing
A technique used by individuals with visual impairments in which one hand maintains contact with the environment in order to establish a straight line of travel or to locate specific objectives along an environmental line.

transciption
The process of transferring thoughts and ideas into words and then putting them on paper.

transition planning
In connection with special education, the development and implementation of activities designed to prepare students with disabilities for postsecondary options, such as work, college, or supported living; transition activities are individualized and are typically designed to address skills or knowledge relevant to the students' postsecondary goals.

transition specialist
Professional who collaborates with and acts as a liason between numerous individuals and agencies in order to ensure that students with disabilities enjoy successful post-secondary transitions.

transitional bilingual education
An instructional method used with English Language Learners (ELL) in which academic subjects are taught in the student's native language until sufficient English is mastered for transition; also referred to as early exit programs.

transliteration services
Services that assist students who are deaf or hard of hearing with their communication needs; can be provided anywhere the student is located, such as the classroom, the playground, the library, the soccer field, or the science lab.

traumatic brain injury (TBI)
Injury to the brain not present at birth or resulting from birth trauma that often results in total or partial disability; may affect cognitive, sensory, or motor functioning.

Trigger Phase
The second phase of the behavior cycle (acting-out behavior cycle), during which student misbehavior can be triggered by a concern that is not addressed; such concerns can take place either within or beyond the school day.

triplegia
A condition of paralysis in any three limbs.

tunnel vision
A severe limitation in peripheral vision; limitations in the width of the visual field.

Turner's syndrome
A chromosomal disorder in females caused by the absence of an X chromosomes in any or all of the individual's body cells; characterized by a short physical stature, webbing of the skin of the neck, a broad chest and underdeveloped breasts, infertility, eye and bone abnormalities, mental retardation (in some instances), and heart defects.

twice-exceptional student
Term used to describe a student who both has a disability and who is gifted.

two-way immersion
Method of language instruction in which academic content is provided to all students in two languages (e.g., Spanish and English); also referred to as dual-language immersion.

tympanic membrane (eardrum)
The anatomical boundary between the outer and middle ears; the sound gathered in the outer ear vibrates here.

type I diabetes
A disease caused by an inadequate secretion or use of insulin and resulting in excessive sugar in the blood and urine; manageable through diet or medication.

underrepresentation
The Low or non-presence of a group or groups of individuals in a special education category; smaller numbers than would be predicted by their proportion in the overall school population.

unexpected underachievement
A description associated with learning disabilities wherein poor school performance cannot be explained by a student's intellectual potential.

unilateral hearing loss
Hearing loss in one ear only; potential for significant negative effect on education process.

unit plan design
A plan designed to help teachers to organize what will be done in the classroom as a means of helping students to achieve whatever long-term goals have been set for the class.

universal design
Barrier-free architectural and building designs that meet the needs of everyone, including people

with physical disabilities.

universal infant screening
The process of testing all newborns to determine whether they have or are at risk for a disability; specific term associated with newborn screening for hearing loss.

universal screening
The practice of assessing every student with a brief screening tool.

unlicensed assistive personnel (UAP)
Personnel who stand in for school nurses and cover nurses' responsibilities in their absence.

upper-hand-and-forearm self-protective technique
A self-defense method in which one arm is used to protect the upper body, specifically the head and shoulders; often used in conjunction with trailing or with the lower-hand-and-forearm self-protective technique.

Usher syndrome
A genetic disorder characterized by nonprogressive sensorineural hearing loss, retinitis pigmentosa and progressively restricted field of vision, loss of the sense of smell, and impaired balance and motor skills.

videodisc instruction
An alternative to computer assisted instruction (CAI) in which instructional discs contain narrated segments of visual images.

vision specialist
Professional whose major role is in the special education assessment and education intervention of students with visual impairments.

visual accomodation
Any of a variety of modifications made to printed materials (e.g., enlarged print, increased contrast) that render them easier to read.

visual acuity
How well a person can see at various distances.

visual cortex
Part of the brain that functions to process electrical signals from the optic nerve into visual images.

visual efficiency
How well a person uses his or her sight.

visual field
The range at which an individual can see objects centrally or peripherally; the total area that a person is able to see without moving his or her eyes or head.

visual functions
The abilities of the visual system, such as visual acuity, visual field, color discrimination, dark adaptation, and contrast sensitivity, as measured by performance on standardized tests of sight; a reference to the extent to which vision is used.

visual impairment
Any level of vision loss that affects an individual's ability to complete daily tasks; term often used to describe both blindness and low vision.

vitreous humor
The transparent, gelatinous substance that fills the eyeball between the retina and the lens of the eye.

vocabulary
The words known by a person; a knowledge of words and their meanings.

vocational rehabilitation
Any of a number of types of program designed to help adults with disabilities to obtain and hold employment.

vocational training and education
Job training or employment counseling offered to students who wish to enter the work force after high school.

voice disorder
Any of a number of disorders that negatively affect an individual's ability to produce speech.

voice recognition software
Computer software that allows a user to issue spoken commands to his or her computer; particularly useful to those whose disabilities prevent them from manipulating other forms of computer interface, such as a keyboard or mouse.

William's syndrome
A rare genetic condition resulting from deletion of material in the seventh pair of chromosomes,

and characterized by mild to moderate mental retardation, heart defects, and elfin facial features.

word identifcation fluency
A test in which a student is asked to read as many words as possible in one minute; this test must be administered to each child individually.

wraparound service
A service delivery model whereby all of the student's needs are met through the coordination of the education system, mental health agencies, social services, and community agencies.

writing
A test in which a student is asked to write for three to five minutes in response to a story starter; the student's score is the number of word pairs that are grammatically and semantically appropriate and spelled correctly; this test can be administered to a group.

year-end achievement test
A test administered once a year, often near the end of school, that offers an indication of a student's overall progress for the year; an example of summative assessment, annual achievement tests focus on the outcomes of student learning.

year-long planning
A method of instructional planning that allows for continuous, sequential, integrated, and cumulative learning.

Young Autism Program (YAP)
Program developed by Dr. O. Ivar Lovaas at University of California, Los Angeles, in which behavioral principles are used to reduce problems associated with autistic spectrum disorder (ASD); sometimes incorrectly called the ABA program.

zero reject
The core principle of IDEA stating that no student with a disability, regardless of its nature or severity, can be denied an education.

zero tolerance
Popular term used to designate (and promote) school policies that address incidents of drug or weapon possession with automatic suspension or expulsion.

Index

Installing REA's TestWare®

SYSTEM REQUIREMENTS

Microsoft Windows XP or later, 64 MB available RAM.

INSTALLATION

1. Insert the Praxis II Special Education TestWare® CD into the CD-ROM drive.

2. If the installation doesn't begin automatically, from the Start Menu choose the RUN command. When the RUN dialog box appears, type d:\setup (where d is the letter of your CD-ROM drive) at the prompt and click OK.

3. The installation process will begin. A dialog box proposing the directory "C:\Program Files\REA\Praxis_SpecialEd\" will appear. If the name and location are suitable, click OK. If you wish to specify a different name or location, type it in and click OK.

4. Start the Praxis II Special Education TestWare® application by double-clicking on the icon.

REA's TestWare® is **EASY** to **LEARN AND USE**. To achieve maximum benefits, we recommend that you take a few minutes to go through the on-screen tutorial on your computer.

SSD ACCOMMODATIONS FOR STUDENTS WITH DISABILITIES

Many students qualify for extra time to take the Praxis II Special Education exam, and our TestWare® can be adapted to accommodate your time extension. This allows you to practice under the same extended-time accommodations that you will receive on the actual test day. For more information about how to customize your TestWare® to suit the most common extensions, email us at *studycenter@rea.com*.

TECHNICAL SUPPORT

REA's TestWare® is backed by customer and technical support. For questions about **installation or operation of your software**, contact us at:

> **Research & Education Association**
> **Phone: (732) 819-8880 (9 a.m. to 5 p.m. ET, Monday–Friday)**
> **Fax: (732) 819-8808**
> **Website: *www.rea.com***
> **E-mail: info@rea.com**

Note: In order for the TestWare® to function properly, please install and run the application under the same computer administrator-level user account. Installing the TestWare® as one user and running it as another could cause file-access path conflicts.